PARENT
GRIEF

The Series in Death, Dying, and Bereavement
Consulting Editor
Robert A. Neimeyer

Davies—*Shadows in the Sun: The Experiences of Sibling Bereavement in Childhood*
Harvey—*Perspectives on Loss: A Sourcebook*
Klass—*The Spiritual Lives of Bereaved Parents*
Leenaars—*Lives and Deaths: Selections from the Works of Edwin S. Shneidman*
Martin, Doka—*Men Don't Cry . . . Women Do: Transcending Gender Stereotypes of Grief*
Nord—*Multiple AIDS-Related Loss: A Handbook for Understanding and Surviving a Perpetual Fall*
Rosenblatt—*Parent Grief: Narratives of Loss and Relationship*
Werth—*Contemporary Perspectives on Rational Suicide*

FORMERLY THE **SERIES IN DEATH EDUCATION, AGING, AND HEALTH CARE**
HANNELORE WASS, CONSULTING EDITOR

Bard—*Medical Ethics in Practice*
Benoliel—*Death Education for the Health Professional*
Bertman—*Facing Death: Images, Insights, and Interventions*
Brammer—*How to Cope with Life Transitions: The Challenge of Personal Change*
Cleiren—*Bereavement and Adaptation: A Comparative Study of the Aftermath of Death*
Corless, Pittman-Lindeman—*AIDS: Principles, Practices, and Politics, Abridged Edition*
Corless, Pittman-Lindeman—*AIDS: Principles, Practices, and Politics, Reference Edition*
Curran—*Adolescent Suicidal Behavior*
Davidson—*The Hospice: Development and Administration, Second Edition*
Davidson, Linnolla—*Risk Factors in Youth Suicide*
Degner, Beaton—*Life-Death Decisions in Health Care*
Doka—*AIDS, Fear, and Society: Challenging the Dreaded Disease*
Doty—*Communication and Assertion Skills for Older Persons*
Epting, Neimeyer—*Personal Meanings of Death: Applications of Personal Construct Theory to Clinical Practice*
Haber—*Health Care for an Aging Society: Cost-Conscious Community Care and Self-Care Approaches*
Hughes—*Bereavement and Support: Healing in a Group Environment*
Irish, Lundquist, Nelsen—*Ethnic Variations in Dying, Death, and Grief: Diversity in Universality*
Klass, Silverman, and Nickman—*Continuing Bonds: New Understanding of Grief*
Lair—*Counseling the Terminally Ill: Sharing the Journey*
Leenaars, Maltsberger, Neimeyer—*Treatment of Suicidal People*
Leenaars, Wenckstern—*Suicide Prevention in Schools*
Leng—*Psychological Care in Old Age*
Leviton—*Horrendous Death, Health, and Well-Being*
Leviton—*Horrendous Death and Health: Toward Action*
Lindeman, Corby, Downing, Sanborn—*Alzheimer's Day Care: A Basic Guide*
Lund—*Older Bereaved Spouses: Research with Practical Applications*
Neimeyer—*Death Anxiety Handbook: Research, Instrumentation, and Application*
Papadatou, Papadatos—*Children and Death*
Prunkl, Berry—*Death Week: Exploring the Dying Process*
Ricker, Myers—*Retirement Counseling: A Practical Guide for Action*
Samarel—*Caring for Life and Death*
Sherron, Lumsden—*Introduction to Educational Gerontology, Third Edition*
Stillion—*Death and Sexes: An Examination of Differential Longevity, Attitudes, Behaviors, and Coping Skills*
Stillion, McDowell, May—*Suicide Across the Life Span—Premature Exits*
Vachon—*Occupational Stress in the Care of the Critically Ill, the Dying, and the Bereaved*
Wass, Corr—*Childhood and Death*
Wass, Corr—*Helping Children Cope with Death: Guidelines and Resource, Second Edition*
Wass, Corr, Pacholski, Forfar—*Death Education II: An Annotated Resource Guide*
Wass, Neimeyer—*Dying: Facing the Facts, Third Edition*
Weenolsen—*Transcendence of Loss over the Life Span*
Werth—*Rational Suicide? Implications for Mental Health Professionals*

PARENT GRIEF:

Narratives of
Loss and Relationship

written by
Paul C. Rosenblatt

BRUNNER/MAZEL
· Taylor & Francis Group ·

USA	Publishing Office:	BRUNNER/MAZEL *A member of the Taylor & Francis Group* 325 Chestnut Street Philadelphia, PA 19106 Tel: (215) 625-8900 Fax: (215) 625-2940
	Distribution Center:	BRUNNER/MAZEL *A member of the Taylor & Francis Group* 47 Runway Road, Suite G Levittown, PA 19057-4700 Tel: (215) 269-0400 Fax: (215) 269-0363
UK		BRUNNER/MAZEL *A member of the Taylor & Francis Group* 27 Church Road Hove E. Sussex, BN3 2FA Tel: +44 (0) 1273 207411 Fax: +44 (0) 1273 205612

PARENT GRIEF: Narratives of Loss and Relationship

1 2 3 4 5 6 7 8 9 0

Printed by Edwards Brothers, Lillington, NC, 2000

A CIP catalog record for this book is available from the British Library.
∞ The paper in this publication meets the requirements of the ANSI Standard Z39.48-1984 (Permanence of Paper)

Library of Congress Cataloging-in-Publication Data

Rosenblatt, Paul C.
    Parent grief: narratives of loss and relationship / written by Paul C. Rosenblatt.
      p. cm. -- (Series in death, dying and bereavement, ISSN 1091-5427)
    Includes bibliographical references and index.
    ISBN 1-58391-033-6 (alk. paper) -- ISBN 1-58391-034-4 (pbk. : alk. paper)
    1.Grief. 2. Bereavement--Psychological aspects. 3. Children--Death--Psychological aspects. 4.x Children--Death--Psychological aspects--Case Studies.5. Loss (Psychology)
I. Title. II. Series.

    BF575.G7 R673 2000
    155.9'37'085--dc21   99-053853

ISSN: 1091-5427
ISBN: 1-58391-033-6 (case)
ISBN: 1-58391-034-4 (paper)

CONTENTS

PREFACE

This book is about what parents who have experienced the death of a child have to say about the death and their experiences as a result of the death. Based on intensive interviews, the book explores the narratives of 58 parents in 29 couples or former couples. Among the elements common to the narratives are the death and the events leading up to it; death rituals; parents' experiences of a chasm between themselves and others; individual and couple grieving; the continuing connection with the child who died; the interplay of grief with the couple relationship; parenting other children after the death; finding (and failing to find) supportive relationships with family, friends, and community; learning what to say about the death; the search for meaning in the death; and the impact of the death on the parent relationship with God.

Woven into the parent narratives are a number of constants, such as the fact of the death, the importance of understanding the death, the sense that there is an objective reality, the feelings of connection to the child, the concern about what others (particularly the spouse) were, and are, doing and saying related to the death, and a social and economic world that gives little latitude to grieve or even to be different from others.

This book is intended for grief scholars and professionals who work with bereaved parents. It lays out issues that will come up with many bereaved parents. These are important things to listen for; these are the domains of language within which problems will be framed and solved; these are the tools available to bereaved parents and those who want to help them talk and to solve problems connected to the death and make sense out of everything.

How This Perspective Differs from Others

The perspective taken in this book assumes that the people who were interviewed are experts on their own experiences and realities and that there is enormous value in taking what they have to say seriously and understanding it in its own terms. This book is not about pathology. In fact, evaluating bereaved people in terms of pathology can lead us to miss the ways that what seems pathological in one perspective makes perfect nonpathological sense in another (Stroebe, Gergen, Gergen, & Stroebe, 1992; Stroebe et al., 1999).

This book does not use the theory of grief work as a frame for asking questions or writing about what the parents had to say. Although all parents talked about their efforts to heal, come to terms with the death, and find a path from their deepest and most engulfing grief toward something else, I think imposing a model of healing (or adjusting or coming to terms) on what they said would obscure the many parts of their narratives that are not about trying to travel such a path. The book is also about social construction. Parents had a lot to say about not only their individual and relationship struggles to construct realities but also the ways their spouse and others have helped or frustrated them in coming to these realities.

Many of the words in this book are words said by grieving parents. I think the reader can understand much more of the nuance, complexity, feeling, ambiguity, and paradox of parental bereavement when reading what bereaved parents have to say. Also, when parents' words illustrate or document the points I make, the reader is in a better place to know what I mean and to decide whether my statements about what the parents said are warranted.

Scholars who write about narrative do not necessarily agree (Chase, 1995). Reflecting that disagreement, I worked with blurred boundaries around my own definition. For me, parts of the interviews were definitely not "narrative." For example, part of every interview involved a discussion of the consent form that laid out the purpose of the research and the interviewees' rights. Part of every interview also included brief answers to demographic and genealogical questions and brief clarifications/negotiations of meanings (both the interviewees' and the interviewer's). Almost always there was a discussion of whether the interviewer wanted something to drink, was comfortable, or wanted something to eat. Often there was a discussion of the interviewer's research goals and of the interviewer's life in relationship to the research. None of that is what I would call a bereaved parent's "narrative."

However there were, in every interview, statements that fit my idea of narrative—a long segment of talk (by one parent or the couple together) that told a story or a series of stories related to the child's dying and death or the individual's or couple's life since the death. Those long, storied segments have what, following Gergen and Gergen (1987), I consider the elements of narrative. These segments give a sense of something to be explained or of moving toward an end-state. They are chronologically organized flows of events or experiences, with markers of story beginnings and endings (or of reaching the present), with coherence, and with statements about characters and settings.

Interviewees also made statements that fall between what I think is clearly a narrative and what I think is clearly not. These may be elaborations on a narrative, brief comments on what the spouse said, brief responses to an interviewer's question, or parenthetical statements inserted in a narrative but not obviously connected to the flow of events in the narrative. Interviewees may consider such comments integral to the telling of their story, but if they do not say that, I cannot know. I cannot say that these segments are narratives, but in some places I have used what people have said in such statements to elaborate my narrative analysis. I use those statements because I think they help in understanding specific things in a parent narrative and because I am never sure, once the storied relationship has been entered in the interview process, that anything said by a parent is not part of the narrative. Even the parenthetical statement asking me if I want a drink of water may be part of the narrative.

This book offers an analysis of parent narratives. It is only one of many possible ways of analyzing the narratives of these parents. The aim of my narrative analysis was to understand parent meanings and why meanings came in the packages they did. I acknowledge that there are many possible ways of analyzing parent narratives with those goals in mind. My approach is not the only legitimate one. And the interviews elicited from each parent or parent couple constitute only one of what may be many possible sets of narratives concerning the child's death and aftermath of that death.

The couples who were interviewed were volunteers. Through advertising in a diversity of places, I hoped to recruit same sex couples and couples in which at least one partner was a person of color, but every couple in this study is white and heterosexual. That is an unfortunate limitation of this book.

☐ Quoting Parents

In quoting parents I have changed or omitted names (of the parents, children, and others) and other crucial identifying information. When the second parent started speaking while the first was already speaking, I have put what the second said in parentheses. Sometimes I have included every word and sound in a quoted passage, because I think there is something interesting there even if I do not comment on it at all in my words about the quoted passage. But often I have eliminated restarts (either where the same words were uttered more than once, or where the person started to say one thing and then changed to something else without completing the statement that was begun), stuttered sounds, sounds like "uh" and "er" that have little lexical meaning, and many instances of "well," "I mean," "and then I said," "like I said," "whatever," "and stuff," "or something," "you know," and a dangling "so" at the end of a sentence. Also, I often omit parts of what people said within a statement I quote. I do so to keep this book from being twice as long as it is and in order to maintain focus on the topic I am discussing or that I thought the parent being quoted was discussing. Following standard usage, where I have omitted part of a sentence, I have inserted three ellipsis dots. Where I have omitted a sentence or more, I have inserted four ellipsis dots. Occasionally I have changed a quote from an ungrammatical form to a more grammatical form. I did that when I thought the grammar was irrelevant to the issues being discussed and that the new grammatical form would be easier for readers to understand.

It is always worrisome, in a book making assertions about language and lived experiences, to omit a piece of what has been voiced. What has been omitted could mean something to some readers, even if it seems to me to be redundant or irrelevant and distracting. I hope readers will trust me and that the book will seem useful and valid despite my editing.

In this book, a good deal of what I and the other interviewers said has been simplified or omitted. I have abbreviated many of our questions and eliminated almost all of our comments that punctuate what the people who were interviewed said ("uh huh," "mm," "yes," "I see," etc.). I know editing interviewer words means that I limit aspects of language and social construction processes that could potentially be very important. However, in the interests of space and readability and with a focus on the bereaved parents, it seemed to be a reasonable thing to do.

This book is my reality, not necessarily the reality of the people interviewed. Even when I quote them, I am selecting and editing what they said and applying my meanings and interpretations, my emphasis, and my context. I am trying to write what will serve the interests of bereaved parents. I hope that in the process I have not offended the bereaved parents who agreed to be interviewed, have not distorted the meanings they intended to convey, and have not lost too much of the context, process, personal variability, and realities as they would construct them.

Paul C. Rosenblatt

ACKNOWLEDGMENTS

This project benefitted from financial support from the Agricultural Experiment Station of the University of Minnesota and a year's sabbatical leave from the University. My two department heads during the course of this project, Hal Grotevant and Jan Hogan, helped with money, interest, and an environment that values qualitative research. The University of Minnesota Libraries were a fabulous resource throughout this project.

I had excellent interviewing help from Terri Karis and Anna Hagemeister.

Over my years of working on this project, conversation has been invaluable to me. Among the many people who helped me to construct my realities and keep moving forward were Sara Wright, Janice Nadeau, Shais Rosenblatt, Mike Baizerman, Anna Hagemeister, Kathy Rettig, Terri Karis, Margaret Stroebe, Henk Schut, Tim Barber, Jim Holstein, Jay Gubrium, Don Campbell, Kathy Gilbert, Paul Lasley, Ramona Oswald, Jennifer Daniel, Ronit Leichtentritt, Carolyn Tubbs, and members of the National Council on Family Relations Research and Theory Workshop who were involved in a discussion of this research in its planning stage.

To the bereaved parents who allowed me to know so much about their experiences I am infinitely grateful.

CHAPTER 1

The Narratives of Bereaved Parents

Grieving involves the construction and voicing of narratives (Harvey, 1996). This book is about the narratives of parents who have experienced the death of a child. Based on intensive interviews of 58 parents in 29 couples or former couples, this book is about what the parents had to say about the death and what happened to them in the aftermath of the death. The 29 couples reported 33 child deaths, including one stillbirth. The children who died ranged in age up to 33 years, with the median age at death being 3. The interviews occurred from 8 months to 35 years after the death, with a median of 7 years after the death. The interviews almost always lasted at least two hours and ran up to about four hours at a single sitting. (See the Appendix for further methodological details.) In every interview parents told their emotionally intense stories about what had happened.

As I wrote in the preface of this book, "narrative" can be defined as a spoken or written connected description of a succession of events or experiences that includes a sense of something to be explained or of moving toward an end-state, markers of story beginning and ending (or reaching the present), coherence, characters, and settings. Much that people say I do not call narrative. It is too brief or disorganized. Often when people might have a narrative to tell it comes out as much less than what I would call a narrative, more like a simple declarative sentence or a collection of fragments of a narrative.

Sometimes, on the spur of the moment, people can spin a narrative that is new for them, but I think typically narratives come out of considerable reflection about an event and considerable experience at developing the narrative over repeated tellings. I think many narratives are about what has been significant for a person. So it is not surprising that bereaved parents have narratives to tell about their child's death and the aftermath of the death. The death is an enormously significant experience. (Conceivably it might not be for some parents, but I have not met such parents.) The death and its aftermath provide much that most parents think about repeatedly and at length, and for many parents there develops considerable experience at delivering those narratives to others. So this is an area of life for which it makes sense to study narrative.

☐   Domains of Bereaved Parent Narrative

Common Domains

When parents talk about a child's death and their grief, much of what they say falls within a limited number of domains of narrative—including the domains of the dying process (if there was a process), the moment of death, funeral rituals, religion, relationships with friends and coworkers, grieving, and couple difficulties over differences in grieving. Each domain provides a coherent vocabulary and focuses on certain frames of reference, certain aspects of social relationships, certain areas of meaning and understanding, and certain ways of labeling and talking about feelings and thoughts. Each domain enables a bereaved parent to name and organize realities and experiences and to focus attention, thought, and the flow of words. Each domain includes an account of the parent dealing with problems that need resolving and questions that call for answers, and each offers stories about routes to solving problems and answering questions. For example, a parent turns to physicians and the medical literature for answers about medical problems, and to prayer, clergy, the Bible, and other religious writings for answers about religious problems.

Areas that Never or Hardly Ever Become a Domain

The major domains of narrative that came up often as parents talked about their child's death and the aftermath of the death are defined by chapter titles and section headings throughout chapters 3–14 of this book. I can conceive of many other domains the narratives of bereaved parents might conceivably include, but it says a lot about the limits of culture, relationships, and experience of the parents who were interviewed that there is little or no interview material in the other conceivable alternative domains. For example, no bereaved parent related the child's death and their experiences resulting from the death to current events (for example, what was going on in Congress that dealt with medical research or accident prevention, natural disasters or military conflicts in the news that led to the deaths of children, or national debates about corporate power and product safety or corporate power and quality of health care). No bereaved parent related the child's death and the aftermath of the death to world history, a religious ideology other than their own, the chemistry of body decomposition or any other scientific way of knowing other than that having to do with how it came to be that the child died, or any text in world literature other than the Bible. No bereaved parent offered narrative about demography, politics, astrology, the cost of things bought for the child that will never be consumed by the child, or a specific film, play, or television drama. Nobody contextualized the death in terms of evolution or natural selection or as issues of public health.

Almost nothing was said about the larger societal context of the death. For example, the parents whose child died of SIDS or a condition present at birth or of cancer or some other disease never talked about how the society could or should put more resources into medical research to understand, prevent, or cure those conditions. The parents of children killed in accidents involving automobiles did not talk about the cost in lives and health of the U.S. being so reliant on automobiles. None talked about what to make of public transportation being minimally available and under-used, the possibility of cars being built that would be much less likely to lead to fatalities, the possibility of more stringent and effectively enforced limits on speeding or other unsafe driving acts, or the possibility of safer engineering of streets and highways. For deaths involving farm equipment, it was almost the same. Only one parent talked about the ethics and politics underlying building a piece of farm machinery that was so dangerous. All the rest of the families whose child died in an accident involving farm machinery or automobiles seemed to take the engineering and business ethics underlying a piece of machinery involved in a fatal accident for granted.

Almost nothing was said about the larger societal context for parent grieving. For example, nobody talked about the death as a community death. To bereaved parents communities do not seem to mourn much or long; they do not seem to acknowledge in the same way parents do that this is a death that will affect them for decades. Nobody argued that society should change so grieving people have permission and support to burst into grief anytime, anywhere. Nobody argued that pressures not to grieve long or in public served capitalism in the sense of minimizing the disruption of economic activity. Of all the thousands of ways parents could conceivably talk about, contextualize, and give meaning to a child's death and its aftermath, relatively few came up.

There is a safety in not bringing in certain conceivable domains. Keeping things focused locally, rather than on what manufacturers, Congress, or the public at large might do keeps things more manageable. It is hard enough to deal with oneself, one's spouse, and others in the immediate environment. It seems very, very difficult and quite possibly fruitless to take on Congress, a corporation, an industry, or a society-wide way of life. In fact, the few couples who tried, through lawsuits or lobbying legislatures or school districts to take on matters related to their child's death found it energy draining, emotionally demanding, and frustrating. For most couples, almost any way of thinking and acting that calls for taking on large, distant, and powerful entities can seem far beyond their available emotional and energy resources.

Relations among Common Domains

Some of the narrative domains that bereaved parents use in talking about the death and its aftermath overlap with others. For example religious languages, languages of blame, and languages of anger all deal with issues of how the death came to be, whether it should have happened, whether it was a good thing, and how the parent should feel about the death. Also, some of the domains are functionally linked—for example, anything that happens can be understood as having a relationship to a couple's marriage, to God, or to parents surviving their children. Since the domains of narrative overlap, it is possible for a bereaved parent to move among domains or to combine domains while talking, even within the same sentence. Typically, though, a parent's narrative seemed to stay for sentences or even paragraphs in what seems to me to be a specific domain. That was an indication that it makes sense to separate the domains analytically.

From another perspective, the narrative domains were not necessarily well linked to other domains. Repeatedly, with every parent, a narrative in some domain would end rather than flow into some other domain. A question had to be asked in order to begin the flow with a new domain. Perhaps that is only an artifact of the question and answer organization of the interview and the implicit turn-taking requirement in the cultural models of conversation and of interview. But in some interviews there were times when the narrative would continue for five or ten minutes or longer and would flow from domain to domain without prompting by the interviewer. So some people, some of the time, were not stopped by the question and answer nature of the interview or the cultural models of conversation and of interview. I think the stops in narrative were, at least some of the time, about the ways that some domains are not well connected to others. Bereaved parents do not necessarily hunt for linkages, and life may be lived in ways that compartmentalize experience so that nothing happens to link one area to another, for example, to link marital sexuality with funeral ritual.

What Is Gained from Organizing Narratives in Domains

What parents gain from functioning largely within what seems to be a relatively small number of narrative domains includes a manageable organization to reality about the death and their grief. When life-dominating events can be defined and described within a relatively small number of domains, there is more of a sense that one can achieve some competence and expertise in thinking and talking about things, and there is an economy of thinking and figuring things out. There also is a sense of where to focus attention. With too many foci, it might be hard to focus on anything. But people need to focus in order to figure things out. Thus, having a small number of domains aids in evaluating past, present, and possible futures, and provides a basis for choosing futures, and a way to put into words what can be very messy, complex, confusing, and ambiguous.

There also is likely to be a relatively small number of narrative domains because a person's language and culture offer a relatively small number of dominant domains. The choice of culturally dominant domains of language means that the parents are using culturally meaningful (and perhaps widely shared) rhetorics for constructing realities (Shotter, 1993, p. 6) with others. The choice of domains that make sense in their culture puts them in a position to persuade others (and themselves) of the validity of what they have to say (Shotter, 1993, p. 6). It means they can pick up print sources dealing with death and grief and find material relevant to what they have been talking about. It means they can go to support groups or counselors and engage in conversations that make sense in terms of what they have been thinking and talking about. And the culturally dominant domains probably link well to what they have thought, said, and heard in the past, long before the child died, about life, death, emotional pain, and relationships.

There are risks to relationships with others in taking on society about big issues. One is no longer like the others around one, and in some sense one can be seen to make the community an enemy. For example, a couple who sued a state agency over regulations that mandated child-endangering designs on public fishing piers faced enormous community hostility because their suit was a claim on taxes paid by everybody and because it seemed to some that they were trying to profit from their child's death.

☐ What Can Be Gained by Studying Bereaved Parent Narrative

Parent narratives represent parents' realities in their own terms, what they have thought about, and what is important to them. The words and organizing ideas parents use in talking about loss and grief shape their grief and create it. Their narratives define their needs, become the medium for defining paths to take and not to take, and are the tools available for problem solving. Narratives are not rare or abnormal attributes of verbal production but are predominant and central in people's lives; left on their own to talk about their lives, people generate narratives (Polkinghorne, 1988). Social researchers may ignore people's narratives or try to silence or abbreviate them in the interests of moving to some sort of precision (Mishler, 1986), but narrative is at the core of what people have to say about what is important to them.

At the couple level, language is what they must use as they work out or fail to work out shared realities about the death and differences between partners. If there are couple difficulties, their narratives may be a source of the differences and will certainly reflect and help to define their differences and the paths to coming to terms with them. Thus, parent narratives provide a window into parent relationships and into why those relationships may be rocky.

Parent narratives lead the parent and the listener away from some places. An astute listener would do well to pay attention to what is not being said. What do parent narratives deflect attention from? I think often what is not said includes things too painful or threatening to deal with. I also think that it often includes things that might be better (for the bereaved parent, for the couple relationship, for society) to attend to. From that perspective, the gaps in what bereaved parents have to say are, in a sense, invitations to help the parents find new sources of strength, insight, support, and problem solving. But also in those gaps are warnings to those who would help that these are areas that might be dangerous to enter.

By attending to the language of bereaved parents, we will be better able not only to understand the complexities of their grief process and their couple relationship, but also to listen to them, understand them, communicate with them, help them if they want help, and understand aspects of U.S. cultures that have a major impact on the grief process.

In the domains of parent narrative are the languages and concepts for addressing their experience that presumably seem to parents to be culturally legitimate and to make the most sense. From that perspective, the domains of parent narrative point to the areas in which those of us who write about bereavement probably will find the most acceptance professionally and in the public for our theorizing—because these are the domains that count the most with the most people in U.S. society. On the surface, it seems a lot more sensible to theorize about areas that many parents discuss (for example, how medical information supports or undermines the grief process). It seems a lot less sensible to theorize about areas that parents never or almost never discuss (for example, how medical and religious ways of knowing dying and death make it almost impossible for parents to describe a child's dying and death purely in terms of what they see and hear).

☐ What Parents Say Is Rooted in Culture and Community

The narratives that bereaved parents use are a product of their culture and time (Smart, 1993)—the words and concepts available to them, languages for creating narrative, and the social systems in which they exist. Their narratives are a representation of the culturally important issues for bereaved parents, the tasks, roles, rights, and responsibilities for grieving parents as they are defined in their culture. The analysis of bereaved parent narrative is necessarily an analysis of parental bereavement in the context of culture. The narrative domains address the needs, tasks, and concerns that are defined and created for bereaved parents by their culture(s)—including what to do about solace, about getting along with those who are not bereaved, understanding how the death came about, dealing with personal pain and a partner's pain, continuing to relate to the child who died, and continuing to function in an economy and country that does not grant most bereaved parents a bereavement leave of absence.

The language bereaved parents use comes from the cultures and communities in which they exist. No parent who was interviewed developed neologisms to deal with their child's death and its aftermath, and none turned to a language other than English in speaking with the interviewer about the death. I do not suppose for a moment that people are exactly the same with a visiting interviewer as they would be by themselves or with someone else, but I also do not suppose that they are or can be entirely different. I think they cannot avoid saying a lot to an interviewer that is part of their everyday language and thoughts and that is linked to the cultures and communities in which they have functioned and now function.

One could argue that people's choice of domains came out of the structure of the interview and the interviewer choice of questions. And it is true that many of the domains identified through the titles of chapters and chapter sections in the book are in areas that most people were asked questions by the interviewer. But many people brought up these topic areas without prompting, and the interview questions asked of most parents represented a sense of what previously interviewed parents had brought up. Also, some of the topics represented in the chapters were not brought out by direct questions—for example, upbringing and other sources of how parents came to grieve, parent metaphors for grief and the grief process, and parent learning what there is to say. Also, some areas of questioning in the interview schedule yielded material so sparse that it is not worth writing about in this book—for example, parent health problems related to the child's dying and death or the influence of the grieving of other family members (their parents, siblings, in-laws, etc.) on the parent grieving.

The ways people speak about grief, understand it, express it, and feel it are inseparable from the cultures and communities in which they have been and are embedded. So are the ways my research assistants and I interview and the ways I analyze the interviews and write about them. As we interview we are providing emphases, words, concepts, and perspectives that feed into and shape the narratives we are told. That makes my written narratives here about people's narratives products of my cultures and communities.

Although everyone interviewed in this study was a native speaker of English, they represent a range of cultures in that they differed among themselves in how much they were connected to the world of psychology, social sciences, therapy, Christianity, Judaism, spiritualism, medicine, and the popular grief literature. Although the few immigrants in the study were from English speaking countries, the interviewees represent a range of cultures in that some were only one or two generations removed from family members who spoke languages other than English at home.

A sign of the times is how the languages of social sciences, theories of the grief process, grief popularizations, support groups, and grief counseling have entered everyday narrative of grieving individuals (Brice, 1991a; Gubrium & Holstein, 1998; Holstein & Gubrium, 1995b; Wambach, 1985–86)—for example, words about stages in grief or about the importance of expressing grief feelings. The following interview excerpt provides an illustration of the ways people used language from grief popularizations. The popularization was not so real for this couple that they could remember the details, and yet it was real enough to give them a language for organizing some of what they had to say about how they grieved.

Stan: I can't even remember how many stages, there's a specific number of stages of grief that they figured out and, what's it like, seven?

Joy: Yeah, five or seven or something. There's denial. . . .

Stan: Yeah, I can't remember but (*Joy:* denial, guilt, anger, probably five) whatever. I think we pretty much went through most of them the same.

Except, I think I was more angry than Joy was. I was pretty angry at the lady [who caused the fatal accident], I was angry at [my brother-in-law], and I just know I was angry at a different time. Maybe it was longer than Joy was. Otherwise, we pretty much coincided with the different stages....

Joy: I would say probably the first stage for me was denial. I remember I used to be out and I would think "Well, when I come home, Jenny will be there." I don't know how long that went on.

Stan: I think we went through a lot of it just kinda numb.

Joy: That's really how I remember the first part, being just really numb.

Stan: Yeah, just kinda days ran into days and

Joy: I remember just actually physically hurting, like my muscles ... physically ached. I had never physically ached like that in my life.

Stan: And you're just drained.

In my experience, bereaved people almost never say, "I have no words to say what I feel." This may be because without words one does not feel or it is hard to know what one feels. People are captured by the words they use. Things get shoved aside or never are created if language cannot be used to describe them or perhaps think them. Not having words one would not know that one does not have words, and having words one would not know what one would get to if one had different words. My guess is that for most people the words start out, at best, only dealing with a part of what could make sense to them, fit their experience, and have meanings that seem to them to be culturally acceptable. I also believe that people generally come to think, feel, and act in ways that fit their words. So even though they start out imprecisely and knowing (or with a potential to know) that the words do not say it all, they are likely later on to feel that their experiences and feelings are fully captured by the language they speak.

I think on the rare occasion when bereaved parents say "I have no words to say what I felt" they are talking about feelings they have not talked about before, as in the following quote, where Joy fishes for words for something she remembers but maybe never talked about.

Joy: I remember just feeling, I don't even know what the word is, when [my husband] was home, at the beginning. I don't know even what I was really afraid of. That something might happen with [our son who survived the accident that killed our daughter] or ... that I wouldn't be able to handle by myself.

☐ Parent Grief Is Relational

What bereaved parents say is relational in many different senses (Brice, 1989). Their grief is about the end of a relationship with a living child and the end of an anticipated future relationship with that child. Their grief is also about a struggle to continue a relationship with the child. Their grief may be about the end of relationships with others who were linked to them via the child. Their grief is told in relationship—in an interview setting where the interviewer is always present and where, in most cases, the spouse is present. Their grief is storied in ways that make it seem to be something that comes from and is intended to be talked about in relationship. In fact, Brice (1989) said that the bereaved always mourn *to* someone, that a dialogical relationship is necessary to provide the existential place in which to mourn. Moreover, relationships with God, the community, spouse, family, friends, coworkers, religious congregation, surviving or subsequently born children, physicians and nurses, and possibly the police, a support group, and many others are important in parent stories.

The relational aspects of talking about grief in the interview context can be understood in many ways—for example, cocreating realities, playing to an audience, choosing language to fit who is present, censoring what might not be appropriate for the audience, being reminded of things by those present. It could be partly a matter of performing a selection of all that could be said, but not changing what is firmly in memory to tell. Talking about grief seemed, for some parents, also to be a matter of coming to new realizations, new realities, new senses of self or what happened, and new senses of the spouse.

At still another level, parent grief during the interview was in some kind of relationship to parent perceptions of who would be reading what I wrote—grieving parents, practitioners who work with the bereaved, and researchers and teachers whose work focuses on grief. Where that comes out most clearly in the interview is when parents offer advice for other bereaved parents. But it is hard to know whether parents ever forgot, in the interviews, that anything they said could help or be judged by many other people.

☐ The Language of Grief Theories

Theories, like narratives, invariably mask, simplify, and focus selectively. Grief theories educate us and shape our realities, though they do not say a tenth of what could be said if we were trying to account for all that we might conceivably claim is part of bereavement. Some grief theories may seem only to be low level empirical generalizations or very general guides to use in helping the bereaved. And yet grief theories define grief, providing us with a set of lenses that focus our attention.

A central symbol of what grief theories gain and lose for us is the issue of defining "grief" or "bereavement." The reader may expect and even want a definition of grief or bereavement. But defining grief is in some ways self-defeating, because there are many different kinds, forms, and expressions of what might be called grief. What might be called grief is fluid, changing, socially defined, and compounded of many things that come and go, change in meaning and intensity, and overlap with many other things that might or might not be productively considered part of grief. Also, grief theories generally deal with individual feeling and action, and I am not willing to grant that grief is only, or even primarily, an individual phenomenon. I think it makes sense to talk about griefs that are couple, familial, or community. However, I also think we can do great mischief by pretending feelings and thoughts are shared that are not (see Gilbert, 1996). Perhaps it would be best if we had different terms for different kinds of griefs—for example, individualgrief, familygrief, communitygrief.

I think there is no essential grief. What might be better defined are areas for an observer to begin to look. But the observer must recognize that the observer's own realities deserve no more privilege than the realities of the people observed. In fact, if we are ever to understand other people's experiences of grief, we must be open to the diversity of their understandings and experiences and the ways they differ from anything our theories tell us to look at or anything we have ourselves ever experienced. One thing that is gained by focusing on the narratives of bereaved people is that we back away from essentializing the language and experience of theorist and observer and open ourselves more than we might otherwise to the complexity, diversity, and fluidity of grief as people talk about it.

A related matter is that the language of theory is a generalizing language—one size, one concept fits all. Why not assume we are so different from one another that the theories that fit some of us are unlikely to fit many others? Instead of believing in or working toward grief theories that will fit all bereaved people or toward a single concept of grief or a single concept of the grief process (Stroebe, 1992–93), we might be better at understanding others if we work with a diversity of theories and understandings that we do not assume apply to everybody. I believe that working with narratives is an excellent route to reaching that diversity of theories and understandings of grief. By focusing on a diversity of narratives we draw away from essentializing the theoretical language and concepts we as scholars and professionals use.

I do not want to argue, however, that the language of grief theorists, grief researchers, and grief practitioners is unconnected with the language of the everyday experience of grief. The language of scholars and professionals comes out of their own experiences and cultures and out of their contacts with bereaved people who talk about their experiences.

Although the focus of this book is the narrative of bereaved parents, I do not want to discount the theoretical languages that have been used by scholars in talking about parental grief. One way I deal with the conflict between parent perspectives and scholar perspectives is to try to make use of scholarly perspectives even as I focus on parent perspectives. For example, I try to take the life course perspective (de Vries, Dalla Lana, & Falck, 1994) into account in discussing diversity over time and across couples, even though I do not move explicitly into a life course framework. The theory of grief work (Rosenblatt, 1983a), the dominant though now seriously questioned (Stroebe, 1992–93) theory in the grief field, must be taken seriously, even though the focus on narrative can be seen to challenge that theory. Still, the majority of research studies I cite in this book seem to me to have been carried out within a grief work framework. I also take social constructionist perspectives very seriously (e.g., Gergen, 1994; Neimeyer & Stewart, 1996; Shotter, 1990). The concern with narrative here is certainly constructionist, and yet by privileging the words of the people interviewed as much as I do, I try not to make the social constructionist framework the focus of the book. The focus is the language of bereaved parents.

In this book I focus on couples who were married to each other at the time of the child's death. I do so because I think the entanglement of the marital relationship in the construction and content of parent narratives must be understood. But I do not want in any way to discount the grieving of unmarried parents or of people other than parents who are grieving for a child who has died.

☐ Studying Language Using Language

There is an obvious problem in studying language by using language. My assistants and I have elicited information orally, privileging the language of our interview guide. I have transcribed the oral interviews into my written language, and now I convey excerpts from those transcriptions and my analysis of what people said in my own written language. I am not an invisible, objective communication link but an active elicitor, stimulus, interpreter, translator, summarizer, selector, and advocate, always working with and captured by my own language. I hope that I do not swamp the language, experiences, and realities of the people interviewed with my own language, but I also have no doubt that my language shapes and masks a lot.

☐ Summary

This chapter has defined what the book is about—the narratives of bereaved parents. That bereaved parents have narratives, organized stories about their child's dying and death and the aftermath of the death, is an important finding in itself. Their experience becomes organized coherently, in ways that make sense. Another important finding is that the narratives of bereaved parents generally feature a relatively small and defined number of domains (for example, death rituals and the gulf that the death creates between themselves and others). Although many other relevant domains are conceivable, they came up in no or almost no parent narrative. In discussing the structuring of parent narratives in terms of domains, the chapter speculates about cultural, societal, interactional, and psychological factors that are related to that structuring. As is argued in the chapter, there is much to be gained from studying parent narratives. The next chapter takes the next step in studying the narratives of bereaved parents. It explores the processes, as parents talked about them, of coming to their narratives.

Coming to a Couple Language about the Death

☐ Immediate Pressure to Construct New Realities

A child's death demands that the parents frame, account for, think about, come to meanings about, and talk about the death and its aftermath. To the extent that they were living within a narrative of parenting the child who died and of a future that included the living child, they must come to new narratives that deal with the death and its unfolding aftermath. To accomplish all this, the parents must learn new ways to use their language.

Often parents are upset with physicians who give a fatal diagnosis. They speak about the lack of emotional support and human feeling. I do not question that physicians often communicate with insufficient emotional support or human feeling, but I think part of what some parents experience as lack of emotional support or human feeling is a lack of sufficient help with the new realities the fatal diagnosis calls for. A parent who receives such help may be very appreciative.

Amy: We *did* go outside of the system ... for a second opinion.... He ... verified where I was at when he said, "You're living in a world that's not natural, and you have to adjust. And you have got to make it natural for the rest of the survival." And it was like, "Yeah, this isn't natural. Thank you for saying that. I need that acknowledgment. I'm going nuts."

The death of a child confronts parents with dreadful demands to think in new ways about events that are probably unprecedented in their experience, and with immensely difficult choices that must be made. The parents may have been asked to make the agonizingly painful decision about how vigorously to try to prolong the child's life. Making that decision and making sense out of it and what happened after the decision was made are enormously challenging matters in themselves. After a child dies, many beliefs, goals, routines, commitments, and relationships become open to question or may no longer seem valid. The parents must deal with issues of how to think of the child and their relationship to the child, what the future will be, how they have been and are parents to the child who died, what their responsibilities are and will be, whether anything can or should be changed, whether they or others have made mistakes, what to do about their ordinary life routines, and who they are as individuals and as a couple. They must relearn the world (Attig, 1990, 1996; Parkes, 1972). To compound their problems, decisions typically have to be made immediately about death rituals, such matters as whether there should be an autopsy (or how to deal with the fact that the law requires an autopsy), which funeral director to call, how the child should be dressed for the funeral, whether to have a cremation, and if the child is to be buried where the burial should be. Deciding about these matters is very challenging when all of reality has been thrown open to question, and dealing with these decisions intensifies questions about reality.

To construct new realities and reconstruct old ones, a parent must have some grounding for thinking, feeling, acting, relating, deciding, and talking. The grounding must come out of language, but few parents start out with language fully in place to deal with a child's death. Moreover, they will be constantly challenged by the language others use, language that pushes them toward realities that seem strange and that may call for perspectives, understandings, and identities that are unacceptable.

Vince: Before we left [the hospital] we had to . . . discharge the body. . . . They were real matter-of-fact. . . . [Imitating an unfeeling, matter-of-fact voice:] "And you, [last name], where do you want the body?" It's like, "How the hell do I know? . . . I woke up this morning; my kid was alive. I don't have a clue what to do next." And they were just so matter-of-fact. They were desensitized to the whole deal. . . . If you discharge bodies all day, well sure. And it's just like an accountant, this bean goes in this pile, this bean goes in this pile, where do you want this bean, mister? . . . Since the infant's under a certain age they gotta have an autopsy. You have to go down to the coroner and do an autopsy, see if there's any *child abuse* . . . and see if the kid was murdered. "What!? Hey, I didn't murder my kid." "Well, it's a state law. You gotta do it."

For all sorts of reasons, a couple whose child is dying or has just died may talk with each other intensively about what confronts them as a result of the death. Among the reasons is that they need both as individuals and as a couple to come to language dealing with the death well enough to make decisions that must be made immediately.

Kelly: At 4 o'clock that Sunday morning, I had [the nurses] call [my husband], ... because of her condition ... being worse, and I knew that we would be losing her. And I wanted him there, because I knew he needed that closure.... He came back to the hospital, and we talked about the possibility of losing her. And we realized that we needed, for the family we needed to have her baptized. And we knew that was completely out of our hands, what was going on, [and that] we would have a complete funeral.

Erika: I guess we tried to include each other with, what are we gonna do this Christmas [the child died just before Christmas], and what are we going to take to church, and what are we taking to the grave.

Barb: We laid there that first night and talked 'til it was time to get up and milk. We didn't sleep.

☐ Numbness and Having No Reality to Draw On

A child's death in some sense ends the world in which the parents have lived (Brice, 1991a, 1991b). Because of the death, the couple is no longer able to rely on major assumptions they have made about themselves and the world (Gilbert & Smart, 1992, pp. 28–32). Without the map, the concepts, or the mental organization to enter a new world, a couple may have little or no basis for talking and thinking about the child's dying or death or reacting to it. Among the signs of this lack of a reality base are numbness and a resistance to the reality of the death that is not only emotional but also cognitive.

Vince: I was at work, and I get this call from the sheriff. "Hi, this is the ... sheriff. You've got a problem. Better get home." And I says, "What's the matter?" He says, "Come on home." ... I hop in the car and ride home. I don't know what the hell is goin' on. Zillion things are going through my head.... Come flyin' down [the street] here, and I see all these cop cars. And "What the hell?!" I ... pull in the driveway, fly in, see all these police all over the place.... "What's goin' on?" Gail says, "[The baby] is dead! Randy is dead!" And I ... wouldn't believe it.

Amy: We came home. Ted didn't go back to work that day, and we just sat. We just didn't know almost how to react.

As Gilbert and Smart also found (1992, pp. 32–34), some parents talked about the sense of being in a dream, that things were floating or were not really happening. One way to understand those feelings is by understanding that the parents lacked language that could give them a firm base for dealing with what had happened.

Joan: Everything felt kind of like a dream, I guess, like it wasn't really happening. And I always thought that even after Alex died, I thought that this all seems so unreal. . . . A lot of times I just felt like I was floating through the day and into the next day, and then into the next day, and it was all just kind . . . of a blur, just kinda all melting into everything.

To the extent that adult memory is encoded in language, it is another sign of the lack of having come to a language that some bereaved parents cannot recall much from the time immediately after a child died.

Karl: I don't remember anything from that time. I don't remember a thing. . . .

Kathy: Whatever we did numbed us, yeah. (*Karl:* Yeah.)

Karl: I don't remember what it was.

Kathy: I don't remember much either. . . . I think we were just like in another dimension, and operating along side ourselves, and just kind of going through the motions of being alive. But not really there, 'cause we don't remember that much.

Karl: And I never realized that. We have not talked about this. And this is the first time I've tried to think, "What were we doing (*Kathy:* Yeah), during those times?" And I don't remember a thing from then. . . . We'd kind of withdraw from each other too. . . . We were like in different worlds for a long, long period of time.

"Going through the motions" is a common report from early in bereavement (Hogan, Morse, & Tasón, 1996), and with it comes a sense of being detached from experience and not being attuned to what is going on outside or inside oneself.

☐ Shared Couple Narratives

Resonating with Nadeau's (1998) research on couple and family meaning-making in bereavement, all the bereaved couples who were interviewed, even those who had rocky relationships before the death or who had later on separated or divorced, told of together trying to come to shared ways of talking about the child's death and its aftermath. They brought to the new situation a common general language, a common culture, and years of experience together. But coming to shared narratives was not automatic or simple.

Searching for What Is True and Right

All parents displayed what could be called a psychological essentialism (Gergen, 1994) in that they talked as though there is a real reality to be known and told. All said, in one way or another, that they had been and were searching for what was true and right about the death, their grieving, and their couple relationship since the death. That does not mean that the parents always achieved a firm reality. In fact, many narratives included accounts of doubt and uncertainty. Although they worked hard to make sense of what happened and what was true and right, quite a few parents talked about feeling uncertain in the days, weeks, and months after the death. At that time they were worn out a good deal of the time, distracted, disorganized, and in other ways not in a good place to think things through or carry their side of a couple interaction about the death and its aftermath.

Erika: I was tired a lot, very tired.... I could sleep so hard, without dreaming.... Grieving is so exhausting. I was so tired, for a long time. That whole first year seems kind of a blur....

Chad: She went to bed at seven o'clock....

Erika: It was very hard to concentrate. We're all forgetful, but it was just so hard to remember things. That's why that first year, a lot of it is a blur. What did I do? And what did I say? And what did you say to me?... And we did what? Or where did we go?

Chad: I had to *re-a-lly* push myself to sit in the office, just to pay the monthly bills....

Erika: Everything was overwhelming.

Chad: Yeah. To just sit down and do (bang on table) something was just hard to do.

Another part of the uncertainty some couples experienced in trying to develop clear realities about the death and the aftermath was that they had a sense that the marital relationship was not a trustworthy or solid place for grounding realities about the death. Questions about the marital relationship reinforced uncertainties arising from the death about how they had lived their life and what the right things were to do. (However, even in their questioning of the marital relationship, couples typically came to shared narratives.)

Hannah: We've always had marital problems, *always.* And Fred's always been kind of controlling and ... I've always been kind of enabling.... I don't do that. I started taking care of myself, and there's a lot of resentment, and my therapist told me that sometimes those things surface when a major trauma happens. And you just never deal with them until something really big happens.... The arguments we have in the last 12 months have been because when Fred gets angry ... he'll say really cruel things. (*Fred:* Yeah.) ... He came home one day and he said, "When I came home today I was hoping I'd find you like I found your son, and then my problems would be over." And those are the kinds of things that just stick.

Fred: You get a call at work and it starts a big argument, or you leave the house to go some place or do something and it's a big, nasty, you know, she's tellin' me this stuff and this stuff and this stuff. And I run away; I will leave. Then when I come home, yeah, I'll say something like that. I'm still angry, when you walk in the door and she starts in on you again, and yeah, I say something nasty. Then I feel sorry for her, but it's said and done. And you can't take it back.... That is probably the biggest thing ..., and it's remembering things that I used (his voice sounds husky) to do, and then remembers that she used to do, the bad things.... It's not ... remembering the laughing, the joking, the happy times, the stuff we used to do for enjoyment. All the good stuff is gone. It's just the anger, the hateful stuff, the stuff that should be swept under the rug....

Hannah: We never dealt with the bad stuff before either.

Fred: But no, and now it's all the bad stuff, not the good stuff. There is no good. We don't even think of talking about anything that's good.

Marital Conversation about the Death

The Spouse as Primary Conversation Partner

Although parents differed enormously in how much they said that they had talked with their partner about the child's death, many parents said that the person they talked to the most about the death was their spouse. This was especially so for the first months after the death, when much of reality about the death and about individual and couple reactions to the death was being formed.

AH: With whom would you say you talked the most about Randy's death?

Gail: The first six months, a year, two years, I would say [my husband]. If you asked me that after a few months had passed, I would say without any question [my husband]. And since then, that has changed. We talk *lots* about Randy now,... but I do talk more to other friends about, not just about Randy, or where he would be or what he'd be doing,... but *my* feelings, how I see things, how I reflect on things, what I see.... I would say I talk more to friends, certainly my family.... It's not a huge amount either. It's occasionally here and there.

AH: With whom would you say that you've talked the most about Leanne's life and death?

Lance: ... [My wife] ... primarily.

AH: And would you say that you think that [she] knows best where you're at emotionally now with [the death]?

Lance: Yes.

Couples with Little or No Talk

A few couples said that talk about the child who died and the aftermath of the death was virtually absent for long periods of time, either because the man in the couple isolated himself from the woman or because one or both partners felt uncomfortable with couple conversation.

Nick: I didn't know ... that I needed people.... So I've been six years of total or close to six years of total ... by myself deal, where I didn't let anybody in. I didn't let her in. Nobody. My kids in.

Molly: A few times, maybe, we said something and ended up being angry, both of us crying or one of us crying.... We couldn't talk. We still can't. That's why I said there had to be separate interviews. He was very accusatory. I couldn't do it. [The couple had divorced.]

Partners in couples who interacted so little may for a time, perhaps even for years, be emotionally, socially, sexually, and in other ways distant from each other, living more like strangers in the same rooming house than like spouses. The lack of interaction about the death may be a cause of the distance, a consequence of it, both cause and consequence, or both the lack of interaction and the distance may result from other things—for example, a pattern of disrespectful communication (Rosenblatt, Titus, & Cunningham,

1979). However, even with couples who interacted little or who bickered and disagreed intensely over most matters, there were still areas of shared narrative and agreement.

Hannah: Our grandchildren, and we both agree that they're wonderful and we both enjoy spending time with them, and that's probably the only common ground, don't you think? (*Fred:* yeah.) And paying bills, that's (he laughs) probably the only common ground.

It seems that even with little or no interaction shared narratives develop. Every couple interviewed had substantial areas of shared narrative. How couples who do not get along well or who interact little can achieve shared narrative is puzzling, but Book (1996) talks about the ways shared narratives about death can arise in situations where family members do not talk about death. For example, people can learn what others think through what is not said, through impressions, and through application of or generalization from implicit and explicit family rules. They may also overhear the spouse talking with others.

A case can be made that it is necessary to come to narratives about the death that fit adequately with the narratives of other family members. If there is too much discrepancy among family member narratives, that constitutes a threat to the believability and reality of each person's narratives (cf. Hinchman & Hinchman, 1997, p. 121). Then family relationships may become extremely difficult because, in a sense, it is shared narrative that constitutes community (Hinchman & Hinchman, 1997, p. 235).

Narratives of Couples Who Had Talked a Lot

Spouses who had talked a lot with each other about the death and its aftermath spoke about having reached a place where they knew well how one another felt and thought and where they shared many feelings and thoughts.

Jane: We talked a lot and ... I knew we were kinda thinking the same things a lot of times.... I remember for example two years ago, [at a graduation].... There was a family that lives close by here, who have a daughter the same age as *ours* ... whose name is [the same as ours]. And a boy the same age as Adam [would be], whose name is Adam.... *All* these years we've seen this other little Adam grow up. And that day, I remember clearly, that Rob and I just looked at each other, and I knew what he was thinking and (sighs) there were tears in his eyes that if our Adam had lived, they would be graduating together. And it was hard to see this little

Adam graduating. . . . Anytime you do anything really fun over the years, . . . I know that Rob is thinking, or he'll say something that, "Wouldn't it be fun if there were two of 'em here."

Many such couples talked together to the interviewer about the death, their grief, how they dealt with the death, how they felt with it, not in a monologue, but in a shared narrative. One partner might have the primary story line at the moment, but the other would punctuate that line with words of agreement, clarification, amplification, or continuation, saying in effect, "I agree with what is being said and even if I differ in minor ways it is my story too."

Sue: They told us it was terminal right from the beginning. (*Gabe:* yeah) There was never any, they never gave us any reason to hope that (*Gabe:* Yes. Nothing to do.) she was going live. (*Gabe:* Nothing about it.) It was just, "She's gonna die."

Denny: We prayed the day he died, and then I had to curse myself for that, because I said, "Hey, if you're gonna take him," (*Marsha:* "take him.") "take him, 'cause this roller coaster we've been on for 10 weeks is just terrible." One day, "Oh, his numbers are great. He's fine." The next day, "Better get him here. . . ." I said that the day it happened. I'll never forget it. I just, it's kind of . . . should I [have] said that or not . . .?

Marsha: When you start thinking as a parent, you start thinking about not just the life of your child but the quality of life (*Denny:* Yeah). Wearing a bag is one thing, but you wonder, our son was so tiny that there's things like cerebral palsy (*Denny:* Many, many things that can go wrong), mental retardation, seizures. There's a lot of things that can go wrong.

Even when narratives were shared couple productions, there still might be disagreements. It is likely that a couple will not achieve identical realities about a death because part of each partner's narratives connected to the death is an account of the self, the self in relationship to the child, the partner, and all else (Riches & Dawson, 1996). With different selves, partners cannot have quite the same story to tell about the death (Sedney, Baker, & Gross, 1994), and some things may never be said to the partner, never heard by the partner, or never understood by the partner. Partners speak sort of, but not exactly, the same language.

Amy: I think that [grief] is just, there again reminds me of just how personal it is, and how "me" it is, and how, in a lot of ways, how separate it is from [my husband].

Joan: I wouldn't really know that he felt that way until maybe couple of months later, and then he'd say something. . . . Our feelings were kind of our own, unless we wanted to share them. . . . If I'd say, "I'm just having a bad day today" . . . he'd just say, "Okay. Well, let me know if there's anything I can do." We just kinda let each other deal with it . . . , 'cause we knew we were gonna deal with it differently.

The imperfect congruence of partner realities also comes from the vagaries of memories. Sometimes a couple agreed that they did something but were far from agreeing about details.

Rob: For a while we did see [person's name].

Jane: Yeah, a psychologist. . . .

Rob: A psychologist . . . initially just for, well, for the whole family. [Our daughter] was there, and then Jane, and I also did see him for maybe a year or two (*Jane:* Once, I think). Yeah, we went to him for a year or more.

Jane: Really? I don't remember that. How many times did we go?

Rob: Oh, once a month or something like that.

Jane: Oh, I don't remember that at all.

So in the couples who had developed large areas of shared narrative there were differences. In fact, some couples said that without granting each other latitude to differ, they would have trouble getting along as a couple and getting on with their grieving.

Gail: It seemed like, at first, we were just very tight and very close, and we just moved *re-e-al* slow ahead together, and not without each other. We wouldn't move, until whenever the day was that one of us moved a little bit differently. And we started to realize that . . . it was *happening* to us, and it was pointed *out* to us after we went to group and heard it talked about. But certainly we could see that happening to each other, before we went to group. (*Vince:* Yeah.) See it happening.

Vince: Yep. And I feel real sorry for the couples that don't have it pointed out to them, that it's *okay*. I feel really, really sorry for the people that think that they need to be on the same level at the same time. And if one person moves off of that level that they should be criticized. They *shouldn't* be criticized. They need to know that it's okay to be at different levels at different times.

☐ Summary

Typically a child's death brings the death of key narrative structures within which parents have been living. With the death, many of the ways the parents have related to the world and talked about it no longer make sense. That puts immediate pressure on parents to develop new narratives. They are also pressured to develop new narratives in order to make sense of the death, to make immediate decisions concerning the death, and to deal with others talking to them about the death. Typically, a couple will talk most to one another about the death and its aftermath; particularly they will do this early in bereavement. This leads to the development of shared (though not identical) narratives. Even couples who do not talk much after the death or whose relationship is highly conflictful have substantial areas of agreement and overlapping narrative.

As I define "narrative," parent narratives have a temporal quality; what they have to say is organized around the progression of events or experiences. Typically they begin with the child's dying. In the next few chapters, that temporal organization will be respected, making it easier for the reader to track what is typical in the narratives of bereaved parents. So the next chapter talks about what was at the beginning of the parent narratives: the child's dying and death.

3

The Story of Dying and Death

☐ Every Parent Had a Story of the Death

All parents had a story of the child's death. Most told a vivid, detailed, at times intensely emotional story, one that they seemed to know well and that seemed fresh in their memory (Peppers & Knapp, 1980, p. 20), even if the events occurred many years ago. The organizing event of every story was the child's death. Every story included an account of how the child came to die, a naming of characters and an explanation of who the characters were, an explanation of how the death occurred, an account of experiences at the time of the death and in the weeks and months afterwards, a temporal organization, and words about how devastating the death was. The temporal organization, the focus on a central event, and the identification of a cast of characters is consistent with U.S. cultural models for story telling (Cochran & Claspell, 1987; Gergen, 1994). Having a patterned account of events and feelings over time connected to a death is also consistent with U.S. cultural models of a grief process (Cochran & Claspell, 1987, pp. 28–36).

Not only did every bereaved parent tell a story of the death, but consistent with reports from other research (Gilbert & Smart, 1992, p. 39; Knapp, 1986, p. 30; Martinson, 1991; Raphael, 1983, p. 249), many said that they had told the story many times before.

Vince: We have been extremely fortunate running across this group called Compassionate Friends.... We've had the opportunity to tell our story *hundreds* of times. And each time you tell it, it's very therapeutic.... With something like this it's like your storage shelf falls out and all these boxes full of things came unraveled, and each time you talk about it you get a chance to put these pieces back into the boxes and get the shelf organized.

Elaine: I don't think we spent a day alone for what? . . . Six weeks after that? Someone always was here with us. Some people said they didn't think they could handle . . . all those people. But for me and for us, we, you need somebody to tell that story over and over and over. . . . You need people that are willing to listen to it over and over, and I don't mean for months. I mean for years. . . . *You* never get sick of telling it. And that's how you get through that is to tell the story over and over and over.

The story of the death seemed for almost every couple to be a couple story. Even though partner stories are likely to differ (Sedney, Baker, & Gross, 1994), it is striking how much the stories were couple stories, with substantial areas of agreement.

A story of dying has an ending, the death. Some other parent stories have endings as well—for example, the story of the funeral and stories of solving relationship problems that resulted from the death. But many narratives of grieving parents are about events still in process and have a flavor of bringing the listener up to the present but not completing the story. For example, stories of how the couple relationship is different because of the death and stories of spiritual connections with the child who died are often stories in progress.

☐ Common Contextual Elements

Each story of the death began with the fact of the death. The death was the entry into the story, the reason for the story, and the organizing idea to which most elements of most stories related. But once the fact of the death was established, every story moved to a time before the death. Many stories told how the child came to be. For the death of a young child, stories often included details about pregnancy or difficulties in getting pregnant or adopting. For children who were born after a difficult pregnancy, the stories began well before they were born, perhaps even before they were conceived, with parents talking about their hopes and plans for having a child and perhaps about infertility treatment.

The stories provided an account of the child's and parents' travels on a path toward the death, and they always included, early in the story, a description of the entry onto that path, perhaps the first signs of illness or the decisions that led to the child being in a fatal accident. For children who from birth were in very bad health or who lived a long time near death, the story of their precarious life might be much more extensive than the story of their death.

Premonitions and Omens

As with accounts of premonitions or omens with other kinds of deaths (Nadeau, 1998, pp. 132–134), some parents said that they knew with certainty or near-certainty before the death that the child would die. Even stories of some parents who had no reason to think the child would die included parental premonitions of the death, something occurring to the parent in advance of the death.

Wayne: Louise had a premonition, in fact, all week, up until this time. . . . All that whole week, she was *really* feeling super-depressed. And she had me call [our son] . . . about 11 o'clock that night . . . to find out if he was okay. . . . And I *never* do that. When . . . any of our kids [are] on sleepovers, I don't call 'em and ask them if they're okay. But she just wanted me to call and find out if he's okay. So I called him and I talked a little bit and asked him how everything's going.

Some stories referred to omens or striking symbols in the environment.

Joy: Then right around 5 o'clock, which was the time we found out later was [when] Jenny died, there was this really bad storm. . . . It was like black as night out, and I remember sitting at work . . . [with] a really weird feeling that something wasn't right.

Elaine: I really believe there was signs that his life was coming to an end. . . . For one thing and this is weird but it's the honest to God truth, the year before, . . . I was . . . washing dishes one day and all the kids were outside playing and . . . for some reason it flashed through my mind that . . . if I was ever to lose one of these kids, it would be [him]. Now why would I think that? . . . I just "Ohhhh, what an icky thought." You try to get it out of your mind, and I did, and I never thought about it anymore until after that happened. . . . I even told [my best friend] about it. . . . It was such a scary feeling.

The Stories Locate Events in Time

All parent stories placed events in the stream of time. Their stories included temporal markers, particularly seasons, dates, times, and ages, that could help them and others to know the temporal context for events.

Paula: It was Memorial Day weekend.

Al: This one particular day in the fall we were getting ready to chop corn, me, and my boy, and my brother.

Molly: The kids were five and three, and they were playing in the living room.

The location of events in time does not mean that for these parents time had a constant flow. Some stretches of time flowed for the parents in a very different way from the precise markings of calendar and clock.

Bruce: The 10 days felt like six months.

Sally: No, it felt longer, like 10 years.

Angela: We brought [the baby] to the Girl Scout meeting, and all the girls held him and talked to him.... We left the meeting, and he was strapped in his car seat,... I backed the car up in the driveway, and I went to cover him with his blanket.... I saw the blood, there was blood comin' out of his nose (sounding desperately in pain), and he was limp. We got in the house; we called 911. It took *forever* for them to get here.

Alice: It still doesn't seem real, and yet it's a year and a month already, and it seems like yesterday.

The Stories Locate Events in Place and Space

Parent stories of a child's death always mentioned places and spaces. There were geographic markers, room arrangements, perhaps measures of distance; the child and the parents were located within some sort of boundaries. There was a layout. For example, a parental story of a death that involved a freeway included the freeway in the introductory remarks of the story of the death.

Wayne: He went to the sleepover, and he rode his bicycle, and it's across the freeway, on the other side of the freeway from where we are. Do you know this area?... There's a shopping center ... across that freeway.... there's a lot of townhouses over there. And that's [where] this boy lived. So he ... rode his bicycle over there. It must take only about 10 minutes to get there.

As another example of a spatial layout in a parent narrative, here is part of a story of a death on a farm.

Paula: Mom wanted me to go lay down for a while and get a little rest, and she was out hanging up clothes and keeping an eye on Jerry. And she had taken him away from the area where the bull was. We had a bull in an outside ... pen area. And she'd pulled him away from there three times already, and she brought him back up to the clothes line again, and put him on his trike. And apparently he rode his trike around the far side of the house and around the front and went right back down there again. And she heard him screaming and yelled at him to lay down, lay down. And he did, and the bull came at him again.

Characterizing the Child

The stories of events leading up to the death usually include a characterization of the child. The child is not merely a name but a person with distinguishing characteristics.

Joy: I feel like I should tell you a little bit about Jenny. She was the first grandchild on both sides of the family so she sort of grew up in an adult world.... She was just a real happy, joyful, really bright little girl. And she maintained ... a long distance relationship with my brother, which really amazed him.

Bill: He was very popular. He was very athletic.... He was very outgoing. He made friends very easily. (voice cracking, loud exhalation) Maybe too easily.

Part of what parents did when they characterized the child was to say that the child was special (more on this in Chapter 5). A second thing they did was to characterize the relationship of the child to her or his own dying, on a continuum from active planner of the death to helpless victim, and from unaware to fully aware of death coming.

Parents as Players

The language of the stories leading up to the death helps the listener to understand where the parents were at the time of the child's death, and what the parent relationship to the dying and death was—for example, actively trying to keep the child alive, passive witness, troubled decision maker, good parents who were unaware of the danger to the child.

Gail: I laid him down. It had been 10 minutes, and I put a lunch and sat down here next to [our four year old]. And I can remember hearing Jeff in there make the little baby gurgling noises and talk in [a baby way], and then ... the parent [of the child I was caring for] came a little later, ... close to 4:00. And all kinds of things, like putting the kids in the car *before* I went to, *all* those kinds of things, I naturally took on all the *guilt* from thinking that if those things had been different ... I could have gotten him up earlier, and he would have been alive.... That really did eat at me a lot, thinking that was my fault, and I could have prevented that. So when this doctor said, "You cannot prevent it. You can't stop it; you can't change it. It's inevitable. That's it." Then it didn't matter if I went and got him at 2:15 or 3:00 or ... 4:00.

Elaine: We must have asked ourselves to death for years, "If we'd have done this, if we'd have done that, if...." Red ... always blamed himself. "If I would have taught Kyle how to drive the tractor better. If I would have never sent him out in the field.... If we couldn't have got the tractor started. Why didn't we just leave the ... thing alone?" I had taken him to get his allergy shot ... that day, and the gal wasn't home to give it.... If he'd a gotten that ... he'd a went along to [the] football game; he wouldn't have been home. And in your mind and for all practical purposes you know there are no ifs. Accidents happen.... If I'd a been here could I have revived him? Could I have saved him? Just all those things.

In their stories, parents were sometimes desperate and frustrated players, trying to get help or save a child's life while limited by their own hysteria or lack of knowledge, the nonfunctioning of telephones or other crucial equipment, or the slowness of others to provide assistance.

Molly: I tried to call for help, and the phone didn't work. If you have two children, which one do you try to save. I took them out of the tub and laid them on the floor. I was hysterical.... I went outside, and I was screaming and screaming to the neighbor. The neighbor wasn't there.... [I] didn't have a car; nobody was home. Finally, flagged down somebody in the alley. And we each grabbed one of the girls. They were naked, wrapped them up, threw 'em in the car [to] get them to the hospital.... We tried CPR when they were on the floor, which one do you save? I couldn't (sobbing), I couldn't save even one (tears). There was a car accident, the roadway was blocked, police wouldn't move out of the way. We tried to tell them what was going on.... They didn't help us ... just all these roadblocks.

Some parents talked about a struggle over whether to take a child off of life supports or not to resuscitate if the child went into cardiac arrest or stopped breathing. Invariably that part of the story made clear that the decision was shared with physicians and others. Parents talked about the things others said in helping them reach the decision.

Brett: There was one doctor, . . . [who] tried to prepare us to make a decision to take him off life support. And the nurses and everybody started talking to us about those decisions. And it finally got to a point where they had to put him back on [a medicine] that paralyzes him. . . . He had like two or three codes that weekend. That's when we talked with . . . people about taking him off, and we finally decided to take him off of it. . . . My decision . . . was mostly based on who I was trying to keep him alive for. And I kept trying to think that I was trying to keep him alive for him. And I was seeing that there was little . . . hope, and I really didn't care about if he was deaf or deformed or brain-damaged. . . . But towards the end it was obvious I was keepin' him alive for me, 'cause I didn't think I could [handle] him dyin'. And when I finally figured that out (sniffles), with people's help . . . , that's when we decided to take him off the respirator.

And when we took him off the respirator, we got a second opinion. There was a guy in Boston General that was in town, . . . a respiratory specialist, . . . and we talked with him, the chaplain at the hospital, and with our pastor at our church and our friends all the way along. And the doctor, one of the main doctors, . . . he had a son that he did too much surgery, and he tried too long. And he came and talked to me about how he made his child suffer needlessly. . . . When we decided to take him off, I wanted to pull his trachea tube out, but [the doctor] said that he wanted to do it, because that was his gift to us.

The stories often told of things the parent did for the child that were efficacious. Parents were not totally helpless but did some things well—for example, dialed 911, told someone the telephone number of the rescue squad, cut down the child who was hanging by his neck, tried to say the right things when the child talked about suicide, or provided palliative care at home.

Hannah: He walked in the house, and he just looked at me (crying) and he went to his knees, and he said, "Mom, I have no future. There's nothing for me." And I had been watching him, and he was getting more despondent, and I've had a lot of experience in psych, and I had been begging him to go for help. And he kept saying, "No, I can do this on my own." I said, "Sometimes there are things you can't do on your own." . . . I talked to [my husband]. I told him I thought that Tyler was getting more depressed. . . .

I had called the VA and I asked 'em if there was any way that Tyler could (3 second pause, voice shaking) get seen by a psychiatrist. And they told me that I could make an appointment for May. Well, this was in February.... And we said, "In May?... He'll be dead by then. He's really despondent." And they told me they absolutely had no openings.... Tyler's income was too much for him to get Medical Assistance, but it wasn't enough to pay for counseling. So then I called the employee assistance program for [my employer].... and they said, yes, they could see him and, no, it wouldn't cost anything.

Gail: I picked him up, ran out here, and laid him on the counter, and called 911. And of course *screamed* hysterically into the phone ..., "Help me!" And they said they called the paramedics and they were on the way, and they want you to do CPR. And I had been trained in CPR ... (crying), I probably didn't do it the way I should have. I'm sure I didn't. They did stay on the line with me. I think a woman answered first, and I think they put a man on the phone. He kind of talked me through the CPR. In the meantime, [our 4 year old] had somehow crawled out of his car seat, gotten out of the car, and come in. And so of course I screamed at him, "You have to go back in the car. Go be with [your brother in the car]." ... I could hear [the one year old] out there screaming. And [our 4 year old] did. He went back ... and stayed with [his brother]. He did real good. And the paramedics came and tried to revive him. They ran a tube up, pumped his stomach.... I'm pretty sure I had told whoever answered on 911 that you have to call my neighbor to come, 'cause I knew my relatives were too far.... While the paramedics were here, the neighbor came.

Parent stories often included a denial that had the parent(s) done things differently, the child might have continued living.

Erika: About 12:30, 12:15, the phone rang, and it was for David. It was a girl. He was almost six feet tall. He was quite handsome, and he may only have been 14, but he ... was already a man.... This girl called, and I remember you started to go downstairs, and I said, "Don't! You wake him up now, first of all she'll start calling back every night (she chuckles) at midnight. And if you wake him up, he'll be up all night. He doesn't need to get that message till morning." So you didn't go down. (*Chad:* That's so.) The kids had their own phone line here, so she didn't know him that well if she was calling on our line. I figure he was already dead by then. You could tell by the way he looked he'd been hanging a long time.

Cochran and Claspell (1987, Chapter 4) asserted that people live in story; they are not only tellers but participants in their stories. That way of thinking makes sense for these parents. An almost paradoxical aspect of the stories parents told is that the stories are at one level definitely not autobiography; they are about the child and the child's death. But at another level, the parent is present in every sentence; the parent provides the perspectives and feelings. It is not autobiography, but it also is. It is a review of the end of the child's life and the aftermath of that ending; but it is also a review of the parent's life (Cochran & Claspell, 1987, pp. 65–66). Perhaps that is a comment on the relationship of the child and the parent; they are separate individuals, but yet the parent experiences the child in relationship to the parent.

The Social Setting

The parent stories are social. A key representation of that is that in parent stories events leading up to the death always involved others. Typically stories included who was with the child and the parents immediately before the death and at the time of death. Even when children died apart from others, the story still placed others who were important players. The life of the parents and child and the death of the child occurred in a social world. The others were there as significant people in the parent's life, possible helpers, witnesses, those who knew what happened, those who shared some responsibility, those who judged or evaluated the parents, or those who got in the way.

Rosa: My sister came around Christmastime. Wendy was born at March. By Christmas they said she would only probably have a couple of more weeks, and she was really going downhill. And she lived till May. My sister stayed with us from that Christmas until May.

———————————

Denny: [The surgeons] had to go in, and we had ran home to get some clothes and go back for the weekend, 'cause they, another surgery, and they were waitin' for us when we got back....

Marsha: It's a horrible feeling when you see your doctor

Denny: And they're just scrabbling, at the elevator, the social workers hanging out ...

Marsha: Frantically looking for you.

Denny: And he was alive at the time. We got to bring him to our room and spend his last few minutes with him. But that's the worst scene ever. It's very difficult to sit there and be told there's nothing you can do.

Some stories included the words or actions of a government authority, like a police officer or a coroner.

Chad: The coroner came and told us that it was an accidental death.

———————————————

Hannah: There was a cop here ... and then I heard ... him call for the medical examiner, so I knew Tyler (bang on table) was dead, 'cause otherwise they would've called for the ambulance.

The stories often included accounts of what medical personnel did and offered praise or condemnation. The condemnation was most commonly about what the parents felt to be misdiagnosis, insensitivity to parental feelings, practice errors, and cost-cutting efforts that may have accelerated the death, increased the child's discomfort, or even caused the death.

Tina: They put me in a room with a woman who ... just had a baby. And of course I was just like out of it. And then they told me they were gonna transport [our baby] to Children's, and I hadn't even gotten to hold her. And I said, "I want to hold her. I want to see her." "Oh, you'll be able to see her before she goes." Well, they wheel her and here she's in this incubator thing. They did not prepare me for it at all.... "You can touch her. Put your hands in there." Well I'm just hwashsh (sound of horrified disorganization), and so then they wheeled her out, and then they bring in this other lady's baby, and Scott went to the nurse. He said, "You get her out of that room. She can't be in that room."

———————————————

Bonnie: Five weeks before she died, she had flu symptoms, a lot of nausea and vomiting.... She went to several doctors, and ... they didn't take her very seriously, and they'd just tell her to go home and drink, 'cause she was getting dehydrated.... So she'd go home ... with medication to try and stop vomiting, and it just kept on and on. It was just very, very severe. And finally ...

John: Her roommate [who was a physician] ... had her admitted to [a hospital].

Bonnie: The doctors just wanted to give her several liters of fluid, and hydrate her and send her home. And that's when [our daughter who lived nearby] went to the hospital and between [her] and this roommate they said, "We aren't taking her home till you find out what's wrong with her." And so they agreed to keep her overnight, and [when our daughter who lived nearby] ... called the hospital to see how Jill was doing.... they said that they just moved her to ICU.

When medical personnel were praised, it was usually for sensitivity to child or parent, intelligent and competent medical practice, extreme efforts to save the child, or showing genuine attachment to the child.

Henry: First doctor misdiagnosed it.

Rosa: I thought there was something wrong ..., and so I would take her in, and he would say, "(clicking sound) You're ... [over-reacting]. There's nothing wrong with her. She's throwing up because of what you're eating...." I asked for a referral to a pediatrician. He turned me down. I ended up going to a girl friend who was a nurse to say, "Is she okay?" And she said, "No," and got me into a friend of hers who was a pediatrician, who got us into a local pediatrician, who took one look at her and said, "You're heading to Sick Kids. I can start testing, but there's obviously something ... terribly wrong. I've got a good friend who is a gastroenterologist; he'll see you right away." ... And he was ... really good. At the end he would put on a, "Mother is knowledgeable. Please follow her advice," as the opening order, because they would try to skip [medications] or say, "Now she doesn't need codeine," or "she doesn't need this." And then I'd ... say, "Wait a minute. I'm here for antibiotics, but you forgot this, you forgot that (slight chuckle)." ... He was really quite good.

☐ The Story of the Dying Process

In the narratives of parents whose child's dying was spread over a period of time, often several different dying processes are described. There is the process of dying that may be going on long before anyone is aware of it. For example, a cancer may be growing in a child without anyone knowing of it. There may be a process of dying that goes on when someone suspects the child is dying but before anyone is sure. For example, a physician may suspect that a child has a fatal condition but still need more information. There is the process that is ongoing when the physician is sure the child is dying but the parents or other crucial people are not. And finally there is the process that is ongoing when everyone is sure. There may have been a kind of battle over when to label the child as dying. The battle may have involved parents trying not to receive certain kinds of information from physicians, not understanding information, or not agreeing with it. Some parents indicated that it is much easier to live with uncertainty than to know that a child will soon die.

Amy: That first week home [after Noah was born] was probably one of the best weeks of my life, before we went to see the pediatrician, before everybody kept on saying they were still concerned.... It was just the three of us. But it started to change. I started healing, I started being able to walk around more, and our world had grown outside of the bedroom. And I guess I felt real protected.... Anyway, went to the doctor and he said ... he seemed fine, and to anybody who initially met him, oh, he looks fine, I mean, he nursed well. He seemed to gain weight.... Things were going okay. He looked great. And that's why it seemed so strange to think that we should have this concern. Well the pediatrician kept on nagging at me. "Well, I want him to come back in two weeks".... They were thinking some pretty serious things and weren't quite ready to tell ... us. We weren't quite ready to ask.

She went on to talk about the physician consultation session where she and her husband were told their child was dreadfully ill. Note that she said she felt almost angry that her husband would ask the question that led to them thinking of their son as dying. That anger seems to represent her not wanting to experience the transformation from having a child who is not mortally ill to having a child who is.

Amy: We went to the doctor and Ted.... I'll never forget this, said to the doctor, "Okay, what are you thinking?" and he said "Well, a couple of things." He said one was a polio like condition. Nah, you know, immediately I clicked into wheelchair. And then Ted said, "Are you thinking anything life threatening?" ... I was almost mad at him for asking that. And when the doctor responded, "Yes," I couldn't believe it.

Her story then reached the point where they received what she called "a death sentence." This was the point of transformation from having a child who would live a long time to having one who would die soon.

Amy: They said it'll take about two weeks for the lab results.... Thursday ... our pediatrician called us up and said, "We have the results. Can you come in tomorrow morning ...?" So we went in after a night of hell, thinking, "What are we going to hear?" ... We went in, and he said ... it was a neurological disease ... an infantile form of ALS ..., Lou Gehrig disease.... He literally had his medical book open. He was reading it and telling us, and was trying to be as positive as he could. And was trying to tell us what would happen with the muscles and how serious this could be, and he was leading to tell us that there was nothing that could be done, that ... it was a death sentence. And one of us asked him, "Well, do cases such as what he has, do they make it?" And he says, "Well, I just read about one that lived to be about five years old." Um, "Well, are you trying to tell us that he's going to die?" Well, and he, bless his heart, he had tears in his eyes and he couldn't say it.

Dying as a Matter of Learning and Awareness

In parent narratives, dying is often not only a biological process but also a process of moving toward greater learning and awareness both by family members and medical personnel.

Iris: The day after he was born, the doctor came in and told me he had a heart murmur, and that's all he told me at that time, which I was *very* surprised, because we don't have a history on either side of anything like that, but it wasn't too distressing, except that the doctor kept talking and talking and talking. And all of a sudden I realized that he was scared, and then it scared me when I realized how scared he was.... I wasn't able to convey to him how serious I was afraid it might be, till later on he caught on. But then they transferred [our son] over to Children's and started doing tests. And we just found out a little more and a little more and a little more all the time. It was very gradual....

Todd: They found out a little more, a little more at a time too. (*Iris:* Yeah) The first week they determined some things, and ... as they went on they found out other things.... The fact that this is a problem in so few cases, they weren't really alert to it to make the tests.... They were finding things out all through the summer really.

Iris: It was so complicated, and he had so many things wrong, and so many problems, and they were trying to sort out the symptoms ..., (*Todd:* Like one of those 5000 piece jig-saw puzzles, really) what's this caused by and this....

Todd: Sometimes they find out because they were prescribing some kind of medicine that was supposed to help one aspect, and that would throw off something else.

In the stories of some couples, the key to understanding the severity of their child's illness was to learn to understand the language physicians used.

Brett: One of the things that we did is when Alex died, we took him off life support, and coming to that decision was kinda hard, and it was just the way that the hospital talks about death, how many times they say "very" before, you know, he's "very sick" or "very, very, very sick."

So dying is, in a sense, a matter of learning. Small wonder that some parents told about not wanting to know what was going on with their child. To know more about what is going on can be to experience what Amy called a sentence of death for the child.

Metaphors in Talk about the Dying Process

Parent talk about dying is often framed in metaphor, words that draw meaning from other contexts in which the words are used. The metaphors parents chose are instructive. They reveal what it means to parents for a child to be dying and what parents want to do or hope to have happen when a child is dying. Like all metaphors, these metaphors highlight certain perspectives and meanings while obscuring others (Rosenblatt, 1994).

Battle

Many parents used metaphors that referred to battle, struggle, or resistance against something harmful. The child battles to live; the child and the parents battle against the odds or battle to overcome serious problems. The battle may be lost with death, or it may be lost in that the child, the parents, or the medical staff give up before the fact of death.

Brett: I don't know who talked to us about it, but they told us ... to listen to what he was trying to tell us.... He couldn't communicate verbally or even make facial expressions. But at a point it seemed like he was fighting, and then he gave up.... He quit fightin',... like the last two months, he went downhill in a hurry. And I think ... he gave up. (*Joan:* (whispering) He had enough.) Yeah, enough.

Rosa: She kept going septic. And we knew at one point that we wouldn't be able to hold off the infection, that something would go big.

The metaphors of battle highlight that dying is a win-lose situation, that death is an enemy, that the way to deal with a possible death is to contend against it fiercely, that the stakes are very high, and perhaps that one should struggle in anger and with the most formidable weapons available. What the battle metaphor obscures is how much dying may be out of anyone's control and how often it is unclear where or what the "enemy" is. The battle metaphor obscures how much what looks like battle is something else—for example, physicians defending against a lawsuit, coming to a more accurate prediction about when the death will happen, and reducing the discomfort of the patient. The battle metaphor also obscures that often the battle is only defined as such after it is lost, after the parent realizes that the child was dying and then decides that what was going on was a battle for the child's life.

Language of Competition and Odds

Death is something against which to compete. The odds may not be good, but some parents talk about feeling that they must compete, to do the best they possibly can.

Al: I knew damn well I had to keep my head. If the kid had a chance, we had to get him out of there, get him to hospital. So I hollered to [my wife] ... to go get on the telephone. I said, "Now try and keep calm. Get on the phone and tell them where we're at. We've got to have an ambulance here." So I knew I was taking a chance, but I took hold of Tom; I dragged him out of there, and he was alive, yeah, but I didn't know if he had a chance to live anyway.... I knew we had to get him out of there.

For a child who is hospitalized or diagnosed with an illness, the competitors are the parents allied with medical personnel. The parent job may be to find the best doctors available and then stay out of the way as the doctors compete against the illness. Then it is the doctors who are the competitors, with parents as bystanders. Once parents have found their champions, their hired guns, they stand back and hope for the best. The relationship is not necessarily a comfortable one. The hired guns do not necessarily communicate well with those who do the hiring and may act as though they can win when they cannot.

Todd: If somebody's in intensive care, well you gotta be a pretty positive person. You gotta say to yourself, "This is something ... that I'm gonna lick." ... It ... may not have really occurred to [the doctors] to think they were going to lose this, that they couldn't really beat this.... The fact that he went a little longer maybe gave them a certain ... confidence that, "Hey, maybe we're gonna find something here...." I guess I don't feel ... that they were overtly holding back on us. I think it was maybe just that all these other factors were on their minds so much that they really didn't stop to say, "Hey, what's the real score here? What are really the odds?" And I think if we had had a sit-down session with them to say, "Okay, let's figure it out. What are the real odds here?" they might have had to come up with some pretty low numbers. I'm sure they would've.

In accidental death, the competitors sometimes are the parents who, without medical help, must administer to an injured child until professionals can take over. For parents without medical training and without medical supplies and equipment, the choices often seem limited to how quickly to call for help and whether to leave the child where the child is or to move the child into a vehicle and rush to a hospital. Some parents agonized after the death about the wait for paramedics to arrive, feeling that the odds for the child would have been better had the parents not waited but rushed the child to a hospital.

Jay: My oldest son ... said, "If I had only put her in my car and took her to [town], I could make it in 12 minutes to [the hospital]." In hindsight, I wish we would've. She would have had a 50-50 chance.... We just [waited].... The responders finally did come.... The neighbors heard it on the ... scanners. And we got a whole bunch of neighbors in here.... One of them went way down by the highway ... and directed the responders here. So they were helpful ..., but after I found out that it took 36 minutes, she could have been in the hospital.... If we have anything like that ever happen again, we're going to dump her in, or anybod–, any one of us, put us in the car. If she died in the car she was going to die anyway laying down here....

Alice: They waited until the ambulance came,.... the responders did.

Jay: Yeah. But that's not a 911 number, where you have a professional people....

Alice: In your small towns they have

Jay: certain people from different towns.

Alice: They're called "first responders," and they have to take a course....

Jay: That's about all they give.... She hollered she couldn't breathe. She kept on hollering for air. "I can't breathe." But she was filling up with blood.... After we found out the coroner's report, that she had bled to death, in 12 minutes we'd have been up to the doctor. See, that'd made a difference. The doctor said that she had a 50-50 chance then. This way she didn't have any.

The language of competition highlights that there are choices in what to do and that the worst thing is to quit (to forfeit). What the language of competition obscures is how much death is out of anyone's control and how it may be only an illusion to think there was a way to save the child.

Language of Difficulty and Seriousness

Parent stories about the approach of death included metaphors that expressed the difficulty and seriousness of the terminal illness. One metaphor of how the child was doing was how the doctor was doing. Rather than talk about the child's vital signs or labored breathing, some parents talked about the doctors becoming more serious. Similarly, rather than saying the doctors were failing at keeping the child at a certain level of health/illness. sometimes parents talked about the child as a tough case.

Todd: The last week [before he died] things just weren't going right. . . . He was having a hard time with a lot of things. The doctors really got pretty serious about that time. You can tell. Normally they were pretty upbeat, and when he'd have arrest sessions, the doctors were serious, but they were still hopeful. But the last week you got the impression they knew that they had (2 second pause) a real tough case on their hands.

The metaphors of difficulty and seriousness highlight that death is not taken lightly, that physician demeanor is a measure of the approach of death, and that there is in medical care a continuum of difficulty or seriousness. The metaphors of difficulty and seriousness may obscure that the child is a person who is dying and obscure the condition of the child—for example, shallow and irregular breathing or loss of alertness. The focus is on the difficulty experienced by the physician, not on the sick child. The metaphors of difficulty and seriousness also obscure how often death was inevitable, that the child's condition was fatal from the beginning.

Up and Down

In some narratives of child illness, there was a sense of things going up and down. The indicators of health go up and down; the hopes and morale of parents, medical staff, and others go up and down; the mood, alertness, breathing, color, and so forth of the child go up and down. In this situation, "up" is usually good and "down" is usually bad.

Denny: There was a lot of roller coaster days and (*Marsha:* Day by day) it was definitely a day by day thing, but he was doing real well, and we got to Kangaroo Care, which to me still is the highlight of I think both of our lives ... to hold your child that you didn't think was gonna even have a chance of making it and survived open heart and many up and down days and kidney failure problems, where if he didn't urinate at a certain time he was gonna die, and you are prayin' for him to pee. . . . There was many up and down days.

Making Sense of the Actions and Words of Physicians

If a death involved a dying process that included physician efforts and physician interaction with the parents, the parent story inevitably included things the physician said. Sometimes a thing the physician said stayed with the parents, justified and explained what was done, and made sense out of the dying and the relationship of the parents to the child's dying. For example, Glenda talked about what the physician said when a child who had been in a persistent vegetative state and who seemed likely to continue in that state for years suddenly took a turn toward death.

Glenda: They kept saying he could go for 60 years,.... have a normal life-span, so it was still a surprise.... We don't know if it was a ruptured appendix,... 'cause he was vomiting blood and appeared to be in distress.... Our doctor came, and we met with the nursing home people.... The doctor's almost first words were, "He's always been in God's hands. Let's let God finish this." So we got all this support.

At one level the physician's words were privileged in couple stories because the physician was an authority and lent credibility to the story. At another level, the physician's words were privileged because the physician provided a vocabulary to describe the child's situation and also perhaps offered the evidence, the things to look at, the signs.

A physician is, however, not always easy to understand. Parent accounts of physician words often included their struggle to understand and believe the physician. Some parents, long after the death, were still trying to understand what a physician meant. This is partly because physicians often are not particularly understandable (because of how they communicate and because what they communicate is technical), partly because parents who are terrified, distracted, and exhausted in dealing with a mortal illness are not good at understanding, partly because initial understandings may not fit what happened, and partly because subsequent events give new meanings to physician actions and words. Some couples who had trouble understanding the physician at first did much better with the help of a family member. One couple, for example, benefitted from the wife's mother, who was a nurse, becoming involved in discussions.

Pete: Paula's mom got into the conversation with the doctor and with us. And she says ..., "Kids, he will never be a whole person if he does survive."

A death opens the parental relationship with physicians to question. If physicians are so great, why is our child not alive and well? So a major challenge for parents following the death was to come to an understanding about physician actions, words, and ultimate competence, and about how the couple could have got the best medical care for their child. In the example that follows, a couple theorized about why physicians did and said what they did when the couple's son was gravely ill. For Iris, one issue was who was more honest, and she also seemed aware that their own hopefulness made them selective about which physician account of what was going on to accept. For Todd, the key issue was what it took for a physician to work on a very seriously ill child. He almost seemed to equate optimism with the highest quality of medical care.

PR: Did you feel that the docs didn't level with you fully about what was going on?

Iris: In a way, yes. In a way, we felt that *they* were so hopeful that he would make it that they were ... kinda in denial. Our family doctor leveled with Todd early on, but nobody else ever really did. And so we always kind of hoped that maybe the family doctor was the least informed. But I think maybe he was the most honest (laughs).

Todd: ... I think part of the doctors', especially the more specialized you get the more they feel that here's something that I can do.... I think they're awfully positive with people.... Otherwise I don't think they could stay in the business, 'cause they have such challenging problems, the people with all kinds of heart problems or whatever.... If somebody's in intensive care, well you gotta be a pretty positive person. You gotta say to yourself, "This is something ... that I'm gonna lick." And I don't think it was a matter of them not leveling ... as it was that they were being confident that they could do something. And they certainly did, to the best they could.

Parents did not necessarily concede all medical expertise to physicians. Some parents talked about how knowledge acquired through reading, talking to other medical experts, or working in medical settings, gave them or other family members reason to doubt or challenge a physician.

Glenda: They took the clot out that was causing the pressure, and they were very open about what was going on.... But every other head injury that, and we've known people and have had friends whose kids have been hurt since, (speaking more slowly and precisely) they put a shunt in to drain the pressure.

Ken: They did that, didn't they?

Glenda: No (angry, desperate tone), and I talked to that doctor when he was saying Mark's brain was swelling. I couldn't make them do it, and they didn't do it. And I think he might have had some damage, (speaking almost in a whisper) but he wouldn't have been in a persistent vegetative state. And I have to carry that (pounding the table) for the rest of my life, that those (crying) people who were supposed to know didn't help him. And I *knew*, and I couldn't convince them. And he couldn't explain to me why (still weeping) he couldn't do it.... We'd have a son; I know we'd have a son. He might have a limp or so.... And I feel responsible (crying), that I couldn't make that doctor listen. 'Cause I know I'm right; they know I'm right.... The reason I guess I know this is because I worked there, and I had some in the medical profession say that the timing alone made the difference in his treatment.

Bonnie: [Our daughter Deb] said they had done a chest X-ray and said Jill had pneumonia. And Deb said, "Pneumonia! She has not had an elevated temperature!" Deb was a nurse. She knew that you just don't have ... full blown pneumonia and not have a fever. But they did the X-ray, looked at the X-ray, and it looked terrible. And it was just the tumors. And later on [the physician] said, "Well, it was the tumors that were showing up."

Morality and Agency in Dying

Where there was a dying process, parent narratives inevitably dealt with it. The issues discussed were entangled in the parents' sense of what was moral and legal and their desire for power to make a difference and a fear of that power. It is difficult to know, when parents talk about what is moral and legal and about their own agency, whether those were "real" issues or metaphors for the emotions and thoughts that came with the dying. Consider, for example, the dying talked about in the quote that follows. Does Glenda's fear that somebody would take legal action to prevent the medical staff from allowing her child to die represent fear about that, or about something else?—for example, fear of her own overwhelming grief, fear that she would decide to stop the dying process, or fear that if she did try to stop it she would jump in too late to stop it or that her stopping it would create horrid new complications.

Glenda: I was scared to death that whole week it took. The civil liberties; you don't know what people come out of the woodwork with. I could not have gone through what Butchers went through (*Ken:* no). I couldn't have (*Ken:* no) had the resilien–, it was hard enough to say, "Yes. We're going to let our child die." Even though he wasn't the same person, he was still alive.

Some parents talked about allowing a child to die. In doing so, they typically used a language that said that they were players, even the key players, in deciding to remove life supports or not to resuscitate. Yet the language also made the situation one in which natural processes were allowed to operate. In that sense, there was no moral agency for the parents, other than the agency of passively allowing nature to take its course.

Jack: Eventually when we took him off the life sup–, the machines at the end and just said, "We're gonna let nature take its course," they determined he'd lost everything. He'd lost all his senses in terms of sight, sound, you know, he, if you stroke his head, he would feel your touch, but his brain could not connect it to it being Mom's touch or Dad's touch. He didn't hear the voice that was connected with the touch. All the other senses had gone, and the brain stem had pretty much gone. And so we just took him off the machine and let nature take its course, and he was gone in 20 minutes. (*Angela:* yeah.)

In some narratives about a child's dying, goals became important when the child was very sick. Although parents, hospital staff, and other players might have felt that the only thing to do was to try to keep the child alive, there came a point where the parents questioned that goal and explored who was being served by working to achieve it.

Marsha: To watch your baby go through that, the NICU is a wonderful place, but it's heartbreaking to see tubes coming in and out, and the babies at that age do cry. You know that they feel pain, and at some point you wonder, "Are we doing this for us or for him? Are we doing it *for* him or *to* him?"

Some parents saw the child's agency in the child's dying, even with the dying of a very young child. They said that it was as though the child made a choice to die.

Denny: He was perfect on our anniversary, and then he died the next day. It was like ... some kind of weird thing where he didn't want to die on our anniversary.

Angela: We both believe that Blake died on [the first day he stopped breathing]. He had one foot in heaven, (*Jack:* Oh, yeah.) and was just waiting for Mom and Dad to let him go. And it just took until [the] 7th before we did.

Jack: Yeah.... He hung on for 27 days, just to give us time to accept and let go and learn and grow and love.

☐ The End of Life

Last Contact

As has been reported in other research (Edelstein, 1984, p. 68), parent stories of the death almost always include a description of the last contact with the child.

Wayne: I called him and I talked a little bit and asked him how everything's going, and I said, "Now remember," and he said, "Oh, okay, Dad," and I said, "Now remember," I said, "get some sleep.... You got that game." "Yeah, Dad, I'm gonna do that." So that's the last time I talked to him.

Brett: When they took the tube out, I thought like death was gonna be, I always thought it was ugly. 'Cause sometimes the babies go a long time. I know that we found out it was a political system at the hospital.... They have a thing that they call, "DB," that's "dead baby syndrome," and that's when the baby is still alive but the parents are just keepin' him alive. You could hear ... some of the nurses talkin', and that's what they said about us. Then they would have a death watch, and that's when they take the baby off the respirator. But it can take a week or 3 months or whatever to die.... They started the death watch, but as soon as we took the respirator off Alex, he was gone instantly. He just died. And it seemed like we literally and physically handed him to Christ, or to God. 'Cause it wasn't ugly at all. To me it was kind of a neat thing.

In contrast to the thousands of interactions that are not remembered, last contacts are vividly remembered. Years after the death, there are still crisp memories of specific sights and sounds.

Elaine: When I came down, before I left, he came out of the house. He had changed his clothes, and that's the last I saw him. He had them gloves on. One on each hand, before I left. [Remembering a day eight years previously]

Some stories included a parent theory of the death that gave the death meaning by relating it to understandable, even positive, aspects of the child or of life. For example, here is a couple talking about a son who died in an autoerotic accident.

Chad: We've told you how intelligent he was. He would be very inquisitive and very inventive, and experiments. He had rockets going half way to [town]. You almost had to call the Civil Aeronautics Board because of low flying things he'd sent up.... Him and another guy, I'm sure they were hacking computers when they were (*Erika:* (whispering as he talks) He called the White House one time....) ... nine years old.... He was very experimental. (*Erika:* And you couldn't get angry at him.) And when you think about it (bangs table once), it was a sexual experiment, I'm sure. And ... all of his experiments didn't go right. This was obviously one that didn't.

Last Minutes of the Dying Child

In many parent stories, the last minutes before the death were discussed in detail because the details were considered to be quite meaningful. Some parents said that in those last minutes they found a clear message that the end was near—there may have been a last goodbye, or there may have been a linking with the afterlife and heaven.

The last minutes or the last contact represents a transition point, from living relationship to something else. For some parents, there may also be a kind of test in the last contact, perhaps of their competence as parents or the quality of their love for the child. And in some parent stories there was an aesthetic about the last minutes, a sense that the last minutes could be done beautifully or horribly, gracefully or clumsily, with love and controlled caring or with chaos.

The story of the last minutes of a child who is dying are often filled with awe and with emotional pain. The emotional pain is about the child fading away, the child in physical pain, and parent helplessness. The emotional pain is also often about the limitations of the medical system, physicians who seem not up to the task, willfully ignorant, incompetent, or unwilling to help, ambulance drivers who get lost, or paramedics wasting precious time in order to do things by the book. One couple talked about physicians who would not believe them that their son was dying (of something the parents had seen kill another child).

Kathy: The day he died ... I had an appointment at the [hospital] with him, and I ... noticed the things that just triggered something in me. And I remembered *her* being like that [the] day that she died.... I told them at the hospital ..., "He's dying. I can just tell." They said, "Why do you think that?" ... They thought I was kinda nuts. And these doctors examined him and said, "Well, everything's fine." And I called Karl and told him the same thing. Called our pediatrician and he said, "Well, don't bring him here, if you think that." And so anyway, we were [very] thankful we were with both of them when they died. And he just kind of closed his eyes and died....

Karl: I was holding him when he died, and we were both almost yelling and screaming that, "He's dying!" And nobody was listening to us....

Kathy: "You're nuts."

Karl: "You're nuts. You're crazy." ... We just knew that he really was dying. How did we know?... Something was different; something was wrong. We could feel it. We could both sense it. We didn't have to talk each other into it. We both *believed* it.... We *really* ... felt that something was going wrong, and we couldn't get any help. Nobody would listen to us. That hurt us a lot.... We took that particular day very hard. (*Kathy:* (crying, whispering) Yeah. Oh, we felt really alone.

An issue for some parents about the last minutes was whether the child was in great pain and whether the child knew that death was about to occur. Parents preferred to believe that the child did not near death with physical pain and awareness of dying.

Elaine: Did he know he was going to die?

Red: He would have laid underneath the tractor

Elaine: That was my [concern]. I made Red describe what the site looked like. Was he thrashing with his feet and his arms? That's all I could think of was that he was laying under that thing knowing he was going to die. That was harder for me, I think, than even the death itself. Did he know that? Now whether this was true or what, but we got the nicest letter from the coroner, and he had said that he felt that Kyle was knocked unconscious.... He said that he really felt that Kyle never knew what, that that had knocked him enough, that he was not really conscious and then the compression on his chest would no longer allow the lungs to expand and he actually died of suffocation.... That just really bothered me. How helpless he must have felt, and where are these people that are supposed to protect me?

Last Words

With children who were old enough to talk, some parent stories included the child's last words. The last words might be said at the moment of death, at the moment of last losing consciousness, or at the last parting of parent or child.

Jay: Now [our son-in-law] said that, when he first got down there, she woke up and she said, "I love ya." That was her last words.

Ken: The last thing he said to us was, "Don't worry. Everything will be all right."

I know from reading many 19th century North American diaries for my book, *Bitter, Bitter Tears* (Rosenblatt, 1983a), that in the past people paid close attention to the words of the dying in order to learn whether they had achieved religious salvation and perhaps to learn more about the next world. My impression of what contemporary bereaved parent narratives make of a child's last words (and immediately above are two examples) is not often about salvation but is often about the child being a good and loving person and the relationship between child and parent still being appropriately caring and connecting.

The Moment of Death

Parents always spoke about the moment of death. In some stories, the parents were present. In others, they were not but learned about the last moments from others or reconstructed it based on things they knew and believed. The moment of death was, in the stories, a dividing point between one set of possible futures and another, between a relationship with a living child and a relationship with a child who is not alive, between one era and another, between one state of mind and another, between being like most other parents and not being like them. It was the point in the story where the child moved from the world of the living to somewhere else. The moment of death was also the point of telling the story.

In some stories there seems to be more than one moment of death. For example, a parent might tell about the moment when the child's body could not continue to breathe or to pump blood without mechanical assistance, the moment when a physician considered the child to be dead, and the moment when the parents learned of the death. Each moment would mark the transition from one place to another for the child and parent, and with several such moments in the story there is a rather blurry period of time in which the child is not alive but not fully dead.

Barb: [The doctor] come out and asked us if we wanted to donate parts. Tom had massive head injuries. And we both said, "No," so then, I don't think it was five, ten minutes he come back out. He said he'd give us time to think about it. And then we just said, "No," so then like five, ten minutes later he come out and said he was dead.

It is striking that, even years after the death, the moment of death was typically placed in a context that included a lot of details. The details were certainly not all of what parents could say (for example, almost nobody said what they were wearing, though quite a few people talked about dressing for the funeral; nobody said what they had eaten at their most recent meal; and nobody said what was in the national and international news that day). The details typically included the date, time of the day, who was present, where the child and parents were, and crucial medical facts.

Erika: It'll be six years at Christmas. He was just about 14 and a half, and it was two days after Christmas, and everybody was up. [Our daughter] had to be up early. She was still 12. . . . She'd gone next door to baby sit, so *we* were up like at 6:00, 6:30. And Chad was up. He'd already gone outside. [Our older son] was up, and David had been sleeping, so I just let him sleep, because nothing new really needed to get done. . . .

Chad: So I'd got up, done some chores, come in, and made breakfast. I went back out again. It was Tuesday, and I was hooking up some cattle trailers. I was hauling cattle on Mondays, but since Christmas was, well, it was Sunday, and Monday was on a holiday, so it was Tuesday morning, and I was just going to go haul some cattle . . . to the . . . auction. . . . I was going to stop in the house and ask David if he wanted to go along. . . . As I was hooking up the trailer, Erika came running out and said David was in the bathroom. We can't get the door open. So I came in the house, and the door was locked. And [our older son] was down there, working with the door. I just took my jack knife out, and used it as a key. Opened the door. And there was David, slumped down, hanging from the (bangs table once) shower curtain. Died from . . . asphyxia.

Lisa: It was a Friday. He came from school about ten after three. He came in the house and ran for the bathroom, said, "I got to go to the bathroom." He never went to the bathroom at school, because all the boys gave swishees (chuckles). He didn't like that. So he always held it until he got home. So he came in, went to the bathroom. He was fine. And 10 minutes later he came in from his bedroom, and he says he had a really bad headache. So I gave him some Tylenol, and he laid down out here on the couch. And he just, "God, it really hurts really bad." So I had a nephew that died of a brain tumor, and my sister always told *me*, "If your kids ever have a headache, there's a reason for it. You call the doctor. . . ." He was complaining that it hurt really bad. So I called the doctor's office, and they said, "Well, give him some Tylenol and 7-Up, and if he can sleep, he should be fine." So, "okay," so he went in and laid down on his bedroom, and fell asleep, and that must've been, I don't know, five o'clock by then. And he got up and went into the bathroom and threw up. And I thought, "This is the flu," really bad headaches, throwing up. Then he went back in and laid back down again. And he said that the light was so bright that he couldn't see. He says, "Shut the light off." So I shut the light off and closed the door.... He wanted to sleep. Well, I went in there, and he was unconscious. I tried waking him up, and he never woke up. So then I dialed 911. Sent a friend of ours, I think it was, did Becky come out to the garage? 'Cause I don't remember much after that. From what Becky told me, a friend of ours was here. She ran out and got Nick. I was calling 911, and Nick and Becky came in, and they started giving him mouth-to-mouth, and that's all I remember (embarrassed little laugh). From there, the ambulance came, and they took him down to ... County Medical Center, and he drove in the ambulance with him. Got down there, and he was brought in for a CAT-scan right away, and then we didn't hear anything almost all night, except for, "He's still in surgery." That's all we kept hearing.

Nick: Then the [doctor] came out, and ... said that he ain't gonna make it, I guess, that was it. And then in the morning they said, well, "We gotta keep him on this thing for 24 hours," and he was brain dead.

The fact that the moment of death can be defined in different ways means that family members may disagree with each other or with medical authorities about when the death occurred.

Alice: She died on the way [to the hospital]....

Jay: That's what *they* said.... I'll always say she died here.

For some parents, the death was not a death until a physician said it was. For example, Molly's daughters may have been dead while still at home, but she was desperate to get them to the hospital and did not consider them to actually be dead until a physician said they were.

Molly: The kids were ... playing in the living room and broke a lamp.... I didn't want the kids to be hurt. So I put them in the bathtub (crying) to give them a bath. Give them a bath, so I could vacuum up the glass in the living room.... While I was vacuuming, [the older child] got ahold of the hair dryer and dropped it in the bathtub, and they were electrocuted.... Flagged down somebody in the alley. And we each grabbed one of the girls. They were naked. Wrapped them up, threw 'em in the car and get them to the hospital.... At the hospital we carried them in and they stuck me in a little room. They started working on the kids. They came back in and said they were both dead.

Reconstructing the Dying and Death

Some parents have to reconstruct the death of the child. Perhaps they witnessed the death, but the events were too traumatic and confusing for them to assimilate them in a way that allows them to develop a narrative about it (Neimeyer & Stewart, 1996). Perhaps they were not present at the time of death. In either case, they have to reconstruct the death, using what they know, what they believe or assume to be true, and their skills at gathering and understanding evidence.

Erika: We knew that . . . if there's a light to go to, and if there's a split second that David could have changed things and come back, he would have gone ahead, to see what was. So he's a lot more fortunate than most of us would be. He died in a way that he wasn't scared. He didn't know he was dying. It must be awful to watch a child of yours suffer, and know they're going to die, and have to tell them they're going to die. So he died painlessly and without any fear, so we probably won't be that fortunate, so you want him back, but that's given me some consolation.

The reconstruction Erika described was not framed as a reconstruction but as certainty. It included beliefs about David's curiosity or will to live, deductions about how he felt and what he knew at the moment of death, comparisons, and the belief that things were as good as they could have been. Constructed realities around a child's dying may often have those qualities—certainties, comparisons, hopefulness. But they also may include crucial uncertainties.

Stan: I don't know how much stock you can put in what a 3 year old remembers or says, but I still have questions as to really how it happened. . . . Why [my brother-in-law] didn't see [the car that crashed into theirs], and [our son] said that they were arguing and, like I say, I don't know how much stock you can really put into what a 3 year old remembers. I still deal with that; every once in while that comes up as kind of: I wish I really knew what happened.

Paula: I guess that's the one thing that bothers me is why and how he got through the fence.

Some efforts at reconstruction involve interrogation of others, but sometimes interrogation may be blocked by family processes. In the following example, people "getting pretty testy," the parents "getting a little mad," and Stan "trying to calm everyone down" may have deterred Joy from getting as much information from her brother-in-law and sister as she wanted.

Stan: I guess when Joy was starting to get angry with [her brother-in-law and sister], she … wanted to dig deeper and really find out why this happened, and I remember … we were over at her parents' house and the whole thing came up and everyone was getting pretty (laughs) testy. Her parents were getting a little mad at her for bringing it up, but this was something unresolved in her. And I was trying to calm everyone down (laughs). That's probably about the only time that I was really worried that something was gonna explode (laughs). And somehow it got calmed down, although it never really got resolved. So I think it's probably still in the depths of everyone, just that kinda nagging question…. I guess it's something I don't think we'll ever find out, unless maybe if it's on somebody's death bed,… and they want to get it off their chest.

Reconstruction may be aided by autopsy information. Sometimes what parents get from the autopsy information is not only a story about the death but a story about who or what was responsible for the death. Parents may feel extreme guilt about a child dying, since society and they themselves define parents as the people who have the greatest responsibility for the child. So the reconstruction may involve the development of a story that says the parents did the best they could and were not responsible for the death.

Gail: [The doctor who went over the autopsy information with us] I think more than *anybody* else, even more than each other, reassured us that we had done nothing wrong. We knew that, but it was like *he* gave us the permission to feel strong enough about that,… to feel that we had done nothing wrong and we'd done everything right. And that it was out of our control.

Vince: And there was nothing that we *could* have done to change it. I think … that removed *my* guilt about whether it's me or whether I felt she was a bad mom…. There's lots of situations in couples where in a case like this,… if the wife is home and the husband isn't, there's an awful lot of opportunity for the husband to say, "Well, why the hell didn't you do this?! It probably would have saved the kid's life."

☐ Naming the Cause of Death

Parent narratives always name a cause of death. Conceivably a parent might wonder what the point is of knowing why a child died; the only important point is that the child died. However, parents thought in terms of causality and talked as though there were lessons to be learned and judgments of right and wrong to be made about the death. So the cause of the death was an important piece of information.

The cause that was cited always was at least in part material—something medical, genetic, physical, or physiological. If the death was accidental, the story also included an account of how the accident came to happen or why, after careful investigating, the accident could not be explained.

Some parents engaged in a great deal of detective work to find a cause—for example, consultation with genetics experts or close personal inspection of an accident scene.

Red: One of the biggest things is to try and figure out why or how. You drive yourself crazy. . . . The tractor was laying upside down. We tipped it back on. It was . . . in third gear, which is probably four miles an hour, so he was not speeding. . . . He come and he made the big turn. He lopped over past the center of the road and he made a big arc and went down the ditch. Now why? He'd driven it before. . . . He had tremendous allergies, especially of bee stings. Was there a bee flying around and he panicked? We have no idea. . . . Once he was down there he drove 100 feet in the ditch before he tried to get back up. . . . If he went another 100 feet, it's right. . . . Then we thought . . . maybe . . . something was wrong with the steering, and he couldn't turn. . . .

Elaine: And then he ended up actually, . . . his back landed on a hump.

Red: The only spot in that whole ditch where he would have died from the accident was within about a ten foot span where he went in. The ditch sloped up and the tractor was laying where there's enough room underneath it, but right there there was a hump of ground. . . . If he'd been ten feet either way.

In another example of the detective work some bereaved parents carry out, Kathy talked about the death of two children from the same mysterious, unnamed malady.

Kathy: They were failures to thrive. Whatever was wrong with them was incompatible with life. They just both died at about the same time. . . . Both lived about as long. And they looked more like each other . . . than us. But not like a Downs Syndrome. . . . We [saw] a genetics specialist at the U too, and she had seen him while he was alive, and afterwards she came up with what she thought was probably what they each had, an autosomal recessive genetic disorder, that each of us carries a bad gene. You only have 25% chance of each baby that that might happen. . . . It's obviously lethal. There's nothing you can do.

Parental consent to a do-not-resuscitate order could be considered a cause of death, and some narratives talked about parent guilt about the order. But typically parent stories that speak of such an order emphasize the child's physical conditions as a cause of death and as reasonable justification for the do-not-resuscitate order.

Tina: We *knew* that she'd never sit, she'd never walk, she'd never talk, she'd never eat. We knew that she had lung problems, heart problems. And at that point, from a medical [standpoint], she could have had a heart transplant, but they couldn't have done anything with her lungs. She never would have been able to get off the respirator.

☐ What Ifs

It was very common for the stories bereaved parents told to include "what ifs" about things that might have prolonged the child's life (cf. Klass, 1988, p. 28). Parents wonder whether other courses were possible that could have led to the child continuing to live, at least a while longer. The "what ifs" can be considered a report of ongoing or past thinking about what they or someone else could have done to make a difference. And, in a sense, the "what ifs" are a way of the parents continuing to parent the child by continuing to think about what would have been best for the child.

Paula: The First Response Team was coming around the corner. And they did what they could, and we had to wait for the ambulance.... It seemed like that took forever.... The sheriff ... was here, but they said, no, we had to wait, because the ambulance was on its way....

Pete: It was like 20 minutes for the sheriff to get here, and the ambulance was at least 10 minutes later. (*Paula:* Really.) And the thing that ... *really* griped me about the whole situation was why the sheriff said we had to wait for the ambulance.... One advice I'd give to any farm couple ..., if you can see that you aren't going to do any physical damage to your ... loved one, put him in your vehicle and go into town. Forget ... the sheriff and the ambulance.

Paula: ... I rode in the ambulance with 'em, and he went into cardiac arrest on the way.... They worked on him for, oh, almost an hour at the hospital. And they couldn't get him back.... He had head ... and chest injuries.... We feel there was kind of a waste of time waiting for the ambulance.

Pete: And the ambulance crew took the blanket off of him that the First Response crew had put on him to warm him up and keep him from shock.

And it was almost as if there was a conflict between the two (*Paula:* Umhm) services there. . . .

Paula: They would not take him in the First Response Team's stuff. They had to use their own blankets. . . .

Pete: Rather than worry about sorting it out afterwards, and (*Paula:* Yeah) you're talking about minutes in situations like this.

Jane: The only thing we were regretful of . . . is that because he was six weeks early, he had been part of a program . . . for premature babies. . . . He was doing so well and was so much ahead of the markers for premature babies that when he was about two years old they dropped him from the program. . . . I wish . . . that he [stayed], because they're much more closely watched . . . ; maybe the [tumor] would've been caught sooner. And if it had, it would've been better, because by the time we did find out about it, it had metastasized. . . .

Rob: Whether it was treatment or bioinfection or radiation, his lungs became destroyed. . . . The cancer was actually gone when they did autopsy. It's just his lungs . . . wouldn't function. . . . The one doctor indicated later that *he* knew there was a higher chance of this, although it was still very slim. . . . We wished that he had let us know that at the time . . . , 'cause we would've been more focussed and observant. . . . Adam was very solid. . . . The tumor probably had been growing for a period of time there, and it was just that that's what firmed up the stomach. . . . You didn't think about it 'cause he was very healthy. He didn't have colds, ear infections, or anything else. You just don't think about it. . . . So you would've wished you had recognized it. Well, maybe it shouldn't be so firm and so solid as it is.

☐ Metaphors for Death

Metaphors for death were common in parent narratives. Those metaphors, like all metaphors, emphasize certain things and obscure others (Rosenblatt, 1994).

Amy: She never lost a child.

Denny: [The nurses] are just incredible. I don't know how they do their job, because what they have to go through is, they do lose babies, and I don't know how they can possibly deal with it.

The metaphor of "losing" a child may imply that the child might be recovered, that the child is not gone forever; there is hope of reunion. The metaphor may highlight a sense of the parents continuing to search for the child. Saying one has lost a child is also a way of saying than one has less than one had before—like losing a possession. The metaphor highlights that death affects the parents (it is their loss) and obscures such grim aspects of death as pain and physical damage.

Erika: We have a wide circle of friends and acquaintances and we've made more, expanding on the type of death David had.

"The type of death David had" distances the son from the death, maybe makes it sound more like a cold, and it puts the emphasis on something other than him being dead.

Brett: One of the things that we did is when Alex died we took him off life support, and coming to that decision was kinda hard.

To say that "we took him off of life supports" is to stay away from saying we killed him, but is certainly a way of saying we were part of making something happen that stopped him from breathing and stopped his heart from beating. Calling it a "decision" obscures how much the death was out of parent control or the control of any human.

Brett: Towards the end, [my wife] accepted the fact that to let him go before I did.

"Letting him go," while the child is alive, may imply that a parent has some control over whether or when the child dies, but that obscures how much the child's dying is out of parent control. "Letting go" also refers to the emotional and cognitive connections that are part of a parent's feeling desperate to hang on to the child. In that sense, "letting go" highlights how a parent can decide to abandon desperate efforts to hold on to the child and be more accepting emotionally of the child's dying. I believe the metaphor obscures how much, even after "letting go," parents are still strongly connected to the child and hopeful of miraculous improvements in the child's health.

Jane: When Adam passed away I was not able to handle having a lot of kids around anymore.

"Passed away" can be a polite way to refer to death, but it may also be a way to distance painful and disorganizing feelings. The metaphor of "passing away" highlights the child's passage from nearness to the parents to far away, while obscuring emotional, biomedical, and other aspects of the child's death.

Gail: First thing out was, "Where do we send the body?" He was no longer our baby; he was a body.

In this statement from a discussion of how offensive a hospital official was in demanding that they arrange to have the child's body moved to a funeral home, the word "body" is part of what was offensive. The hospital official pushed the parents to think of their child as a thing, with the word "body" a stark statement that the child is not living and no longer a person. Instead of a person there are only remains, and those must be disposed of soon. The metaphor "body" obscures the humanity of the child and the human connections of parents and child.

Rosa: You hold your breath when they get on a bus every day, 'cause if it was to happen again, it would be devastating.

"It" is so vague and nonspecific that the word can be used to speak about what is big and horrifying or about what is unspeakable. Calling death an "it" also makes it a thing, with all the metaphoric qualities of things—for example, existing independently of the speaker, having properties, and being something that can be acted on and can act on people. "It" is also a word reserved for what is familiar, so familiar that it does not have to be described with more specific words.

Paula: They worked on him for, oh, almost an hour at the hospital. And they couldn't get him back.

"They couldn't get him back" to her and to life. "They couldn't get him back" from death, from a journey to death, from a place other than here. Death is somewhere else, not here. "Getting back" also implies that before death the child was already distant from the parent and the world of the living.

Paula: It was just his time.

———————————

Barb: I just think that truly, when it's your time, if I had a hold of his hand and if it was his time there's nothing I could do to pull him back. It would be just, let it go.

By saying, "It was just his time," a parent says that death occurs at an as-signed time, a time assigned by a higher power, so it is out of human power to prevent. Death is the ending of an assigned time period. Believing that absolves the parent and others of responsibility for the death and provides the meaning that God knows what He is doing, even if it is unfathomable to humans.

☐ Summary

Every parent had a story of their child's dying and death. The stories were always detailed and had a temporal organization, a cast of characters, an explanation of how the death occurred, and an account of events leading up to the death and following the death. The narrative was typically a couple story, with spouses talking together as though they had shared views of what happened and how to understand it.

Every narrative about a child's dying moved to a time before the death. Often the narrative told how the child came to be and the path traversed toward the death. Some stories included premonitions or omens. The narratives located events temporally (in terms of the calendar, the clock, and things going on in the family at the time) and spatially. Every narrative characterized the child, and typically the characterization included a sense of how special the child was. In setting the scene for the account of the death, parents were always players in the story; the story was about the child dying but also about the parents.

Parent stories reflected parent efforts at understanding what happened. That understanding was complicated, in some accounts, because there were several different dyings. There might be several different dyings because there might be stages in parents realizing how close to death a child was, stages in parents understanding what they were being told, or stages in a child's deterioration. In some sense, dying, in parent narratives, could be not so much a physical process as a matter of parents (and perhaps physicians) learning things and becoming more aware.

Parent efforts to make sense of the dying process often included efforts to make sense of the words of physicians. However, physicians were not the only basis of understanding. Parent efforts to make sense of the dying process, when there was a dying process, included metaphors for the process, for example, speaking in terms of "battle" against a disease. Like all metaphors, these metaphors highlight some things and obscure others. And in that highlighting and obscuring there are interesting things to learn about the parent experience of a child's dying. As part of that understanding, parent stories always dealt with matters of morality and agency—questions of what was wrong and right, questions of who or what had a role in causing the death.

In parent narratives the last minutes of the child's life were considered significant and meaning-filled, with the meanings not only about the child, but about the parents as parents and about the transitions of child from alive to dead and of the parents from being like most other parents to having a dead child. Some parent stories of the last minutes also dealt with questions about possible pain for the child and possible child awareness of dying, with parents strongly preferring that the child not feel pain and not be aware of dying. If a child said last words, those words were also a part of the narrative, with the last words being taken as reflecting qualities of the child as a person and qualities of the parent-child relationship.

The moment or moments of death had an important place in parent narratives. For parents who were not present at the death and for those who were present but not able to grasp what was going on, there were accounts of their efforts, in some cases long term and strenuous efforts, to reconstruct the moment of death.

Parent narratives inevitably named the cause of death. In that naming there were lessons to be learned and judgments of right and wrong to be made. As with the moment of death, there might be considerable parent investigative effort put into learning the cause of death. Related to this, parent narratives often included "what ifs," consideration of how if certain things had been different, the death would not have occurred, would have been delayed, or would have been different in some ways.

Parents used various metaphors for dying and death. For example, death might be an "it" or a "passing on." Examination of these metaphors suggests what parents choose to emphasize and to stay away from in talking about a child's dying and death.

Parent narratives flowed from talking about the dying and death to talking about the death rituals that followed the child's dying, and so those rituals are the focus of the next chapter.

CHAPTER

Death Rituals

Rituals at the time of the child's dying and death have a prominent place in many parent narratives. The rituals came with culturally attached meanings and created meanings as they were planned and carried out. These meanings applied to the child, the dying, the death, and the parents' relationships with the child, family, community, and God. The rituals were also important to many parents because they were a connection to the child and were central to redefining the parent-child connection.

☐ Baptism

Baptism is a death ritual when a young child is extremely ill, has not been baptized, and is a member of a family that considers baptism prior to death of great importance. Narrative about baptism is then narrative about life-threatening illness or approaching death. And when a parent talks about being asked by hospital staff if a seriously ill child has been baptized, the parent is talking about a message that the child may die very soon.

Angela: They wouldn't let me see him when I got to the hospital. Then all of a sudden this clergy person comes up and says, "Has your son been baptized?" (voice shaking) And I said, "No, he was scheduled to be baptized on Sunday in church." (crying) And he said, "Well, I think you better have him baptized right now." And I just, I collapsed. (crying) And Jack hadn't gotten there. And I'm like, "Oh, my God!" (crying) And he was all bloody.

Some parents who knew a child was near death talked about having the child baptized, almost as part of the funeral ritual. In their narratives baptism was a kind of goodbye.

Kelly: At seven o'clock that Sunday morning we called [my husband's] parents, my parents, had them come down to the hospital, 'cause we knew they needed to be there ... to say goodbye to her. At nine o'clock we had her baptized.

☐ Autopsy

In some narratives, autopsy seems to be a death ritual (DeFrain, Martens, Stork, & Stork, 1990–91). It is a first step in dealing with the remains of the deceased, a basis for giving certain kinds of meanings to the death, a way of legally defining the death, and a step toward the mortuary and the grave. It is also a way of asserting that society's right to a child who has died has precedence over parent rights. Parents can be upset about that, but they also can accept and understand how an autopsy is appropriate.

Wayne: They took Will down to the morgue, and he was really banged up.... We weren't able to *see* him for like two days....

Louise: We wanted to see him (*Wayne:* Yeah ...). We didn't want to ... have to go identify him, but we wanted to see him (*Wayne:* Umhm) that morning....

Wayne: They wouldn't let us do it.... They had to do all this testing (*Louise:* Yeah).

Autopsy information may be incorporated into parent narrative, providing perspective on what they did or did not do.

Jay: After we found out the coroner's report, that she had bled to death, [if we had driven her to the hospital ourselves] in 12 minutes we'd have been up to the doctor. See, that'd made a difference. The doctor said that she had a 50-50 chance then. This way she didn't have any.

☐ Police Inquiry

Following accidental deaths and many deaths at home, there is an inquiry by the police or sheriff's department. At one level, it is a ritual of officially recognizing that the death has occurred and officially releasing the corpse of the child to the funeral director or parents. At another level, a level that receives substantial attention in the narratives of some parents, it is an official defining of the death, addressing matters of guilt, blame, and responsibility.

Al: A policeman met us at the hospital.

Barb: Deputy sheriff or something.

Al: . . . Asked us all about it. . . . The sheriff himself was here at the scene while we were gone to the hospital. Talked to Dad, and that's all there was to that. Just it had to be reported, and they had to investigate to see whether it was an accident. . . . When we needed it, we got the paperwork. . . . The sheriff . . . talked to me that night for a long time. Well, you gotta give them the whole story on what happened. . . . He said, "Don't worry about a thing. Just concentrate on trying to get your life back together." And they just ask you totally, diagram and the whole damn works as to how it happened.

☐ Organ Donation

In the narrative of one couple, a ritual that gave meaning to their son's death was organ donation. They talked about feeling that it was a way to have good come from the child's death.

Wayne: They used about three different things of Will's. . . . (*Louise:* He was already dead). . . . They couldn't use his heart and so on, and they couldn't use some other vital things. That would've been great for somebody, but they wanted to get whatever they could use. And I know, I remember the eyes, the corneas.

Louise: The corneas and the heart valves and tissue.

The interest of various groups in society to promote organ donation may blur the moment of death for some parents, because that interest leads to mechanical prolongation of heart function until the parents have responded to a request for permission to "harvest" organs.

Barb: They hooked him up to the machines when they got there, and I don't think we were there half an hour till [the doctor] come out and asked us if we wanted to donate parts. . . . We both said, "No," so then . . . like five, ten minutes later he come out and said he was dead. But they had kept him going just because of parts.

☐ Wakes, Visitations, Funerals, Memorial Services, Burials

The death rituals that parents emphasized as they told about a child's death were those occurring after the official release of the body to the family. The rituals typically included a wake or visitation and a funeral.

As they told their stories, one of the things that a substantial number of bereaved parents emphasized about the death rituals for their child was how difficult everything was.

Al: Your head's not working right anyways so that we left most of it up to [the funeral director].... We had it at the Lutheran church ..., and people couldn't all get into that. And so then you go through that,... and hell, you don't even know what is going on, at least I didn't anyway. A lot of it I can't remember. I just don't know what the hell even took place.

Dealing with Funeral Directors

Some parents talked about the ritual of picking out the coffin for the child. They might talk about the shock and unpleasantness of having to make choices and carry out economic transactions as a result of the child's death, about the small size of the coffin, about feeling manipulated by, put off by, or helped by the funeral director, and about struggling not to be exploited. Some talked about the effort to understand what was going on in dealing with the funeral director. Some talked about the effort to pick out a coffin that seemed right for the child.

Angela: We picked out this little white cradle. That's what I called it. It's actually a casket. But I've always called it his little white cradle. (*Jack:* Yeah, it's probably more cradle than casket. It didn't have a lid to it.) Well, it didn't then.

Red: [The funeral director] took us aside ... and he said, "Now don't let your emotions get carried away now. You can spend $10,000 on a casket. You can buy a nice casket for $1000 and spend the money on a bull." ... He was real helpful that way.

Elaine: But the kids made that choice—on which one he was going to have. (*Red:* the casket.) Yeah, they said, "Oh, we want that white one there. That's the flashiest."

Letting Others Know about the Death

In the narratives of some parents, an important part of the ritual that follows immediately after a child's death is communicating to others that the death has occurred and that there are bereaved people who need acknowledgment and support (Ruiz & Atwood, 1996), and that there will be a funeral, visitation, and/or wake to attend. Some parents talked about the telephoning that had to be done to let others know that the child had died.

Wayne: All that morning we were on the phone calling ... people, telling them that Will died that morning (*Louise:* umhm). And that afternoon, and then the other people were calling other people and so on.

Candy: For some reason, ... I found strength to do all these things that day [he was killed]. And I called ... to tell the minister ... to go tell my father, and I have a couple of aunts who live in town to tell them. I made a lot of telephone calls that day.

One of the things that goes on with such telephoning is that the person doing the telephoning gets many chances to develop and crystalize important parts of the story about the death (Ruiz & Atwood, 1996). However, the parents do not necessarily do much of the calling. For example, the friends of an adult child who died might be the most active telephoners.

Bonnie: This was the fourth of July weekend, and she died at two in the afternoon, and by Sunday, these friends of hers ... called everybody.

One story about the use of others to inform the closest relatives was about a ritual that had gone bad because the information about the death was transmitted insensitively.

Elaine: Our son [Ron] ... had been playing football and he was only 14 months older than Kyle, and they fought like cats and dogs but they were their best buds.... This should of never happened but it did.... Ron was to get off the bus in [town] at the church 'cause [grandmother] lives [there] and they just walk down.... Red's brother said that he would go up and get Ron off the bus. Well, if that's what he would have done that would have been fine. But he sent his daughter who is a year older than Ron.... You know, a school bus full of kids. Here's this girl waiting for Ron at the church. And well they're just giving him the business like you wouldn't believe, so he comes off the bus and he's just laughing and all that and he gets in the car and she said, "I don't know what you're laughing about. Your brother was killed today." That's how he had to find out.... So insensitive.... Why did they send her?

Meaning-Making in Funeral Decisions

Some parents talked about decisions they made about how to do the funeral that helped to make the funeral meaning-making in a positive way for themselves or for others in the family. Thus the processes of preparing for the wake or visitation and of choosing meaningful things to put in the coffin with the child were important parts of the death ritual for some parents. Those things communicated what was special about the child and gave an opportunity for meaningful participation to family members who might otherwise feel distant from the ritual.

Pete: I still got his ... toy tractor underneath the bed....

Paula: Yeah, well, no, he had two of 'em, (*Pete:* Yeah.) because one—

Pete: Yeah, the smaller one we (Paula clears her throat) put in the casket with him (his voice is shaky), and [a friend] put a horse in there that he played with

Paula: over at her place, and [our older son] had gone through the encyclopedias, at all the flags of the different countries for the nationalities that we have in our background, and made a flag on paper for each one, and he put them in the casket. And (sighs) his teddy bear went in there too.

Elaine: Our kids were real instrumental in helping us plan his funeral and picking everything out and down to the clothes he wore.... I wanted my sister to go get him a new pair of pants and a new sweater ..., [but our older daughter] ... said, "Mom, why would you put a sweater on him? He'd hate it.... Why can't he wear the outfit he had his picture in that you just thought he was the cat's pajamas...." And I said, "... because it's in the wash." My girl friend came out [and] ... took care of all that.... Then ... the kids ... picked out a white casket for him. They said the rest weren't flashy enough for his body.... They picked out all the songs.... They did it totally different from what I would have done.... They looked at it from his point of view, on what he would have wanted and what was best for him. And that's the way it should have been.... The kids had picked out all the pictures and then they had tables full of pictures [at the visitation]. They had all his most prized possessions there.... It was getting close to the end of the visitation, and all of a sudden, here comes [our middle daughter] doing cartwheels, right in front of the casket, all the way across. There wasn't anything wrong with it, but here this kid, and I could have just about died. But those kids picked out everything that went in his casket. [The youngest] drew him pictures that went with him. They took a picture of our car and then put that in there.... All of that was real important for them to just do that, to get through that whole process.

Louise: Having the kids do posters. [The funeral director] suggested the pictures.... He said get your girls a piece of tape or have them write whatever they want on the [posterboard], draw pictures, write, whatever. And they did.... We had them hanging above [the] casket ..., three ... big posterboards.... I think it was to help the girls, but I decided that since they did those for Will, that [the posters] should go with Will (laughs). And I told this ... man ..., "When the funeral's over, before you close his casket, I want those ... in there." He looked at me ..., "All three of them?" And I said, "Is there a problem?" He said, "Nope!" (*Wayne:* (laughing) No, nope.) And I remember just out of the corner of my eye, I was trying not to watch, (chuckling) they were shutting his casket, this poor guy (*Wayne:* (chuckling) Trying to stuff this in there) has these three big poster boards that he rolled, and he was trying to do it without (*Wayne:* Moving him)....

Wayne: He had other things in there besides. He went with the (*Louise:* A lot of his friends brought things) luggage (laughs)

Some parents talked about giving meaning to the child and to the death through their choice of funeral music.

Wayne: When you're dealing with [a] ... child's death, it's a whole different ball game. In fact, at our funeral,... that's the song that we played ..., "Take Me Out to the Ball Game."

Louise: ... What we were trying to do is to make it, we knew there'd be dozens of kids there (*Wayne:* Umhm), to make it—

Wayne: To make it ... not cold. Make it a little bit ... less morbid, and kids could relate to that (*Louise:* Yeah). When they played that song, I'd say 90% of the audience cried.... It was (*Louise:* Yes) just a perfect time for this. It was an upbeat song for [our] little baseball player.... [His] whole team got around and dedicated his uniform, and he went with his uniform on. And they ... retire[d] his number.

Funeral Attendance

Many parents said it was touching and important that so many people attended the funeral. Parents who talked about heavy funeral attendance usually interpreted it to mean that a lot of people supported them and cared about the child.

Denny: You find out who your friends are.... There was over 300 people, and the guy said he's never seen that many people for a 10-week old baby that a lot of them didn't even get a chance to see, so it makes you feel like you got a lot of friends, a lot of people that care about you.

Wayne: The church was ... very large ..., and it was *packed*. With all these organizations he belonged to,... it was just *extremely* crowded (chuckles).... Then when they had the ... procession from the church door to the cemetery,... it ... was like a dignitary that died.... They had to wait about 20 minutes for all the cars.... My brother made the comment, "Geez, I hope I don't die next week." He said (laughing), "I'm gonna have about 15 people." He looks back (still laughing), and there's thousands of people back. So it was kind of amazing, the turnout, which obviously made us feel pretty good, that they all came out to see him.

Bonnie: Great funeral. Even at the funeral home, there was just a *long* line of people. We'd greet them .... but we just couldn't keep up, and I would look up and the lines kept coming and coming and, boy, I just couldn't believe the support.

One parent said she was glad for heavy attendance at the funeral because it enabled her to get the initial condolence conversation out of the way with so many people.

Elaine: I never believed much in visitations. I have always looked at them as kind of barbaric and ... archaic. But I see that differently now because as much as you need to have a grieving process, other people need that too. And like I said to Red, "I couldn't stand for the next year running into people and having them paying me their condolences." It gives them a chance to come and pay their condolence to you, so that you can kind of get it all. That would be horrible, if every time you went to get groceries, every time you went anywhere, somebody would be [offering condolences].

A few parents, however, were cynical about the heavy attendance or qualified their enthusiasm about it, because they felt that afterwards most of the people who attended the funeral distanced them.

George: There was a lot of people that had come to the funeral. It was packed. It was just short notice. They found the body at about midnight. It would have been Saturday AM, and I think it was that following Monday

... that we had the funeral. And we didn't put anything in the paper, but there was an article in there with a picture of Nils.... Steph was in the real estate business at the time and—

Steph: And most people were mortgage company people, real estate agents, other type companies (*George:* yes) that I've worked for, abstract companies. They *all* were represented. And I thought that was great....

George: [My friend who had lost a child years before said not to] build a false sense of security, because after the funeral and everybody has a good cry, and you get a card,... these people are essentially out of your life....

Steph: They want to get on with *their* lives. They don't want to live through your misery.

Words Said During the Funeral

Some parents told of feeling touched by how others defined their child through things said at the funeral.

John: There must have been 30 of them that stood up and gave a testimonial for Jill, recognized what she had done for them. Very, very touching (small laugh), never (sniffs) dreamed that something like that would be possible, I guess. Very emotional service.

Bonnie: A very emotional tribute to her.... So many that got up said that, "Jill was my best friend."

Burying the Child in a Meaningful Place

Typically children were buried. For some parents it was important that the burial be in a place that seemed friendly and nurturing for the child. Denny, for example, talked about burying his two children in a cemetery for children and finding comfort in the appropriateness of the symbols in the cemetery.

Denny: There's a lot of neat markers in Babygarden.... This flier is swinging in God's playland, and different kind of sayings and teddy bears and different things on these markers that kind of want to make you think that maybe there is some kind of playland ... there.

Many parents said that they wanted the child's body to be close to the bodies of meaningful others. For example, Steph talked about how much it meant to her that her son was buried with his paternal grandfather.

Steph: He's buried with his grandfather, which I feel very good about, George's dad, 'cause George's dad was cremated, that they buried the urn, so there was space there for his coffin. So he is buried with his grandfather, which he never met.

Louise talked about being able to get a burial plot next to the one in which her father was buried and her mother would someday be buried.

Louise: I wanted him to be in [our] area, and I didn't even know the name of the cemetery.... Fortunately there was a plot right next to my parents, so that's where he's buried.

For some, the issue was not *whether* to bury the child near someone significant, but *which* significant someone to choose.

Elaine: My mom and my dad and my brother were all buried together, so then we decided at the time you just couldn't hardly handle the thought of him being alone somewhere, so we buried him in that plot with my family. And now you think, "Did we do the right thing? Should we've put him some place where we could be?"

☐ Rituals Beyond the Funeral

In some narratives, death rituals continued beyond the funeral. One such ritual was a well-attended meal immediately after the funeral. At one level, it was a way of feeding close family members and friends who had attended the funeral, of communing together, and of facilitating the bringing of food to the bereaved (as gift, as support, and as symbolic nurturance). At another level, it was a ritual involving others helping the bereaved and the bereaved accepting the help.

Rosa: I'd been a nursing supervisor. The people I had supervised came up to the apartment ... [for a] luncheon right after the funeral. They just came into my house, shooed us out, straightened everything, set everything up.

For some parents, the first Sunday church service after the funeral was a ritual of community support.

Elaine: We went to church on Sunday morning and church was packed. You could not have put another person in. We always sat in the second pew from the front, always, always, always. And when we got to church on Sunday morning, people were standing in the back of the church, ... and there was no one sitting in that pew. ... I'll never forget that. ... He never thought that he had any friends. That was another thing he was going through. He didn't have any friends and all this. That day in church, oh, geez, the side aisles were full, the center aisles were full, the outside of the ch—, you know, I looked up at Red and I said, "And he thought that nobody cared for him."

For some parents, reading condolence cards was a ritual that extended for days or even months after the funeral.

Elaine: We opened cards for what, ... three nights? We as a family opened every one, read every one. We read every one individually.

For some parents visiting the cemetery was a ritual of caring for the child, marking their continuing relationship with the child, and including the child in the family.

Denny: We visit the cemetery and we decorate it for Christmas and Valentine's and birthdays and just whenever we feel like going. It's close to home. It's nice that they are that close.

All family rituals can be funeral rituals after a child dies, in the sense that the family must relate to the child in some way as they carry out the ritual. Some parents talked about trying to leave the family rituals as much as possible the same, with the child or symbols of the child included. Sometimes they made changes, and the changes could be quite difficult. Quite a few couples who had other children talked about symbolically including the child who died in the family Christmas rituals.

Paula: We ... started a tradition ... after Jerry's death, at Christmastime. ... The kids all have stockings that they hang. In fact we all have 'em. ... Everybody's got their names on 'em. And Jerry's stocking gets (clears throat) filled with a Christmas ornament for each of the other kids. To be from him, just as a remembrance.

In a sense, part of the ritual of dealing with the child's death is making the decisions about what to do, during the first year after the death, with each family ritual (Klass, 1988, p. 11; 1999, Chapter 4)—Christmas, the child's birthday, July 4th, Thanksgiving, and so on. This can make the first year's rituals especially painful and especially creative.

☐ Summary

Death rituals were prominent in the narratives of many parents. These rituals might include baptism, autopsy, police inquiry, and organ donation, all of which gave meaning to the child's death. Connected to the rituals of wakes, visitations, funerals, memorial services, and burials were rituals of notifying others of the death and of funeral planning. As parents talked about various funeral rituals it is easy to see how, for many parents, rituals helped to define the child, the death, changes in the parent-child relationship, and much else.

A number of parents talked about difficulties they experienced in dealing with and participating in death rituals. And yet they generally felt positive about the attendance of others at funeral rituals and the meanings they and others communicated during the funeral rituals. In some parent narratives, the rituals continued beyond the funeral, including, possibly, meals for funeral visitors, the first Sunday church service after the death, reading condolence cards, visiting the cemetery, and redesigning family rituals throughout the year to take into account the child's death.

Although parents who thought a child was dying could have strong grief feelings prior to the death, one could say that the initial death rituals defined the onset of parent grieving. As one way to understand parent grieving, the next chapter explores the metaphors parents used in talking about grief. That exploration helps us to know the meanings and understandings that parents said were at the forefront as they grieved.

5

CHAPTER

Metaphors of Grief Feelings

Feelings are integral to the direction and mood of parent narratives, the goals the parents talk about in their narratives, the difficulties they say they encountered, the approaches they say they took to the difficulties, and their explanations of what they did. One key to understanding how feelings shape and are integral to parent narratives is to look at the metaphoric nature of the words parents use to talk about feelings. As parents used the word "grief" and other words to describe their feelings, certain metaphors recurred. Those metaphors highlight certain aspects of parent grief and obscure others (see Rosenblatt, 1994, for a comprehensive discussion of metaphor). Through that highlighting and obscuring, the narratives focus the listener and the speaker on certain ways of conceptualizing parent feelings and away from others.

The metaphors of grief discussed in this chapter refer to how parents talk about feelings. The metaphors of the grief process discussed in Chapter 7 refer to the process parents say they went through in coming to terms or dealing with the death.

☐ Grief is an Entity

As parents talked about it, grief is an entity, a thing. As an entity, it has a reality, a solidity, and a potential impact on the bereaved person, other people, and things. For example, in the following quote, Amy uses "it" to make grief a thing, and "it" pushed her to roots that she never thought she had.

Amy: You get beyond, it's so *deep within*, I mean it's such a, well words never can explain, but it's so deep. And that heaviness is so deep that that's almost far more difficult than crying.... A sexual relationship is very deep but grieving is deeper than that. Deep, deep, deep, deep, deep.... You find out that you have roots that you never thought you had, and you go to those roots.

When seen as an entity, grief has boundaries, limits, and other properties, and it can be distinguished from things that are not it. This highlights that the parent who feels the grief knows what it is and experiences it as a palpable, almost weighty presence. But it obscures the ways that feelings of grief may be vague, fluid, blurred together with other feelings, changing from moment to moment, and not clearly distinguishable from other feelings.

Perhaps making the grief so palpable makes it easier to make grief part of a narrative. It would be hard to make something vague, changeable, and blurred a focus for narrative or even a substantial adjunct to narrative. Perhaps in the generation of narrative, the requirement for a "good" story gives a character to feelings, but perhaps too the demands for structuring experience in terms of narrative actually shape feelings to be more distinct and constant than they would be if a parent were dealing with the experience without coming to a narrative.

As an entity, grief can be contained (the grief is inside the person) and possessed (it is someone's grief). As an entity, grief can also contain things—including the bereaved individual (Klass, 1996, 1997).

Brett: She was in her grief.

As an entity, grief can be evaluated by standards applied to entities. For example, it can be of greater or lesser magnitude, and it can be judged in terms of its neatness and coherence.

Fred: [My grief is] just completely different than hers. Hers is a mess.

Making grief an entity may make it harder to recognize the ways that grief can be so indistinct and amorphous as to be beyond words. And in the application of the word "grief" and related words, those of us who write about grief may make it seem that there is more commonality and uniformity among bereaved people than there actually is. There are very likely many different kinds of "grief."

☐ Grief is Emotionally Draining

PR: Did Noah's death affect your sex life with each other?

Amy: Oh, yeah.

Ted: ... I think we were just too emotionally drained.

Stan: You're just drained. You don't really feel like—

Joy: Really, if we wouldn't have had [our surviving child] to get us up every day, I don't know how, what would have been the motivating factor.

The metaphor of "draining" highlights how grieving is associated with a loss of energy, upbeat feelings, a sense of purpose, and life-meaning. This draining, in turn, saps the couple relationship and makes life less interesting and less rewarding. The metaphor of draining provides a tone and an organizing concept for narratives that explain what went on in the early weeks and months after the child's death—the couple relationship, events at work, parenting of other children, relationships with friends and neighbors, and so on. The parents were limited in what they could do because they were drained.

☐ Emptiness and Holes

Parent narratives often connect feelings to the child's absence. With the child missing from the physical environment, a metaphor that encompasses both that absence and parent feelings is the metaphor of something missing. The emptiness is in the physical, social, and emotional environment, both present and future. Also, as indicated by others who have written about grief (Brice, 1991a, 1991b; Cornwell, Nurcombe, & Stevens, 1977; Rando, 1986, 1991; Raphael, 1983, p. 229), the emptiness is in the self. Many parents talked about feeling empty or about having a hole in themselves.

Chad: Obviously you've got a real strong common bond now, if it's nothing other than your grief for the big empty spot you've got. You've both got the same empty spot.

Hannah: It's like somebody has got into your body and pulled a piece out, and you really don't need it to survive, but you know that hole is there. . . . It's always, always there. I can't imagine anything worse in the whole world. I know that we're going to survive it. But there's something missing; there's just a hole there.

Rosa: It's a gaping hole, and you feel like part of your heart's amputated, and that you're just going to have to learn to live with this gaping hole, that nothing ever makes it better. But you learn to live with this giant loss.

So the child is not merely missing from the physical environment but also from inside the parent. The metaphor thus highlights how children are inside parents and how feelings of grief are in part for what is missing from inside the parent.

The hole is also in the family (McClowry, Davies, May, Kulenkamp, & Martinson, 1987) and in the parent's roles and relationships.

Rosa: I'm really jealous of women who have daughters, because that's the big hole in my life. I'm from a ... fairly matriarchal family.... Men are there for breeding and making money.... The relationship bonds are between women. The strong bonds, the bonds that will always last are between women. And my mum's close to her mom. My mom and her sister are really close. I'm really close to my sister, and there's a sense that I won't have a daughter to be close with. That's hard.... I'm the first born daughter of a first born daughter, and my first born was a daughter. And she's gone. I feel like the pattern is broken.... There's the hole in the family.

Although for some parents the hole or emptiness inside implies that healing is impossible (some holes can never be filled), others saw the hole as something that could heal, get smaller, or become armored.

Gail: When we get together with people from Compassionate Friends, we talk about when this first happens to you, you feel that you have a very large hole in the middle of your chest, and the wind blows through that. Everybody can see it.... [If] you go to a meeting, and there's new people there, ... you know those new people have that hole in their heart, in their chest, and as time goes on, a lot of that closes up. Part of it out of self-defense. You have to; you can't be that vulnerable.... Part of it because time's going on and you [have dealt] with some of it, and gone through some of the healing process and actually have healed some of that hole.

Joy: I think we come to realize that [our little daughter] can't ... fill the hole that [her sister] left, but she's like this healing balm poured into it.

Elaine: My heart.... will never heal, but the hole gets a little less deep.

Perhaps there is a kind of parallelism in people's thinking so that if the child is no longer physically present than it makes a lot of sense to use metaphors of other things no longer present. The metaphors of emptiness and holes thus play off of the child not being present. But the hole/emptiness metaphor obscures how the child's death, in a sense, does not create a hole or emptiness but fills up all space, thoughts, emotions, and dreams so much that there is little room for anything else.

☐ Part of Me Died

Another way of connecting narratives of the aftermath of the child's death with the child's death is to use the idea of "death" metaphorically. Some parents talked about the child's death as having created a dead place in the parent (Cornwell, Nurcombe, & Stevens, 1977; Hocker, 1988; Klass, 1988, pp. 12–14, 1993). This metaphor implies that the child and the parental role in relationship to the child were part of the self (Edelstein, 1984, p. 39), that the damage is beyond repair, that the child was part of the parent, and that the parent is, in a sense, like the child who died (has, in some sense, joined the child through a kind of dying).

Kathy: Those feelings are really right up on the surface of both of us, and time doesn't really make that any better. We decided to go on with our lives, and to continue, because you basically don't have much of a choice, but it never feels okay. It never feels right. And there's always a part of us I think that each of us feels, part of us died with them.

Angela: Part of me died when Blake did.

Bruce: I'm not going to be able to survive another loss. . . . A very large part of me died with Mike. And another part went with this last loss.

Statements like these highlight how a part of the self died, a part, for example, that loved, was innocent, and was optimistic. They also highlight how the part of identity that was tied to the child died. Also, to the extent that the child and the parent were not separate beings in the parent's thinking, the child's death means part of the parent died (Brice, 1991b). And this dying of part of the self is not just an observation, but a feeling. Parents who say that part of them died are talking about a feeling of irreparable loss and of lifelessness.

What is obscured with the metaphor of part of the self dying is that the parent continues to live and is constantly faced with the challenge of what to do with that life—the parent is not free of the responsibilities, duties, opportunities, needs, and so on that an actual death would terminate. But in a sense, it is the paradox of the awareness of continuing to live while missing so much that makes it clear to the parent that part of the self is dead. It is the indifference to so much that used to matter, the lack of positive feelings, and the continuing sense of loss that help to make the metaphor of part of the self dying seem so apt to some parents.

☐ This Child Was Special

In the narratives of most parents are metaphoric statements that provide a measurement of magnitude of loss and intensity of feeling. One kind of statement that says the loss was great and the parent has very strong feelings about the child's death is a statement about how special the child was. I would call these statements metaphors, and such statements are consistent with what has been reported in other writings on grief (Raphael, 1983, p. 274; Rubin, 1993); bereaved parents say wonderfully praising things about the child who died. How could they not when they are telling others and themselves how much they have lost? I do not want to discount in any way the truth of what these parents say, but in statements like the following I think the parents are not only speaking literal truth but also metaphoric truth.

Wayne: He was always a straight A student.... Everything he did he had to be the best in, not because we told him to be the best in, but because he felt that's how he wanted to.... One of the top hockey players in the state.... He played the piano.... He was very musically inclined....

Louise: He was very well liked by his friends. He [had] lots of friends.... When he'd go to their houses, their parents all just loved him. He wasn't like a normal kid you bring here that comes and he goes down the basement. He was *so* personable, a lot of charisma, and he ... got along with adults so well, and yet with kids, that their parents all just thought he was a great friend to have, 'cause he just had such a good sense of humor and his teachers all loved him and just a really neat kid, really easy to get along with.

John: [Jill] ... went out to California, and she got a job,... started working in the [furniture] department, and she became their top retail sales person. She won (*Bonnie:* Many months) sales-person-of-the-month.... She was friends of everybody.... She drew people.

Joy: She was just a real happy, joyful, really bright little girl.... She was a really special child from the beginning. She taught herself how to read....

Stan: She was ... very special, very smart. She used to read to her kindergarten class rather than the teacher doing it....

Joy: Jenny just loved everybody.... I remember even from the time she was a baby she'd reach her arms out to anybody.... None of the other kids have ... been like that.... So many people after the accident ... thanked us for sharing her with them.... The school psychologist that tested her for early admission called her Nobel prize material.... She was a little gymnast. She was pretty much a natural.

Hannah: Tyler always tried to excel in everything, and he was probably the most sensitive of our ... kids (crying). Very sensitive, very giving. He used to go ... to the nursing home and play cribbage with the old people. And he loved little kids. And he was kind of our family peacemaker.... He would bring home animals that people left on the street and ... find homes for 'em.... At school he would befriend kids that nobody else liked, because he said, "... Everybody's got to have one friend, Mom." ... Everybody who met him said there's just something very special about him.... When he would laugh,... it just came from the bottom of his soul. And he's also a kid, no matter what I cooked, "Mom, that was great." ... He's teased his sister just unmercifully. But boy, if anybody else ever did anything, he would just be ready to knock 'im.... If he was alive now, [our daughter's] boyfriend that took off when he found out she was pregnant, Tyler probably would've hunted him [and] would be in jail....

Fred: He was six foot tall and all muscle....

Hannah: ... I was mending clothes one day, I said, "If I had a sewing machine with an open arm I could mend these ... without taking the seam out," and a couple of days later there was a sewing machine on my table (crying). And when CD players first came out, "Wouldn't it be nice to have a CD player...." I came home and he had bought a CD player, and he told me (still crying), "I'm going to be really rich someday, Mom, and you're going to come home, and there's gonna be a beautiful car in the driveway. It's going to have a red bow on top" (still crying). That's kinda what I miss, is the sensitivity.... There's a young man that walks around the neighborhood.... The kids call him "Crazy Bob." And I'm sure he's probably schizophrenic.... He's kind of a nuisance, but he doesn't do anything to harm anybody ... (crying). The day after Tyler died he came to our door and ... said, "I just want you to know Tyler was really a nice guy. When I was really cold, he'd give me a ride in his car.... Nobody else ever did that for me."

What Hannah said about Crazy Bob are like things said by many parents. Many talked not only about their own reasons for thinking their child was special but also about how much others valued or cherished the child and thought of the child as special or outstanding. The opinions of others validate a parent's own sense of how much has been lost and provide what can be taken as a more objective, outsider's view.

Iris: [The nurses] really liked him. He was a really pretty baby, and a real pleasant personality, and everybody just really liked him, loved him.

Value for these parents is determined by, among other things, the reactions of others. These narratives are thus offering information about the child's value as measured by the evaluations of others. The language could be taken as one of societal values, but I think the place where scores were most determinedly kept was the hearts of these parents. They were saying that the child was very central in their own lives (Braun & Berg, 1994) and that they valued the child very, very much.

Loss of the Parent in the Child

In some narratives, one way the child was said to be special was that the child represented genes, personality, values, and other things passed on to the child by the parent. Because of this, the loss of the child also meant a loss of parental self. Talking this way was also another way of saying how great the loss was to the parent, particularly if what was lost was what the parent had been wanting to pass on to a child.

Tina: When I was a baby, I had this real dark olive skin, and I had just black, black hair. And that was the kind of little girl I wanted to have. Well, wouldn't you know, dark skin, and she had black hair. She was like *everything* I ever wanted. And so I think that part of it sort of added to the intensity of it.

Some parents used this kind of metaphor to talk about how the loss was shared by both parents, with the child who died combining aspects of both parents.

Glenda: [He combined the] patience of you and the extrovertedness of me. [Talking to her husband]

The metaphor of the loss of the parent in the child highlights how children are, for many parents, a kind of immortality, or at least a potential continuation of something of themselves beyond their own death. The metaphor also highlights that the loss is in some sense a loss of the parent, not of someone totally separate from the parent.

A Death So Bad It Kills

A few parent narratives included a story about a child's death causing another death in the family. I am sure that such deaths happen, but one could also say that saying the child's death caused another death is a very powerful metaphor. The second dying becomes a way of expressing how much the child's death made life not worth living or how much it disrupted somebody's functioning as a living organism.

Elaine: That night [of Kyle's death, my husband's] dad, or the next morning his dad had a massive stroke and then died three weeks later.... It was really hard for him and even the nurses had written in the chart that he was so despondent over his grandson. Like he said, "I'm 85 years old. Why didn't it happen to me?"

Red: ... He was close with the boy. He was out here all the time.

Elaine: Yeah, yes. See, this farm has been in Red's family ... 100 years. And Grampa would always come out before we owned it and paint the buildings and ... put a rock foundation under this old granary.... Those boys were with him all the time, helping him. And he'd take 'em home ... [for] supper. He'd have them in the back seat of [his] car. It was really hard on Grampa. It really, really was. It just was kinda more than he could take.

The metaphor of the child's death causing other deaths in a sense high-lights how life can lose meaning and hearts can be broken when a child dies.

☐ A Loss So Bad My Grief Was Out of Control

In many ways, control is a common theme in stories about grief (Cochran & Claspell, 1987, p. 70; Klass, 1988, p. 25). Many parents use the metaphor of control in talking about situations where they struggled with grief.

Tina: It's ... really hard to get a grip ..., because ... you're not controlling your emotions. Your emotions are being controlled by this thing that's just out of control, the pain and stuff.... One of the goals that I had kinda set out for myself when I was first going through in the first six months was I wanted to get to a point where *I* could control my emotions about it, and my emotions weren't controlling me. So if *I* wanted to talk about her and cry, that was okay, as long as I made the conscious decision, because initially I couldn't do that. I *had* no control over my emotions.... This was something I did for myself, and I'm at that point now where again *I* can

control my emotions. They're not controlling me.... It took a lo-ong time
to get there, but that's a good feeling.

The metaphor of feeling out of control and the metaphor of moving to
gain control of emotions highlight how the child's death was out of the
parent's control and that the parent is powerless to restore the child to
life. The metaphor also highlights the great impact of the child's death
and the great power of parent grief feelings and the ways it seems that
in their grief they are unable to do most of what they would normally have
done. The metaphor obscures how even very early in grief people exercise
some control of feelings (Schwab, 1990)—for example, they may be able to
distract themselves with exercise, household chores, or by medicating the
feelings (Cook, 1988).

There is a paradox in parents offering narratives about being out of
control, because in a sense stories are a way to gain control over events
and feelings (Harvey, 1996, p. 11). Parent stories about being out of control
are in a sense part of their taking control, even if the stories speak of being
out of control.

☐ The Language of Pain

All parent narratives included words about pain. Their words about pain
spoke a literal truth, but they were also metaphors, drawing from the
language of physical pain to express the injury, ache, and shock felt as a
result of the loss.

Amy: I was so exhausted that for a couple of months I was sleeping like 12
hour nights. And I ached.... My body ached, my heart ached. That was the
first time that I ever ... physically felt a broken heart. And I had this ...
pain in me, and ... it was as though somebody took me by the ankles and
just slapped me against a brick wall, pretty hard, a number of times. That's
how the rest of my body felt.... It was ... an emotional thing. It was a very,
very physical thing, too.

Words about pain imply that what parents do with physical pain they also
do with emotional pain—cry, grimace, moan, desire healing, desire help
from someone (physician, nurturing family member), use pain killers, and
do what is necessary to become healed. There is an implication of something
damaged, that the pain of grief comes from damage to something—including
the self, the family, and the future. Pain is a powerful teacher. It says
whatever one did it is best not to do that again.

In parent narratives there was often a sense that in public situations, particularly after the first few days of bereavement, they were expected to mask or hide their pain, to minimize it in the presence of others. Small wonder then that often the most extreme actions expressing pain were saved for private moments (Cook, 1988).

Erika: I remember exactly the first time [my husband] left me alone in the house for an extended period of time. And I really needed that. I needed to just wail by myself, to just scream at the top of my lungs (crying), where I probably didn't want to do that in front of him.... I thought I'm going to be very, very, very selfish. I don't want to have to think about my scaring him, or he'd try to comfort me. I just have to *scream!* And I was glad he left me alone for a little while. I didn't want to be alone altogether. But right then I needed it.

The pain parents talked about was not only about the death but also about how people close to them reacted to the loss. By putting it into the language of pain they highlighted how lack of support from others can have the same effect as physical pain.

Tina: With my mom and dad, it really hurt me a lot. There was just sort of this feeling that someone dies and they call your dad and he activates this stuff he needs to do on their life insurance policy. And "Oom, dump," end of thing. They go to funerals and reviewals, and it's no biggy. I still to this day have a *very* hard time, and will *only* go to a funeral or a reviewal if I absolutely, positively have to.

☐ The Language of the Body

In quite a few parent narratives there was a sense that grief was embodied (Brice, 1991b; Lauterbach, 1994), that grief was contained in or expressed by the body. That probably should not be surprising when a dominant metaphor for grief is a body metaphor, "pain," and when the pain that comes with a child's death is intense, long term, and pervasive (Cochran & Claspell, 1987, p. 67; Hogan, Morse, & Tasón, 1996). But the embodiment metaphors were not merely of pain, but also frequently about connections to the child. Here is what seems the most obvious and detailed example among the couples interviewed.

Kathy: I felt bad when my babies weren't healthy, 'cause I've always been healthy, and couldn't give them that. And I remember I couldn't eat for a long time. I just didn't feel right to eat when they were dead, and I had gotten sick after that, and I remember I went to a doctor, and he weighed me. I was less than 100 pounds, and I don't think I'd ever been, and I didn't even know. I was kind of just so numb. One day I was at school and a kid accidentally stapled my hand, and it was bleeding, and I didn't feel it. He said, "Miss . . . , Miss . . . . your hand is bleeding." I looked over and said, "Oh, yeah." I was so numb from everything.

Her numbness was not only of thought and emotions but also of body, a way of saying that "not even my own physical pain or body health matters when my children are dead." Not eating can be taken as a statement about not enjoying physical pleasure when a child has died or not being attuned to the body's hunger signals. But not eating may also have something to do with her dying children not being able to take in much food. And her husband had trouble eating also. His eating disorder anteceded the deaths of their two children, but it became more serious after the deaths. Thus, for two parents whose children in a sense had starved to death, there was a kind of starvation that could be taken as expressing their continuing links to the children and their empathy for the children.

Kathy: Karl has had some problems [sexually]. . . . He's had some problems with eating disorders, and that diminished his (3 second pause) drive a lot, and I think after the kids died, he was even worse. He was just emaciated. . . . He was delirious at times and really in bad shape physically and consequently emotionally too, I think, just because of lack of food. . . . He still has an eating disorder. . . . That's . . . been a lifelong thing with him, but it got particularly worse during that time. . . . I don't think he had *any* sort of a drive then. He was just barely walkin', don't you think? If you could remember that. Is that accurate, or? (*Karl:* Yeah.) And I was taking care of him. . . . Like going to the emergency room. . . . I thought of him more like a child. . . . He was literally a bag of bones, and I remembered what he used to look like, and [it] broke my heart to see him that way, and people would say to me too that this was all going on at the same time, "Why aren't you feeding him? . . . You must not be making what he likes." . . . That obviously had nothing to with it.

He (and she) confirmed how much thoughts about personal eating were entangled in thoughts and feelings about the children not being able to eat enough to thrive.

Karl: One of the main problems that we had with the two children was the feeding. And trying to feed them, and get them to take the four ounces of fluid. (*Kathy:* umhm) And it used to really bother me to the extent that here I can eat anything I want, and at that time I was pretty much still close to okay.... It just didn't seem fair to me that they couldn't eat, and that they weren't able to survive because they couldn't....

Kathy: I don't think you can understand that unless you actually are holding your child, and trying to get food into them, and they (*Karl:* It would be every other hour) can't take it....

Karl: Hour after hour. We were doing it *all* the time.... We really wanted to do that. We really wanted to be as close to them, and to provide for them.... It was her turn. And then it was my turn. And you'd get up and you'd try to feed them, and you'd want them to do well *so* bad. And they just couldn't consume food.

☐ Deep Depression and Suicidal Thoughts Measure Grief

Narrative about deep depression and possible suicide is, among many things, a way to measure loss, grief, and pain. It is a way of saying the loss is so vast, has laid me so low, and that the feelings accompanying it are so devastating that life may not be worth continuing. From that perspective, it would be difficult, perhaps even pointless, to dissuade a grieving parent from talking about deep depression or suicide. The parent is telling how much has been lost and how strong the feelings of grief are, so to persuade the parent otherwise would diminish the child who died, the loss, and the grief.

Glenda: If I ever really truly believed this really happened, and he's never coming home (she starts crying) I think I will go crazy. I have enough pills on hand. I can do it. [My husband] knows it, and I know that's a terrible thing to say, but it's part of my inner opting out anger, whatever, depression, is, I can be in control of that. I can choose to do it anytime (sniffles). Because I, I, I think if I ev—, I haven't accepted it yet. If I ever truly believe it, I still don't accept it, I probably will.... And maybe just saying it is healthy and then one doesn't act.

In saying, "If I ever truly believed this really happened," Glenda did not doubt the death of her son. I think she was saying if she ever really "accepted" the death in the sense of no longer grieving her son, then life is not worth living. There is a paradox in what she said, the idea that she will commit suicide if she stops hurting. But what she said is consistent with ideas that deep depression and thoughts of suicide are a measure of a parent's loss and of how much the parent continues to care about the child who died. Speaking of and having those feelings mean the child and the death of the child continue to matter very, very much.

☐ The Anger of Grief as Metaphor

Language about any feeling may include words that measure the intensity of the feeling. For example, a narrative about anger may include words about how loudly a person talked or about anger so great that things were thrown and doors slammed.

Wayne: [Louise] had some real bad temper tantrums. It would build up inside her. And she would lose it, and sometimes she'd be throwing ... things. And that door got a work out, slamming it, 'cause she (*Louise:* leaving) wanted, she'd want to leave, and get out, because ... she hated the house. She hated what [was] in this house. She hated the rooms in the house.... She'd slam the door and leave.

Parent narrative about anger in bereavement can be, like narrative about other grief feelings, a measure of how much was lost when the child died and how great the parents' grief is. Whether Louise's anger is directed at Wayne, the child who died, someone perceived to have caused the fatal accident, herself, society, or some other entity, her verbal and nonverbal expressions of anger can be understood as measuring the magnitude of her loss and grief.

☐ Guilt and Blame as Measures of Loss and Grief

Many parent narratives speak of feelings of guilt. They say their guilt feelings arise for many different reasons (DeFrain, 1991; Edelstein, 1984, p. 70; Johnson, 1984–85, 1987, pp. 31–54; Miles & Demi, 1983–84, 1991–92) including guilt at surviving, doing something that might have directly caused the death, doing something that may have caused God to take the child, having been a less than sterling parent, not being loving enough in the last encounter with the child, participating in medical decisions that may have hastened the child's death, and about not being there for the child while the child was dying. The following quotes give a sense of parent narratives about guilt feelings.

Al: You'd be surprised what you think about and what you go over and over and over.... I ran over him, and you hear these stories on radio and TV about people being jailed. This runs through your mind, where here I am. I killed somebody, and even though it was accidental, and yet I'm still out here. I can do what I want to.... I don't give a damn, you're still associated with what you do. I know for a long time I don't think she understood what the hell was going through my head but (*Barb:* Did you?) Yeah. I did. I just didn't know what the hell to do about it.

Red: I spent a lot of time blaming us. I rolled that tractor twice. And I haven't even been out shopping for a different tractor. [Shouldn't have kept it,] because it's so dangerous. I very seldom ever left the kids drive it. . . .

Elaine: He always felt that he had put monetary value over Kyle's life. . . .

Red: Yeah, I went to buy a tractor that was $3000, and I thought, "Geez, I can't afford that."

Words about blame and guilt, like words about anger and other feelings, can measure how terrible the child's death was, how much was lost, and how strong the parents' feelings are. In the quotes immediately above, Al suggested that perhaps he should be in jail and Red said that he had "spent a lot of time blaming us." Both the idea of jail for causing an accidental death and the notion of blaming that lasted "a lot of time" say, among other things, that the guilt and the blaming were heavy and long term because the child's death was so significant to the parent.

☐ The Language of Money

With money such a widely used basis of measurement in U.S. society, it makes sense that some parents would measure the magnitude of their loss and the strength of their grief in terms of money. One way to do such a measurement is to think of life insurance payments after a death as a measure of loss and feelings. Thus, for a child who had died to be deemed worth little or no money in insurance payments could be taken as diminishing the child, the parent loss, and parent grief. Parents could be very upset when an insurer said parents could not collect on a child's death, because the judgment that no compensation was due to the parents seemed to say that they had not lost much.

Al: (Crying) I have ... insurance on the farm and us. I had backhoe insurance covering me for operating ... the machine, covering anybody. So when Tom was killed, these policies didn't pay off. There was a loophole. . . . The backhoe policy would not pay because he was an immediate member of the family. . . . He didn't have any value at all.

The proceeds of a wrongful death lawsuit can also provide a measure of the worth of the child or the magnitude of parental loss and pain. Suing for a lot of money is a way of saying how great one's loss and pain are, and how great one's anger is (Rosenblatt, 1983b). [A lawsuit also is a bid to assess liability, to measure someone's responsibility for the death.] Some parents contemplated lawsuits directed at physicians, strangers who were involved in an accident, hospitals, HMOs, and manufacturers of equipment or structures involved in an accident. Some parents took at least the first steps in suing.

Unfortunately, lawsuits can be seen by others as a measure of the greed and materialism of the parents who are suing. For example, one couple sued because of the design of a pier that their son fell from and drowned. Some people in their hometown took the suit to be a measure not of the couple's loss and grief but of their greed and unwillingness to take responsibility for how they supervised the child.

George: This fishing pier ... was not designed with children in mind.... The rail system with three horizontal members. That works just wonderful as a ladder for a kid, or wonderful for a kid to fall through.

Steph: Yeah, because there was enough room through the bottom two (*George:* yeah) for them to reach down.

George: ... You could not *build* that type of a rail system in a residential application.... You couldn't get a permit for a rail system like that in a ... shopping center ..., but it's judged safe for a lake.... After losing Nils, I recognize this could happen to somebody else. And I had this good friend of mine, the attorney, and he had a bright idea. He said, "Well, maybe we could change things." So I thought we were going after the [state department of natural resources]. It turns out [our town] had to be named in a lawsuit (*Steph:* So was the state).... Some people thought we were being opportunistic, I suppose. Just by the tone of their letter ..., "How come you weren't looking after your kid?"

Steph: ... Well, we basically just wanted to get it changed (*George:* yeah) so it didn't happen again (sighs)....

George: Some people thought we were in it for the money, which was not the case.... I'd already made up my own mind if I got the goddamn money that wasn't going to go in my account.... There would've been a memorial for Nils.... The last ... thing in the world I would want to do is somehow financially gain from the loss of my son. I'd rather burn the money.

With selfish interest so obviously an alternative interpretation when parents try to use money metaphors in assessing the magnitude of their grief, it is no surprise that every parent who had mentioned thinking about suing or who received insurance payments as a result of a child's death backed away from the money metaphor. They downplayed money in their narratives, and some talked about converting the money to uses that seemed more for other people than for themselves, for example, for a monument honoring the child.

☐ Summary

Parent narratives included many different metaphors for grief. These metaphors highlight some things about the parent experience of grief while obscuring other things. For example, as parents talked about grief, they made it an entity. As an entity, grief has substance and impact. Making grief an entity makes it easier to talk about grief as though it is something distinct. It might even be in the nature of narrative that grief has to be made something palpable and distinct. But by making grief an entity, there may be an obscuring of the ways it is vague, unbounded, ever changing, and hard to know.

As parents talked about grief, they used metaphors like "emotionally draining," "emptiness and holes," and "part of me died." An analysis of these and other common metaphors parents used for grief helps to understand what grief was like for the parents. The draining metaphor, for example, helps to understand how much parents felt drained of energy, purpose, joy, and life meaning. The emptiness and holes metaphors, highlight how the child is missing from the parent's daily life and also from inside the parents. The emptiness and holes metaphors obscure, however, how much the child and the child's death fills the parent to overflowing.

Other metaphors analyzed in this chapter include metaphors of how the child was special, metaphors of parental pain, body metaphors, feeling metaphors that measure the magnitude of parental loss and of parental feelings, and money metaphors.

This and the previous two chapters have focussed on the beginnings of parent grieving—the story of the child's dying and death, the death rituals, and what grief felt like to parents. The next chapter continues the exploration of what is present at the beginning of parent grieving, focusing on an aspect of the relationship between parents and others that emerged when the child was dying or immediately after the death. In various ways parent narratives spoke of a chasm that opened up between the parents and rest of the world. In the narratives of most parents, one of the great challenges of early bereavement was to make sense out of and do something about that great gulf they experienced between themselves and the rest of the world.

CHAPTER

The Chasm Between Grieving Parents and the World

☐ The Chasm and Where It Comes From

When a child is dying or after the child has died, what one could call a vast chasm forms between the parents and other people. Consistent with what other researchers have reported (Klass, 1986–87, 1999; Lauterbach, 1994), almost all parents talked about something resembling a chasm.

The chasm seems to come partly from the devastating feelings that engulf parents and that are the essence of grief (Hogan, Morse, & Tasón, 1996). Those feelings make everyone who does not share the feelings seem to a parent to be distant and uncaring. The chasm comes, in part, from society being so fragmented and anonymous that many others do not know of a parent's bereavement, and those who do know typically go on with their ordinary life routines.

Ted: You feel like you're in another dimension that other people can't relate.... You're off somewhere else, and ... you just feel like ... you want to ... scream [and] say, "Don't you realize what's happening?" ... I can remember walking down the streets ... in a daze. And you wanted to just scream out to people, 'cause everybody's going about their business, but you know ... something sure is not business as usual.

_____

Hannah: After Tyler died.... I saw garbage trucks going by, and I saw the mailman delivering mail, and I wanted to go out there and ... just scream at them, "Don't you guys know that Tyler died?!" (*Fred:* Life goes on.) Life goes on, but your life stops (bang on table) right there, for a while. And I was ... really pissed when I'd seen my neighbors going to work, 'cause I sat in this chair for six months, just staring out these windows. I'd watch my neighbors go to work. I'd watch the kids outside playing. And I'd (*Fred:* Kids ... walking to school) be so angry, so angry, because my kid is dead. And none of them were acknowledging the fact that I was, you know what I'm saying? I was really mad. How can life go on when mine's not?

George and Steph talked about the chasm forming because others who knew about the death distanced them.

Steph: People don't want to see you.

George: Like all of a sudden you're HIV positive ... and then they're out of your lives, ... forever gone. It's just (*Steph:* They don't know what to say to you) well, they almost to the last person, I mean you could have a thousand friends and then you lose a child, you can almost bet within probably 60 days you won't have any left, outside of just a few, very, very few.

What George and Steph said was echoed by many parents. The chasm comes, in part, because U.S. culture gives the ownership of grief to parents and not to the whole society and expects the parents to handle their problems on their own.

Some parents said that others, even those who know them well, did things that broadened and deepened the chasm. Sometimes it seemed to those parents that the others acted out of a desire to help the parents get past the loss, and sometimes it seemed to the parents that the others acted that way because it was inconvenient for them to be sensitive to the parents' feelings.

Sally: My mom ... tells me about people having babies. They want my feelings to go away. About the time [our son who died] was born my sisters-in-law on both sides of the family had children. It caused me such pain to have them come to town with their children, to brag about their children, to complain about their children. I had a big fight with one of my sisters-in-law.... "How can you come to *my* town to show off your baby when my baby is dead? And don't complain to me about the work of two children!" Our falling out lasted for years.

When people drop out of a bereaved parent's life, they do not usually make an announcement of why they are doing so. Some parents spoke of their uncertainty about the cause of people disappearing and their conjecture that it was because of the death.

Tina: I lost a friend. I wouldn't say it was *over* this necessarily, but a friend I had known in college, and we've stayed in contact, and after Gina died I called her and told her what had happened, and I never heard from her again. And after about six months . . . I thought, "God, what kind of a friend is she?" . . . I think people just didn't know what to do or . . . say. . . . When you're goin' through it, you feel like everyone's evaluating you; . . . when's the truck gonna come to (chuckling) put her in a straight jacket? . . . It made me mad, because I thought, "Geez, how would they be if *they* went through it? It's awful."

The quote from Tina suggests that others do not necessarily understand parent grief and expect it to be over quickly. Consistent with what Schwab (1990) reported, a number of other parents spoke of the assumption of many people that a parent quickly gets over grief for a child who died.

Woody: Most of them don't realize how long the grief goes on (sounds teary). Most of them think it's over. If they don't experience it, they think in two weeks it's gone.

The assumption of others that parents will quickly get over grief helps to maintain the chasm between grieving parents and others. The assumption offends the bereaved parents and makes it clear that others do not empathize with them. People who assume grief will end quickly may think that parents continuing to grieve are strange and perhaps mentally ill—people who might best be distanced.

☐ First Encounters with Others Across the Chasm

Many bereaved parents said that the first encounters with familiar people and the first returning to familiar social settings were challenging because of discomfort about the social and emotional chasm, a discomfort that might exist on both sides of the chasm.

Chad: You know what one of the *real* tough things to do is? . . . I [used to go] to the local Elks and sit and play a little euchre in the afternoon with four or five guys maybe . . . twice a week. Walk back in that place again. (*Erika:* Oh, I remember that was pretty traumatic for you.) We were old drinking buddies and good old boy network . . . , and it was just *real* hard to walk in that place.

Erika: I bet it was real hard for them to see you walk in, that first time. But I felt so glad that he had done that, because it was one more thing to face.

Chad: It was just one of the things you had to get done. . . . You weren't going to move out of town; you weren't going to sell the house.

Wayne: I have some golf buddies. . . . The very first time that I played golf with them after Will died, . . . that was kind of hard. 'Cause *they* didn't know what to say, and that's why a lot of these people avoid you. They don't know . . . what to say. They have no idea how you're gonna react to what they're gonna say.

A few parents talked about the chasm making them feel as though they were on stage in their first encounters with others.

Erika: The first couple of weeks, the first couple of months, were just such a mishmash of, can barely remember getting along, making yourself go, going to buy groceries that first time was just, if he thought it was hard to go walk into the liquor or the Elks, it was pretty hard to walk in the grocery store, where everybody's eyes go right to you.

In some first encounters across the chasm, others were described as saying things that were hurtful or offensive, for example, religious framing of the death that seemed to diminish the parent's pain or to impose a meaning on the death that did not fit the parent's understandings (Gilbert, 1992). Sometimes such words would leave the chasm unbridged or bridged in a way that maintained or created great distance between parent and other. (See the section on "Sorting" in Chapter 11 for further discussion of this.)

☐ The Part of Bereaved Parents in Making the Chasm

Most parents said that the ways others reacted and did not react to them was of great importance in creating the chasm between them and others. But some parents also saw their own role in creating the chasm. For example, the discomfort others have with bereaved parents may be a reaction to things the bereaved parents have communicated through words or actions.

Gail: [My friend who avoided me all these years] was here [the day after Randy died], and there was a bunch of people in here eating dinner, and I got very angry and threw chicken. I don't think I threw it at her. I think I just threw it on the plate. "Everybody's eatin', and our kid is dead! Don't you care?!" How can the world go on? And she got so scared, and . . . left. . . .

Until her aunt's funeral, and obviously that had bothered her for a long time, [because she] kept on saying, "I'm sorry, I'm sorry."

Some parents said they had a part in creating the chasm through their discomfort with how they thought others would react. A woman whose son born with a fatal birth defect lived for a week talked about wanting to avoid those who had known she was pregnant.

Sally: After we lost Mike, I felt like a failure. I had to change my hair stylist, my dentist, everybody. I couldn't face the people who knew I had been pregnant.

Some parents said that they sought activities that minimized their interaction with others, that they needed distance from others in order to hurt and be strange without the interference of having to tune in to others or worry about their evaluations.

Barb: Tom was killed in September, and I think it was the first part of April I asked [a friend who owns a restaurant] if he just didn't have something I could do, 'cause I just needed something. . . . I washed dishes for three years, and . . . I'll be there four years . . . in April. . . . He wanted me to waitress about six months after I was there, but I was not ready for people. . . . I could do my own little thing back there in the kitchen, and if I wasn't coherent that was fine because nobody (little laugh) noticed. But I just, no, I didn't waitress.

☐ The Challenge of What to Do about the Chasm with Others

As some parents talk about the grief process, a major part of the process involves dealing with the chasm—whether, how, and where to bridge it and where to leave it unbridged. One woman talked about finding a job to escape to and then struggling about what to do about the chasm between her and her coworkers.

Amy: I wasn't working. . . . He could go to work, he could be occupied. I had an empty house. And I didn't know what I was going to do. . . . I didn't want to go back to [teaching]. . . . I couldn't take that intensity, so somebody . . . hired me; I worked at a gourmet deli. It was kind of a mindless deal. But it was a fun atmosphere and . . . an escape. . . . It also felt really awkward that three, four weeks ago my baby just died. Nobody there except the boss knew what happened. And I felt strange about that. . . . Eventually I would tell some people. They couldn't handle it. And they wouldn't talk to me about it at all. And I didn't know what to do with that.

For many bereaved parents, the start of bridging the chasm with someone is that the person acknowledges the death. And the start of bridging the chasm with the community is that the community collectively acknowledges the death. I think that is one reason why many bereaved parents made a special note of how many people attended their child's funeral.

Chad: We had a *lot* of community support. I mean there was (*Erika:* We're very visible.) Well, we'd been in [town] for what, 16, 17 years at that time.... We do know everybody through [sports].... The church was fuller than it was on Christmas day.

The bridge across the chasm is almost always a bridge of words. Being there is important, but I think it is words that establish a shared reality about the death. Among the words that seemed to make a difference were those by others that acknowledged the death and that said the death was often in their awareness. The chasm existed partly because bereaved parents were living with the awesome knowledge, every moment of the day, of their child's death, while the people around them seemed to live as though nothing had happened. When somebody acknowledged the child's death and said they thought often about the child or about the parents' bereavement, that was valuable in spanning the chasm. After the incident quoted above that ended with her friend saying, "I'm sorry, I'm sorry," Gail spoke about the importance of words in bridging the chasm.

Gail: Other people do think about that. That made me realize that other people do think about us. It's not that they forget you. They don't know what to do.... I'd rather have somebody say something stupid to me where they'll get a reaction out of me than to say nothing. That's really hurtful, and they pretend it never happened, and they never say his name, and then they don't ask, "How are you?"

Similarly, Tina talked about wanting words to bridge the chasm and being upset that people avoided talking about her daughter's death and Tina's feelings.

Tina: Particularly with family and friends, I really felt like I was goin' it alone. *My* parents (snorts), nothing.... *My* dad is in life insurance, and ... death is part of his job.... It was sort of ... a nonevent for them. Nobody says anything around her birthday.... Although this year my mom did say something about three weeks after. (mimics the voice of an older woman)

"Your dad and I were talkin'. Just how old would Gina have been?" I just wanted to scream and say, "Well like you care! You haven't asked me about her since the day she died!"

It also can help bridge the gap to have others show strong feelings of grief. One couple talked about their gratitude for the strong emotions expressed by a pastor immediately after the death.

Pete: In a way it helped us too because it seemed like he felt the grief so hard, so much.

If the gap is bridged with someone, there are still issues of the quality of the relationship between the bereaved parent and that person. A parent could feel acknowledgment and sympathy from another person and still not find much support with that person. Chapter 11 deals, in part, with what parents thought constituted supportive relationships and how and where they found such relationships. Also, bridging the gap was not necessarily easy for the parent. Some parents told how bridging the chasm at a first encounter with a friend or acquaintance could bring a bereaved parent back to more intense grieving.

Bonnie: It was hard coming back [to work] because every time I'd see somebody I hadn't seen before, it was just all over again.

☐ The Chasm Between Partners

Chapter 9 provides an extended discussion of the couple relationship, but it is appropriate to say here that some parent narratives spoke of a chasm existing between the two parents (Schwab, 1990). The chasm was understood as arising from many different sources. Not infrequently parents thought the marital chasm arose because grieving created emotional unavailability or because of an unwillingness to have emotions stirred up by the partner. Some parents, like Karl, seemed not to be sure why the marital chasm had developed.

Karl: I think it's truly had an effect on our relationship. I think that the first time, [when our daughter died], we withdrew from everyone else, and ... the second time, [when our son died], we almost withdrew from each other.... It was that little bit deeper. I love Kathy as much now as I did then, but sometimes I find (crying) that (Kathy is crying too) I just back away. We both go our separate lives.... We have been ... backing off from everybody else ..., and (Kathy sniffles) we're backing off a little bit from each other. And I've often thought whether it's, do I blame her? Does she blame me? . . . I don't know.

Some parents said that the marital chasm stemmed in part from the child who died having been a major (or even the major) link between the parents.

Al: The biggest reason I think that people part after a death like that is that you have the problem finding a reason to go on, to keep going.

Barb: Well you're looking for something.

Al: If you've got the kid, you've got something in common. If he ain't there . . . any longer, well, you've lost that, the bond between the [two of you], tying . . . you . . . together.

☐ The Chasm Between Life Before the Death and Life After It

In some parent narratives the chasm is not only between the bereaved parent and others but also between the parent and the whole world. I think that is one reason why firsts, like the first birthday, Thanksgiving, Christmas, or vacation following the death, are so hard. The death has opened up each of those events to be dealt with and understood very differently than they would have been if the child were alive. All couples had stories about how they struggled with those firsts, struggled to cross the chasm between ordinary life before the dying and death and the new life that started with the dying and death.

Erika: We used to really decorate for Christmas outside. Used to outline the house, and [our friend] says, "Well, I know David helped you at that." So she offered to do it, and I say, "We're not doing it." That first year I didn't think we were going to have a Christmas, and he'd been dead almost a year. But it was *really* hard to do that that year. . . . [Our older son] says, "Well, aren't we putting up a tree . . .?" I say, "You want it up? You're going to help with it." But . . . we're not going to have the same thing we've always had. We're going to have to change things. . . .

Chad: We had a Santa Claus . . . up on the roof. . . . He was still up there when David died. . . . That was tough to go up there and take that Santa Claus down. I knew . . . that's the last time it would ever get put up there. And we had all kinds of lights around. . . . (*Erika:* Even part of the barn). Yeah, and those lights out there are the first time. That's his tree. We planted a tree there for him. And that's the first ... Christmas lights we've had. This year. In five years, that's the first time we've ever had any.

In a sense, the chasm Erica referred to is a chasm between personal or familial historical eras. But in another sense she was referring to a chasm that divided her family from families that were not burdened by grief in carrying out the annual cycle of rituals.

☐ Summary

Most parent narratives spoke of the death creating a chasm between the parents and the world. The chasm comes out of a culture that gives the ownership of grief to parents, not society, and that says people should generally handle their problems on their own. It comes out of a society so fragmented and anonymous that many others do not know of a parent's bereavement, and among those who do, many will feel compelled to go on with their ordinary life routines and, if they interact with the bereaved parent at all, to interact as though nothing is different. Some parents spoke of others who did things that broadened and deepened the chasm. Sometimes it seemed to parents that the others acted out of a desire to help the parents get past the loss, and sometimes it seemed to parents that the others acted that way because it was inconvenient for them to be open to the parent's feelings. Some bereaved parents also talked about their own role in creating the chasm. For example, the discomfort others have with bereaved parents may be a reaction to things the bereaved parents communicated through words or actions. Many bereaved parents said that following the death the first encounters with familiar people and the first returning to familiar social settings were challenging because of discomfort about the chasm.

As some parents talked about the grief process, a major part of the process involved dealing with the chasm—whether, how, and where to bridge it and where to leave it unbridged. For many bereaved parents, the start of bridging the chasm with someone was when that person acknowledged the death. The bridge across the chasm is almost always a bridge of words.

Many narratives spoke of a chasm existing between the two parents, and most spoke of the chasm between life before the death and life after it.

Narratives about the chasm between parents and the world indicate how significant the grief process is in relationships with others. The next chapter analyzes how parents explained the grief process in their narratives and how the explanations were used in helping parents to understand what was going on in themselves and in relationship with their spouse and others.

CHAPTER

How Parents Explain the Grief Process

Most of the parents were interviewed at least several years after the death. Typically they had well developed narratives dealing with how they and their partner had dealt with the death. For many, a significant part of the story of the aftermath of the death was their narrative about why they grieved as they did.

☐ Upbringing, Tradition, and Personal Characteristics

Family and Ethnic Foundations

For some parents, part of the story of how they or a partner grieved lay in how they were raised or in personal characteristics. Those explanations sometimes provided an organization to the story of the aftermath of the death, not only answering "why" questions about individual grieving but also accounting for couple differences. For example, some parents (more often men than women) said that they did not go to counseling, therapy, or support groups because they were raised to deal with their problems themselves.

Chad: You're born and raised on a farm, and if something's broke, you can fix it. And you don't *call* somebody. You don't have to get five people to come in to tell you why it's broke or ... how you got to fix it. You just figure out what happened, and you fix it.

Sometimes both partners saw one of them as growing up in a family where, because of genetics, socialization, or something else, emotions were not expressed, and difficult topics were not dealt with openly.

Rosa: At one point, Henry's sister, [after] about a year, ... hugged me, and ... said, "I just don't want to deal with what you're going through. I'm just so sorry." Hugged me and then walked away.

Henry: I know where I get it from. (they both laugh)

Rosa: Yeah, that's his family being close. None of them are really open with their feelings. They're all very ... Irish Presbyterian, very closed, very stoic.

Some parents explained or justified actions by referring to precedents established by their parents.

Angela: It's like I want it; I need it; and Jack knows that.... I'm a very physical person. I want to get hugged. I want to get held. And it's like he can't do that. But he used to be able to do that.

Jack: My father ... is one of the most loving men I've ever known. Probably *the* most loving man I know. And he's just not a physically demonstrative person.

Wayne: I don't think we talked about [things much]. Louise is kind of a quiet person anyway. She's like her mother.... Her mother is very stoic. And so she keeps a lot of things inside her.

Similarly, some parents explained why they stayed together despite serious difficulties following a child's death by referring to family of origin patterns.

Rosa: I don't have an expectation that a marriage is always wonderful and perfect. My parents' marriage wasn't, and it would go through periods of big, not a lot of fun for them, and then they would work it out, and then they'd have *years* of it being wonderful. So I guess it's sort of my feeling that there's always times in somebody's marriage that it's not gonna be everything you want it to be. It doesn't mean you dump it. You just keep working on it and helping it come around.

Breaking with the Past

Some parents explained how they dealt with things since the death by talking about trying to be different from a parent or from family of origin. For example, Kathy explained her independence from Karl partly in terms of not wanting to be like her mother.

Kathy: My mother was a homemaker, and never had worked outside the house. And after they got divorced, she tried to work and wasn't able to hold on to a job. It's not that she's not smart, 'cause she is, but she just didn't know how to work outside the home.

Karl: She didn't want to work either.

Kathy: No, she really didn't want to, and they had been married 20 years, and I didn't want to end up, I think, like her and unable to support my family and unable to make decisions that needed to be made and be dependent on someone. So I'm not, and I guess in that sense that's made me who I am now. And I'm not dependent on him financially or really emotionally either. If he's not there for me, I've got my friends or I'll do something.

Sally talked about her continuing to grieve and to do so openly as a break from her family of origin. In her narrative, her open grieving not only broke with the family pattern but helped to explain her alienation from her family of origin.

Sally: I gave my family a book to read, and gave my sister an article to read. But it didn't help. My sister just glanced at the first page and then said, "I've read enough." They think I'm weird or crazy, that I should stop having feelings and get on with life. It's what they all do. My dad never shows any kind of emotion—love, pride in his children, nothing. My mother is sort of like that too. When I was a kid my sister ran away. I was told not to tell anyone, to show no feelings to others. But ... as soon as I got to school I told people. I've always been a rebel that way.... My mother said, "Have another child," but you can't replace a child. It takes a lifetime to process a loss like that. It will take my lifetime to process the loss of my son. But that I'm so willing to talk about it helps me. It's so in my consciousness. That's the very thing my parents don't like.

Wayne and Louise talked about including their surviving children in funeral rituals and being open to questions from their children as a way to do things better than their own parents did when there were deaths in the family.

Wayne: Both for my father when he died and Louise's father and also for [our son who died], our children were included in the whole process.

Louise: Yeah, because I remember myself as a child how I was completely ignored, and it's like the grandmother didn't mean anything to *us*, and yet she lived with us all those years. She was like a second mother to us.

Wayne: It was wide open, and that's how we are anyway. We're more wide open people.

Character and Personality

Some parents offered narratives explaining what went on in the aftermath of the death by referring to character and personality. That language was used to frame, explain, and justify what went on. By justifying actions, the character/personality explanations may reduce power battles because they seem to say, "This person can only be the way he or she is." For example, in what follows it seems that by having a character or personality explanation for Jack's behavior, Angela is pushed to accept what Jack does and Jack is excused from trying to change.

Angela: I learned a lot by talking to his parents. . . . I got on the phone and I called 'em. I said, "Jack's hurting, and he won't open up to me." . . . His mom just said, "That's the way he's always been. He needs space, he needs time. Just be there for him."

Character and personality are seen as being anchored in other things, anchored in ways that make them hard to change. In the following example, a couple talked about character and personality as anchored in gender, genetics, and family upbringing.

Rosa: You're a man and

Henry: . . . Man and my family was always sort of very emotionally stilted. (*Rosa:* Yeah) And then you're a woman and come from a family that's very emotionally supportive. So we kind of fell into classic roles.

Rosa: Yeah. 'Cause your family doesn't even show happiness that well.

Henry: Look at how my mother dealt with the death of her friend. Basically, just (*Rosa:* Denied that she was her friend). It's kind of like, she done her wrong or something like that. . . . It's almost like she got angry at her for dying (chuckles).

Rosa: For dying.... Wouldn't go to see her when she was dying, ... wouldn't even take her ... food.... They'd vacationed together. But as soon as [the woman] was dying, your mom backed off from her. "She's not my friend. We never were that close...."

Henry: Well, it's hereditary; it's genetic.

Rosa: It's genetic.

Henry: (In a kidding voice) Nothing I can do about it....

Rosa: No, so, you have a family history of running from bad; also they don't really embrace the good all that well either. They're nice people. They're just slightly strange, your parents.

Birth order is another "anchor" for character/personality. Kathy referred to birth order as one way to explain how she and Karl behaved.

Kathy: Karl and I both are the youngest in our families, and we both do things without asking advice. So we (small laugh) just made a decision, and once I make a decision I don't look back. [Talking about trying to have another child after two previous children had died of a genetic disorder.]

Character/personality also has a kind of inertia. If it has been a certain way for a long time, it's hard to change. Some parents explained how they dealt with a death by referring to how they had been for years.

Joy: We really believe that God is in control, and that He doesn't make mistakes, and that we don't always understand why things happen, but we always know that we can trust Him.... I've known the Lord since I was 19 years old, and that's 20 years, and He's just proved faithful ... over and over to me. So that's really where we get our strength.

Marsha: A social worker ... looked at us after the loss of our daughter and [was] very concerned and said, "This can really ... pull people apart," and this person went on and on about ... how devastating it can [be], and Denny and I just looked at one another. It just seemed so odd to us....

Denny: (interrupting) It would be cruel to fight with your mate or pull apart or sit and wallow in your own self-pity....

Marsha: I think part of it is the way you are.... Denny is not your typical hide the emotions and don't talk about it, like maybe some men are.... He's ... just so open and so easy going with his emotions.... It's been easy for us, [and] I think that part of that is because of the way he is.

In another example referring to long-standing character or personality, Glenda explained why she and her husband had dealt with their son's persistent vegetative state, his death, and each other as they had by saying that they were good people, had been raised right, and were doing the right things.

Glenda: We're both pretty much optimists.... So we kind of force ourselves to look for good.... I don't know why some people survi—, and a lot of people don't. They do commit suicide. I'm joking when I say I have the pills, but I truly do.... I could be 400 pounds. I eat like he drinks, to fill up a void. And I think we're both intelligent enough, we know why we're doing it. It's being smart enough to stop doing it. But I think the foundation is there, and he had a real hard, hard life growing up as far as economics, and mine wasn't too much better. And I grew up in a house of ill-health.... I had it modeled for me with my grandfather's Parkinson's disease.... My folks took care of him, and lived with my grandparents and my brother and me. Then my dad had a massive heart attack, and from the time I was 13 my dad was sick for 20 years. So I saw two good role models ..., my mother and my grandmother.... They did what they had to do. And they took care of the sick ones, and they stood by them and ... each other, and didn't walk away from trouble. And you work; and we were both raised to work. And it just drives me nuts when I see copping out.... You don't have to clean your junk drawer (she laughs), but ... you have obligations to society.

Similarly, Nick explained his unwillingness to join his wife in participating in Compassionate Friends by talking about his personal characteristics and upbringing.

Nick: I wasn't ready to talk about him.... I still, six years I still break down ... when I talk about it. So that *then* I was really *completely* devastated as far as the talking about it.... I just couldn't do it. I was hurtin' too bad, and I didn't know ... how ... she could do it. I never understood that. I couldn't. I don't care how many people were there, that kid or kids died.... I had one, mine, and I had my own problem. I don't need to listen to 10 other ... peoples' problem.... That comes back again when I was born, or raised is do things by myself.... If I ever had a problem in my whole life I had to sort it out myself. This is how I did my whole childhood. If I had something, I had to do it myself. And I couldn't go to anybody. So that's how I, four years old and 38, that's how I still do it to this very day.

Using the language of personality or character, it is easy to come to a typology in which some people are good and others are bad. A few parents, in trying to explain how they differed from a spouse in terms of personality or character, struggled about how to talk about the difference without making themselves or their partner look bad.

Joy: Stan didn't read as much stuff as I did. I was more, I don't know, I think I've always been more the searcher than Stan has. He's always been more, I don't mean to say anything bad about him, it's just the way his personality is. I, even when, like when we got into home schooling, I was just devouring the books, and where Stan is just more of a ..., what was the word (slight embarrassed laugh)? Not "complacent," but just happy to find out what he can ... but not really dig into it much.

☐ Parent Metaphors for the Grief Process

There were eight common metaphors in parent narratives about the grief process. The things these metaphors highlight and obscure say important things about grieving as it is reflected in parent narratives. (See Chapter 5 for metaphors for grief feelings.)

The Grief Process as a Measurable Quantity

In some parent narratives, the grief process was talked about as something that could be measured. Most commonly, measurement of the grief process came up as they compared the process of their personal grief with the process of their partner's grief. Often the comparison was associated with talk about couple relationship problems, with one parent upset that the other's process involved too little or too much grief.

Rosa: The first year I probably *grieved a whole lot more* than you.... And I thought I was sort of moving beyond, and I wanted to get the relationship back to where it was.... *Then* you started getting depressed. And it was sort of like, "Wait a minute. *How long are we carrying this* with us?" I talked to the counselor.... I've done a lot of stuff that I viewed as working through it, and you got obsessed with work and quiet and withdrawn.... If I hadn't had the kids, I think I would have left him.

[When it appears in a quote, the metaphoric concept that is being discussed in this chapter is italicized.]

Coming to Terms

"Coming to terms" can be understood as meaning to consent to something, to give in to something, or to reach an agreement (the "terms" of agreement). With any of those three meanings, the metaphor implies that a parent has had dealings with a powerful other—perhaps death or God. In addition, the metaphor implies that a parent has made a commitment to go along with the demands of or has made an agreement negotiated with the powerful other. "Coming to terms" implies that the parent has accepted that what has happened has happened and that now the parent must live with it.

The process of coming to terms is not easy. Some parents say that they only came to terms after the passage of several years and after intense and prolonged work at cocreating narratives about the child's death.

Kathy: About five years ago, one of my closest friends at work, she had a perfectly healthy baby who ... died of SIDS. I just completely fell apart. And yet she ... sought me out for help and ... all of a sudden this woman wanted to know everything about my kids, 'cause I didn't know her at the time when all that happened. And I went to some of her meetings at Children's Hospital ..., talked to her *every* day that whole school year, every morning we just cried.... It was somewhat cathartic for me too (exhalation that is almost a small laugh) I guess, because I understood what she was saying, and she understood that I understood, and that helped her a lot. So that helped me *come to terms* with a lot of things that were too painful to talk about. She's the kind of person that just had to talk about everything.

Some parents see coming to terms as an ultimate goal, but one that they have not yet reached.

Molly: Someday I'm going to have to *come to terms* with it. I feel that someday I'm ... gonna have to just get it all out. Maybe that's one of the reasons that led me to this study, for myself and for other parents. I really do feel a very strong concern about other people.... I don't want them going through as much hell as I had. I don't want them to divorce over the death of a child. It shouldn't be that way.... Sometime in your life you have to review your life and say, "I did okay." You have to deal with every phase of your life, the good and the negative in order to die peacefully. ... Someday I've got to face all of this.

A Journey

Many parents used the metaphor of a journey in their narrative about their grief process. A journey gives a sense of going forward, going through something to someplace else, or going from one place to another. The metaphor of the journey highlights that there is a process of the parent moving from a starting place (for example, devastation, total numbness, or the most intense grieving imaginable) to someplace else. For some parents, the journey metaphor highlights what might be called destinations in the grief process—for example, normality. For other parents, the journey metaphor highlights that grieving is a part of all of life, that whether a person wants to or not, a person must experience loss on the journey of life.

Tina: I think [one reason Scott] and I got into being these graduate parents [in a support group] was we wanted to help other people, because when we started to *go through it,* ... I didn't think I'd ever be normal again. How am I ever going to get through this thing? So I wanted to kind of be out there to show people that you can get through it. It's hard, but you can.

Joy: They told us that Jenny had died.... I really immediately felt God's grace poured out over me because I don't know how I could have lived through that without His hand on me. And from there on, I don't know, it's just been a real *journey....* It's been 11 years, so this didn't just happen overnight, and just the realization of God's sovereignty, in fact I really think the grief process is just the soaking in and the settling of what really happened and making your peace with it.... For the first, I don't know how long, you're numb. (*Stan:* Yeah, you are ...) I really ... felt physically carried. I felt like I was not moving on my own strength....

Consistent with what Knapp (1986, p. 29) reported, the parents' journey through the grief process did not end in forgetting the child or having no feelings of grief. Joy, for example, did not feel that she would ever get over missing Jenny or that she wanted to.

Joy: We haven't gotten over Jenny. We've just gotten used to being without her. I don't think it's anything you ever get over. It's [not] like, "Oh, oh yeah, that's okay now." It's never just going to be okay that she's not here. We'll always miss her; we'll always wonder what she'd be doing now and what she'd be like, and we can accept it ... because God is sovereign, but it's never going to be just that, "Oh yeah, we're over that now, and that's behind us."

The journey through the grief process involves getting on with the journey of life but not journeying without grief. Further on in the journey of life, grief will not dominate daily existence. But the grief does not disappear.

Kathy: Those feelings are really right up on the surface of both of us, and time doesn't really make that any better. We decided to *go on with our lives*, . . . because you basically don't have much of a choice, but it never feels okay. It never feels right. And there's always a part of us I think that each of us feels, part of us died with them. But we *went through with it.* It was very hard. And it still is. . . . The best I can do . . . is just to live with it, to put it in its right place, and to be able to go on and lead a normal life. Everybody has things that happen. I realize that the death of a child is just particularly cruel (voice cracking, sniffles). . . . We really couldn't help each other that much. We had to really find it within ourselves to help ourselves, and it took, well, it's taken, it's gonna take a lifetime, I think. I don't think we'll ever find everything that we need. But we found enough *to go on* and to have fun days and . . . laughs and . . . good times.

What Kathy meant by a "normal" life is interesting. When bereaved parents journey to "normality," they do not reach a normality that is like what they would have reached if there had been no child death (Attig, 1991; Gilbert, 1992, 1996). I think what they mean by normality is that they can live an everyday life—for example, attending to shopping, bills, meals, watching television, work, and perhaps the rearing of other children. The new normality includes laughter, but it also includes recurrent grieving and a sense of difference from parents who have never experienced the death of a child. It also means journeying to discover new facets of the loss— for example, new realizations of what has been missed when reaching the time when the child would graduate from high school or be likely to find a lifetime partner (Brabant, 1989–90; cf. Johnson & Rosenblatt, 1981).

The journey metaphor helped some couples to understand their marital difficulty following the death. They talked about the difficulty as a matter of not journeying together as a couple.

George: Steph did really burrow herself in with alcohol. I had stopped drinking. I read books. I talked to people that had lost children. I went to the cemetery. All that stuff was . . . very, very painful. It was my way of working through it. . . . I've dealt with Nils's death by just absorbing myself with it, reading about it, crying my eyes (Steph sniffles) out. . . . Going to bed at nine o'clock at night and still being awake at five o'clock in the morning when the alarm went off. Going to work, working hard, and then maybe getting together with somebody . . . and talking to him about child loss. Going to the cemetery. Sitting out there, wondering what this is all about. . . . Whereas when she would feel, "Aw, this is painful" (Steph sniffles), she would benumb herself with the drinking. So her (Steph sniffles) grieving process was delayed for years. And then unfortunately a year goes by, and

I'm [going] on with my life. I've regained my perspective.... Nils's death, as horrifying and terrifying it's still, *I can move forward*, or put the past in perspective, and kind of live for today.... I don't know what else a person can do.

In another example of a journey metaphor used in talking about marital difficulty, Bruce described his struggle to get Sally "to move along with me."

Bruce: She became depressed, maybe even clinically depressed. But she wouldn't take medications. She didn't want to get out of bed for weeks, months.... I'd say, "Isn't it enough that we're still married to each other, that you still have me and my love?" She'd say it wasn't. It was very hurtful to me.

Sally: All my dreams were wiped out.

Bruce: Wasn't I a part of your dreams?

Sally: No. (He crosses his arms, looks unhappy, perhaps even miserable.)

Bruce: It was a particularly difficult time.... My wife was always crying, and she didn't want to do anything and wouldn't admit that things were okay because we were together. I was struggling to get her *to move along with me*.

If a parent thinks of grieving or life as a journey, then there may be things the parent can do, such as deciding to have another child, that may lead to continuing with the journey.

PR: Did you plan to get pregnant with your younger son?

Joy: Definitely. We wanted another baby. We wanted a friend for [our son], and we did want another baby.... probably as *a going on*, picking our life up and going on. We probably felt like we needed to do that. If not for ourselves, for [our son].

Some parents had mixed feelings about moving on because they did not want to leave certain things behind. In talking about a physician whose neglect may have made it more likely that their son would die, Denny said that he wanted to continue to challenge the physician's neglect but also wanted to leave that behind to get on with trying to have another child.

Denny: I had a ... bit of anger at this guy who's too lazy to get off his ass and get in and check on my baby. And then Matt goes into surgery the next morning and has to have an operation, where if [the physician] would've got there, maybe more of the bowel would've been saved.... We wrote a letter, and we went to the patient concerns committee.... We get a letter saying he never was told that Matt's condition was that bad. He would've came in. He would've never refused.... The nurse flat out told us he basically yelled at her for waking him up. So ... some kind of board said that he'll be talked to about it, and we get the semi-apology letter for him, and then we told them these other facts that he *did* know about the condition when ... in his letter he denied knowing it. And he was glad we made him aware of it, and he was gonna follow up on that and get back. Well, he's never got back. That part I still have a hard time with.... Is it worth pursuing?... There's times I wanted to wring the guy's neck or something to make it better for the next parent ... and maybe I still will.... In general *you try to move on* to the next pregnancy. [Our daughter who was stillborn] was a new hope and now this new baby's new hope,... You try and let go of the bad stuff and focus on the good.

The metaphor of grief as a journey makes it easy for a parent to think about people being stuck and not going on. For example, Jane talked about feeling disappointed in a support group because so many participants seemed stuck.

Jane: It was helpful at Compassionate Friends,... but I found that a lot of people were very (sighs) oh, bitter and angry. And I just couldn't relate to that. I did not feel that way.... Some people ... were ... kind of trying to maybe probe or indicate were we upset about anything that had happened at Children's.... People were angry about their doctor and were considering suing.... It looked to me like ... they kind of [had] an arrested development. They were there, and they kept talking about that issue. And until that was resolved, *they weren't gonna go on* in the process. And *I wanted to get on* with the process.

The journey parents were on was not through space but through feeling, thinking, and time. One of the ways the time dimension came out most clearly was in how some parents explained their haste to have another child.

Denny: You have a nursery that's already made up.... You have tons of gifts from friends and family, and you have to go by it every day and look at it, and, you know, why wait?

Marsha: You're not getting any younger (laughs).

Denny: Ya, and then we're dealing with the biological clock. (*Marsha:* It's true.) ... She looks 21, but she's (*Marsha:* Yeah) not.

Marsha: Yeah. People would say, "Oh, don't you want to wait longer?" No, wait for what? What can I change? Nothing.... For me it didn't make it any better waiting.... Every month that went by that I got my period was depressing to me. I just ... want a baby (bangs on table), and I wasn't getting any younger, and we want a family, and it's like, "*Let's go!*" (laughs). So, yeah, it's been actually, I think, healthy for us. Maybe not for other couples.... But we were ready for it.

The journey parents were on was not necessarily linear. For some, aspects of the journey seemed circular, a circle which returned them to places, activities, goals, and frames of mind where they were before the death.

Joy: [Our little daughter] was born like 7 years ... after the accident. And to me that was a real high point in the journey. It was almost like we had come full circle. We sort of felt complete again, as complete as we could feel without Jenny here.

Putting Life Back in Order

In talking about the grief process, many parents said that in the early weeks, months, and even years after the death there was a lot of disorder in their lives. The disorder metaphor highlights how confused parents were, how irregular life became for them, how some things that should have been attended to were not, how they might not have clear plans for what to do, how they were no longer sure of who they were or how sane they were, and how their feelings and lots of other things about self and life seemed out of control. To put life back in order requires arranging things, picking up the pieces, creating order, repairing what has been broken, and gaining control of at least some of what is out of control. Some parents talked about putting things back in order and, according to a number of parent narratives, one source of motivation for putting things in order was concern about surviving children.

Elaine: We're very, very fortunate in that we had to *put our lives back in order*. Because you think, how must [our surviving children] feel if you can't get your life back together? How must they feel? "Are we not worthy enough for you to be able to stop it? ... We're still here. Aren't we fulfilling your life enough that you can't get it back together for us?" And that was kind of what brought me around.

For some, progress in putting life in order involved getting in control of something, even if was not their own feelings.

Erika: I announced one day, "I just have *to have control over something.* I haven't got control over anything in this world!" ... So ... I ripped the kitchen apart. I thought, "I'm going to do it one drawer at a time," and I felt so much better. That took a lot of energy though, to put something in order. And then I could remember where things were, and I'd done it, and I felt so good, but it's so exhausting.

Surviving

Some parents used the metaphor of survival to explain how they dealt with the death. A survival metaphor highlights how a child's death is a kind of death for the parent or that the pain is so great that suicide is seriously considered (DeFrain, 1991).

Hannah: I did not think that I would ever *survive* this.... Everybody has their limits. That's why people say (imitating an unintelligent, busybody voice:) "God never gives you more than you can handle." (*Fred:* Oh, sure) Well, will somebody get a message through to Him that I've had enough now.

Some parents said that the death was so awful that if they had not dealt with it they would have been destroyed.

Elaine: You either deal with it or it *destroys you.* Those are the two options that you have.

Getting Over It

Some parents felt that others wanted them to "get over" the death like a person gets over a cold or disappointment that a favorite sports team lost a big game. In that understanding of "getting over it," they would have to have no feelings of grief and might even have to forget the child. No parent who talked about others urging them to "get over it" and who understood that to mean having no feelings of grief or having to forget the child found that advice helpful or reasonable.

Alice: That isn't helpful, when somebody comes up to us and tells you, "Well, you've got to *get over it.* You got to forget about her." ... You can't forget her. You *can't*.... I suppose their meaning is good, like you have to try and get over and go on with your life, but I'm sure they don't mean to say ... "forget about her," because anybody in their right mind would know that you can't forget a loved one; you just can't.

In contrast to the expectation that people can and should get over grieving very quickly (Ruiz & Atwood, 1996), many researchers have found that grief for a child's death may continue a very long time (Lang, Gottlieb, & Amsel, 1996; Rosen, 1988–89), even a lifetime (e.g., DeFrain, 1991; Donnelly, 1982, Chapter 3; Gorer, 1967, p. 121; Horacek, 1995; Klass, 1988, pp. 13, 18–19, 1999; Knapp, 1986, pp. 40–42; Malkinson & Bar-Tur, 1999; McCowry et al., 1987; Paul, 1986; Peppers & Knapp, 1980, Chapter 5; Rosenblatt & Burns, 1986; Rubin, 1993, 1996). In accordance with previous research, a number of parents said that they had not gotten over the death, and some said that they never would. For them, the metaphor of not getting over it highlighted the ways their thoughts and feelings returned to the child and the death and their belief that they would never be as they would have been if the death had not occurred. The child's death had permanently changed who the parents were and their orientation toward life (Rubin, 1993, 1996). The death was not something to get over but part of the parent forever.

Al: You'll never totally *get over it,* but I'm still learning to handle different things, and after a while you realize that everything's not totally against you. It's just life, but you're so damn down over something like that.... You never get over it affecting your life.

Other parents, speaking of never getting over grief, said that they might continue on life's journey, but getting over the grief was not a prelude to, a part of, or a destination of the journey.

Kathy: It's not something that goes away.... You don't move on like you do with the death of a sibling or a parent or a close relative, a friend. You don't move on in the same ways that people expect.... It's forever, and it's so deep that it doesn't feel okay really ever.... It's just something that each of us lives with everyday. And it hurts everyday. I know you can see that when we started talking about the actual incidences or the actual things. Then it's just right there on the surface, and it always will be.... People, our families, don't really understand that. They think we've had the other two and so everything's okay. But you don't replace a child.

Although no parent claimed to have gotten over a child's death or that it was possible to get over it, some talked about getting over specific issues connected to the death.

Tina: One year, the day of her birthday, the Minneapolis paper did a big article on near death experiences. And there was a story in there, this woman, when she was in high school, had a near death experience where she almost drowned.... Years later she owned a company, and she was hiring people, and this woman came in for a job.... In the course of the interview, this woman ... broke down crying.... Her son had drowned in the past year, and her ... marriage had broken up.... And this woman who owned the company said to this lady, she was just distraught [about what] her son had gone through, that the death was painful and awful, which was something I'd always worried about with Gina too. And anyway, so she said, *she* knew right then ... that the reason she'd had that near death experience was so she could share with this woman it wasn't an awful experience. It was a pleasant experience to almost die. So that article ... helped me ... move on to another phase, and I could let go of ... that part of me that just ached because not only did she die, but I just thought she was in pain and it was horrible. Now I know that when she was dying it wasn't.

Many parents also talked about getting to a place where they could, at times, put feelings of grief and thoughts about the child who died aside.

Steph: Christmas was *really* hard for a while. I do tend to forget about him during Christmas, except maybe remembering when he *was* alive and the size he was.... It's easier just trying not to think about, except though when we trim the Christmas tree, there's *lots* of things of Nils on there, things that he made. And that's fine. (*George:* Yeah) I guess I never want to forget that. Yes, *you have to put it aside at some times*, but he was part of my life and I'm (crying) never going to forget it.

Many parents talked about their struggles about whether and how to put aside grief at times in order to live with or engage in fun, silliness, mindlessness, and other ways of feeling, thinking, and being that do not fit with sorrow.

Al: You just gotta learn to handle it.... After time's gone by ... you can look back and you can remember different things that he did, whether it was funny or, you know, and you can laugh about it, whereas before you couldn't. And that's what you've gotta learn to do if you're gonna to live.

Brett: After he died, ... I would feel guilty about havin' fun. And I remember when I was going through counseling, that was something else, that *it was okay to have fun*, it was okay to enjoy your life again.

Healing

Healing was a common metaphor in parent narratives. The metaphor of healing highlights how the parents have experienced damage, injury, and pain. There is also an upbeat piece to the metaphor in that "healing" highlights that some sort of improvement is possible, that there is a process to go through to produce that healing, and that the parent can be restored to a state where there is less damage, injury, and pain. This does not mean that the parent has forgotten the child, but that repairs have happened. There might, however, continue to be scars or the possibility of relapse.

As parents used the metaphor of healing they made clear that the process of healing takes a long time, that a parent may heal herself or himself but there are also healers who can help, and that healing may be facilitated by certain activities. The following narrative is about healing activities. No other parent told a story like this one, though it is like other stories in describing a healing process with a time course.

Molly: I ran into a woman at a convention ..., a music therapist, and she was an enormous influence on my life and *helping me heal....* She was selling [records] at the convention, and her music was [about] death and dying and ... grief, and beautiful song. And I went to buy an album for my sister and I had her autograph the album and as I was going to leave she said "You look so sad." ... I told her what had happened, and she invited me back the next day because she said she was going to perform in front of 200 people. She ... wanted me to be there.... [I] decided to go. She had us singing.... It was a fun concert and very meaningful, very beautiful songs. And she said "I'm going to sing this song for a new friend and I hope she'll understand." ... She starting singing ... a song called "Playclothes," about this mother who had lost a child and how painful it was to fold playclothes. That's it, I lost it.... I got up and wanted to run away and I looked around and the aisles were full.... I remember sitting there and sobbing through the whole song. And after the concert she said, "I didn't mean to do this to you. But I wanted you to know that other people have gone through the same kind of grief. And maybe we could start working together." And I just lost it.... So every time she would go someplace she would send me an invitation to go. I'd show up like a follower of a guru, and each time she would introduce me to the audience and have me tell about the accident and my feelings and experiences with grief. I said to her once, "How can you do this to me?" And she said, "You need to help people and you need to help yourself. You need to heal." I said, "I know you're right." And as I was getting ready to leave, one mom who had just lost a baby came up to me, grabbing me and giving me a big hug, and she said, "Thank you for having enough," I don't remember what she said, nerve or whatever, "to stand here and tell us about grief." She said, "I didn't know what I was going through. I didn't have a clue that it was grief that I was going through. I didn't know what grief was." And that had a big impact on me. For three years I did this with her.

Some parents said that having another child helped them to heal.

Joy: We always say [the son who was born after Jenny died] was our comfort. The Bible says, "Blessed are those who mourn, for they shall be comforted," and [he] was our comfort, because ... he brought laughter and happiness into our house again.... New life, it just really does something to bring *healing* into your home.

Acceptance

Another common metaphor in narratives of the grief process is "acceptance." The metaphor of acceptance highlights that some entity (God, fate) has given the parents something and that the parents should not refuse, resist, or turn away from what has been given. The metaphor of acceptance also highlights coming to the end of a struggle to understand the death, to believe it happened, or to deal with extremely hard feelings.

Amy: I think if I let myself think about it long enough, there's always going to be something that's very unresolved. But over time I've been able to *accept....* If I didn't have the family that I have now, if we didn't continue to have kids, I think it would be different.... I'm busy,... and I've gotta look at other things in my life.... I'm ... more *accepting* and hav[e] just gotten used to the idea, and it's just a part of my life.

For John, acceptance seemed to mark an end to struggles with "what ifs" and with a sense that the death was unfair.

John: I had a lot of [what ifs] at first. But then, I don't know, just (sighs) ... *accepted*, I guess, that whatever happened was meant to be. Just kind of made justification, I guess probably that what happened happened, and if it maybe would've been caught earlier, she probably would have gone through so much suffering and it would have just been prolonged.... She was a strong Christian. She was very athletically inclined. She ran in the marathon;... she'd go running every day; she'd go horseback riding ...; she was always swimming. Very, very good shape.... She ate right.... It's ... hard to believe that something like this could happen to somebody that was in such perfect physical shape. She never smoked, she never drank.... So it was hard to accept.

For Paula, acceptance seemed to mark an end of anger and of questioning why the death happened.

Paula: For a while Pete kind of . . . always asked why? Why now? . . . I still ask why, but the feelings have changed. I'm not angry anymore like I was or I've *accepted* it. You can't bring him back.

☐ Parent Metaphors for a Failed Grief Process

With narratives of successful grief processes were implications about grief processes that failed. Some parent narratives defined what a failure in the grief process would be. A common metaphor for those failures was that of mental illness. The mental illness metaphor highlights that many grieving people behave in ways that they or others think are "crazy," that the pain and disruption caused by a child's death can be so great that a parent can become insane (DeFrain, 1991; DeFrain, Martens, Stork, & Stork, 1990–91), and that a properly functioning mind will somehow get through the grief process. But the metaphor obscures that there is not a clear notion of what proper functioning is, particularly with the death of a child. Here are two examples of parent talk about the possibility of mental illness arising from grief over a child's death

TK: How did you make it through that hard time?

Jay: I don't really know. Just a tough Norwegian, I guess. I don't know why. Somebody with a lesser mental could've been *in a nut house.* . . .

Alice: Talk. I think that's the big thing, talk. If you go off in some corner and mull over things and don't have contact, I think you could drive yourself *over the edge.*

Red: You gotta just quit second guessing it. Otherwise you will *drive yourself nuts.*

Some parents said that they or others used the concept of mental illness when it seemed that grieving was in some way not proper. What was "not proper" might be any of the things that ordinarily are thought of as a sign of mental illness in the culture (Edelstein, 1984, p. 63)—for example, seeming not to be in control of feelings or actions, not thinking or remembering normally, or not engaging in ordinary adult activities (work, self-care, eating, etc.). However, what was "not proper" also might be based on erroneous ideas about bereavement—for example, that recurrent crying weeks or months after the death is not normal or that months of depression are not normal. At the couple level, thinking or talking about a husband or wife in terms of mental illness could drive a wedge between partners, promoting thoughts about commitment to a psychiatric hospital rather than thoughts of providing support and understanding.

Scott: I thought I was gonna have to commit her ... (laughs) to someplace.

Tina: He said that to me one day too.

Scott: Well, so, yeah, I was very concerned. I, like other people, thought, well, "Gosh, you should be moving on."

☐ Summary

Parents' narratives don't just describe the grief process; they explain it; they make it understandable to the parents and others. One way the narratives explain the grief process is to frame it in terms of upbringing, family and ethnic traditions, and personal characteristics. Explanations in these terms helped parents to understand self and partner and to frame marital conflict in the grieving process as not arising from partner malice but from things about the partner that were not easily changed. However, some parents said that they broke away from family of origin precedents, for example, by grieving more openly than was customary in their family of origin.

Parent narratives also framed the grief process in terms of metaphors. Some metaphors made the grief process a measurable property, and being able to measure the process helped particularly in talking about spousal differences in grieving. The most common narrative metaphors for the grief process included "coming to terms with the death," "a journey," "putting life back in order," "surviving," "getting over the death," "healing," and "acceptance." Each of these metaphors implied that certain things were true about the grief process, framed relations with others in certain ways, and helped parents make sense of certain aspects of the individual grief process and of the couple relationship in bereavement.

Some parent narratives also offered metaphors for a failed grief process, with "mental illness" being the most common metaphor for failure. That metaphor could be helpful, but it could make trouble when it led to labeling ordinary grieving as pathological.

As can be seen in the quotes in this chapter, as parents talked about the grief process, they made clear that the process did not mean an end to the connection with the child who died. For example, "getting over it" does not imply, for any parent, ending the feelings, memories, or sense of relationship with the child. The next chapter focuses on the parents' continuing connection with the child.

CHAPTER

The Continuing Connection with the Child

The Child Continues in the Parent's Life

In the narratives of almost every parent, the child continued to be a presence in the parent's life. Death does not break the bonds between the living and the dead (Attig, 1996, p. 174). The child is in the past, but also in the present (Brice, 1989, 1991a, 1991b; Klass, 1988, pp. 18–19, 1992–93, 1993, 1996, 1997, 1999; Sormanti & August, 1997). Many parents continue to count a child who has died as a member of the family (Brabant, Forsyth, & McFarlain, 1994) and continue to speak about the child to others. One can think of parents maintaining contact with the child or with the inner representation of the child (Klass, 1988, p. 50, 1992–93, 1993, 1999) as a way to find solace and an acknowledgment of loyalty and the inseverability of connection (Brice, 1991a, 1991b; Klass, 1988, Chapter 3, 1996, 1997, 1999).

Brett: The grief group ..., instead of trying to forget about Alex and the pain, they helped us figure out how to make him a part of our family.... People ask me how many kids I have. I have three. Two at home and one in heaven. And I'll explain it different ways and try to make people feel comfortable, but I'll never not say that I have three kids. And even our family here, our boys and our extended family *will* treat Alex like he's still part of our family.... We celebrate his birthday, and it's a joyous occasion....

We just try and keep him part of us. And even [our youngest child], and [he] wasn't even around when Alex was born and died, . . . talks about him like he knows him. . . . We put a Christmas stocking up for him every year, and put a Christmas tree . . . on his grave, and . . . try and keep him with us all the time.

Gail: Randy is in our memories. He's in our hearts. He's in our conversation. He's *always* in my thoughts, especially when you do a family thing. [Our younger son] . . . certainly knows about him. . . . [Our older son] I think remembers his death. . . . I think Randy is a *very* important part for [our older son]. When he has to fill out a form . . . in school or scouts or whatever, and it says on there, "List your siblings," he'll list Randy.

When other people do not acknowledge or accept that the child is still in a parent's life, the parent may feel hurt, stung, and angry. The feelings may be partly because the parent wants to be supported and understood, but they also reflect a determination to keep the child from being forgotten or ignored.

Angela: I was very angry at my parents, because my brother's memorial service was put on the day that Blake would have been six months old. "Pick any other day! Why couldn't you pick any other day?" No, they had to pick that day. "Why did you pick that day?" They couldn't tell me. [It] didn't even dawn on them that Blake would have been six months old [that] day. . . . I was angry at 'em. And I wanted them to list Blake in the obituary, "Preceded in death by . . . nephew Blake." And they wouldn't do it.

☐ Remembering the Child

Parents say they do not forget or want to forget a child who died (cf. Klass, 1999; Knapp, 1986, p. 29; Peppers & Knapp, 1980, p. 48). Many parents retain, years after the death, vivid and detailed memories of specific events involving the child. However, some parents also talked about trying to stay away from certain memories. As Klass wrote (1988, p. 67; 1999), memories can be a source of great pain as well as great solace for bereaved parents. Some parents talked about trying to stay away from memories of child illness, dying, and death.

Jay: The memories will always be with us.

Alice: You always think of bad things too. Everybody has bad memories. But you have to try and, *try* and forget the bad ones, and just think about the good ones.

In talking about memories of the child, parents used the past tense almost all the time. But some memories were in the present. In some sense the child was still present.

Kathy: I can smell each one of them. I can hear them; I can see them; and I can feel them. And I always will.

Parent memories emphasize connections between child and parent (Klass, 1993, 1999) and do so in a way that makes the parent seem to have been worthwhile as a parent. For example, when Chad talked about his regrets at not having been in much contact with his son who died, his wife, Erika, talked about Chad being a good provider and said that he should not feel guilty. The couple then had this exchange:

Erika: Now ... what would David say to you when I would say, "Why did I marry your dad?"

Chad: "To get a good looking kid like me." (all laugh)

Erika: As if that's the only reason I married Chad (sounding cheerful). David had those great big brown eyes. He could say that when he was three years old. He had a sense of humor. Well, he was a healthy boy.

They were remembering David in a way that emphasized the positive and how special he was. And Erika tried to relieve Chad of guilt and regret over having had so little contact with David by emphasizing special connections they had with him.

Remembering the child is an act of connection (Brice, 1991a, 1991b; Edelstein, 1984, pp. 68–69). Parents remember the child because of how important the child and the parent role were—and are—to them, and to show that they still care about the child. They also remember the child because their relationship with the child is not over.

Joy: A day hasn't gone by in 11 years that I haven't thought about Jenny, and at times it is just this overwhelming flood of sadness, just from missing. Eleven years is a long time not to see someone you love so much.

Al: Still the hardest damn thing for me is being back here doing work, and I keep looking up to see that motorcycle coming. And I know it ... shouldn't, but I keep looking for somebody to come, and there's nobody to come.

With memories of the child so important, it was common for parents to feel upset or disgusted with others who avoided talking about the child.

Some parents thought that others wanted to protect them by not mentioning the child, but still found it insulting (because others assumed parents did not constantly remember) and a gross misunderstanding.

Wayne: A lot of these people avoid you. They don't know ... what to say. They have no idea how you're gonna react to what they're gonna say....

Louise: What most of them will say is that, like say if it was Will's birthday, and I certainly know it's Will's birthday, and a lot of people I know know it's his birthday. But aside from my mother and one good friend I have who would always send me a card, no one would ever mention it. And their reasoning would be, maybe they'd mention it two days later, but they'd say, "You looked like you were doing okay. I didn't want to bring up memories, remind you." And I thought, "Do they think I don't remember that it's my own son's birthday?"

Al: The best thing you can do is talk about it. And if you know someone that goes through a situation like this, don't evade them. Go talk to them. Don't act like it never happened, because it did. Don't turn your back. It's done. The person's gone, and especially if it is a child, you're not going to forget that child, especially the parents aren't and probably the grandparents aren't.

For many parents, having the child forgotten might be like another death or a further death. So part of the continuing relationship with the child who died was an effort to keep the memory of the child alive (Klass, 1999; Knapp, 1986, p. 29). Remembering is not automatic. Parents may struggle to hold on to memories or to recover them. They may fear that they will lose memories of the child (Malkinson & Bar-Tur, 1999). As an aid to memory, parents hang on to reminders (Riches & Dawson, 1998)—for example, photos, or things with the child's odor—that evoke the presence of the child (Klass, 1993, 1999). They may visit places, like the hospital where the child was a patient, that are reminders of the child. Another way parents retain memories is to tell memories, tell them repeatedly, tell them so often that the story of what is remembered is practically memorized.

Joy: We had cried so often together, and we had "Remember the time Jenny would do this?" Or we'd try to keep memories alive for each other, too, and tell each other that maybe we didn't know the other person knew and experienced. (*Stan:* yeah.) And we still do tell stories about her over and over. It doesn't matter if we've told them 50 times; we still tell them.

Remembering and thinking about a child who died is an act of loyalty (Brice, 1991a, 1991b). Not to remember can seem to be disloyal and unparental.

Denny: It'll never be gone. And I think if it's gone, then something's wrong. One of the facilitators at the group lost one of his daughters, seven, eight years ago, and he said it's always gonna be there, but at least in time, which is true, it has gotten better. It doesn't consume every waking minute and hour like it used to. And I don't want to ever forget.

Some parents had reached the point where they could say that they did not think of the child all the time, but some who said that wondered if it was disrespectful to the child to say that.

For some parents who said they would never forget the child there had developed a sense of unreality about the child's existence and death. It was almost as though, for them, the disembodied memories were not enough to keep the child who died completely real.

Elaine: We'll never forget him, ever. Some days you wonder if it really happened. Did you really have him? I think that a lot. Was it just kind of a figment of your imagination?

A risk in relying on memories to maintain connections with the child is that there is then a conflict of interest between hanging on to memories and hanging on to connection with the child by other means (for example, through prayer to the child or mental interaction with the child). Putting too much into the current connection may make it less clear that the memories are what one would ordinarily call memories. Perhaps they become creations that are products of efforts to maintain a connection. Some parents saw this problem in situations where the parent had tried to maintain, through recounting stories about events, a surviving child's connection with a sibling who died.

Jane: She recalls incidents, and I can't tell if she's actually recalling the incident, or recalling the fact that we've talked about some of these things enough over the years that she just recalls hearing about it.

☐ Keeping Reminders of the Child

In the previous section of this chapter I mentioned that reminders were helpful to parents in holding on to memories. In fact, all parents talked about keeping reminders of the child—for example, photos, toys, and clothing—in order to remain connected with the child. The reminders were treasured aids to memory that helped maintain a sense of who the child was for the parent and also might help to stimulate conversation with others about the child (cf. Riches & Dawson, 1998; Klass, 1999). Many parents also said that they used reminders to maintain an ongoing connection with the child.

Joan: We talk about him all the time.... The boys say, "Alex is with us. He's in our hearts." And we have pictures of him all over. We have his Christmas stocking. When we first put it up, I thought, "We should write a letter every Christmas and put it in his stocking." ... I did it for the first two years, and then didn't do it, and then this year I wrote another letter. It was kind of fun to go back and look at those letters. We've got a hope chest in the bedroom, and it's got all his stuff in it, mainly from the hospital.

Some parents who were eager to maintain the connection of their other children with the child who died said they gave mementoes of the dead sibling to the other children.

Stan: We've given some things away to brothers and sisters if they wanted to take something of hers.

Joy: Just so they'd have something of Jenny's.

Some parents tried to make things that were reminders to them of the child also serve as reminders for their surviving children.

Joy: They'll draw a rainbow, ... [and] if it reminds me of Jenny, (*Stan:* yeah) I tell 'em about it.... The kids will ask us questions about Jenny. If they're eating something that Jenny really liked, we'll tell them that.... [Our youngest child] especially is real in tune to that. I don't know if it's 'cause it's her sister and she can relate, 'cause little girls ... are little pack rats. [She] has all these little purses and containers with stuff in 'em, and I'll tell her, "Jenny used to do that same thing." So she can really relate to Jenny being a little girl like this and stuffing all these things with little treasures, and she ... seems real interested in what Jenny did.... There's a couple of dolls that I saved that were Jenny's, and [our little one] is playing with them now and taking care of 'em. I think it's ... intriguing for her too. There's this little girl that used to be here and now she's not.

Parents are extremely protective of reminders that are important in maintaining connection with the child. For example, they may work to keep a child's room as it was just before the child died (Edelstein, 1984, p. 58), or they may not want visiting children to play with the toys that were fa-vorites of the child who died. That protectiveness of reminders is a sign of how crucially important the reminders are for maintaining parent connec-tion with the child who died. On another level, the things said and done in protecting the reminders say to others that the connection with the child is still enormously important, that the child is very much in the present for the parent.

Kelly: As you can see, her pictures are up. The albums down there are all Leanne's.... Her clothes are still here. Her animals are still here. And Leanne's room is there. You can walk in, see her Barbie dolls, see her animals. The nieces and nephews ... know that ... you have to have permission to play with Leanne's stuff.

Some parents had a child's body cremated and kept the ashes at home. The ashes could be a reminder with great potency and too precious to move out of the house.

Angela: I have his clothes that he died in. Blake sits on my dresser.... He was cremated, and Jack's mom and dad bought this little cherry box for us (crying), and you open it up and in it is his new born picture. It has his foot prints from the day he died, and his Nukers that he had from the day he was born until the day that he couldn't ... breathe and suck anymore. And that's all in that box, and then if you lift all of that stuff up then his ashes are underneath it. But he sits on my dresser. And I have my sister-in-law tellin' me I should put him somewhere, like in a mausoleum, and I'm like, "No, I can't do that." I want him in here.

☐ Creating Reminders, Memories, Memorials

Many parents spoke about finding symbols that reminded them of the child and honored the child.

Joy: There's three things that really remind us of Jenny. One is rainbows, 'cause she was always drawing rainbows on her pictures. And hearts, be-cause she drew hearts too because of just how she loved everybody. She truly loved everybody.... And ... morning glories, because morning glo-ries are her birthday flower. And we'd always plant morning glories, and so whenever we see something with a morning glory or a rainbow or, you know, we'll buy it for each other. You know, a birthday [card] with a rain-bow.

Some couples, alone or with the cooperation of others, created memorials for the child who died, for example, planting a tree, setting up a scholarship, or establishing a balloon-launching ritual for anniversaries of the child's birth or death. Memorials are a way to maintain parent connections with the child and to keep the child in the awareness of others.

Sally: We set up a memorial foundation in his name....

Bruce: We give grants every year to two or three students from the interest on the funds in the foundation.... Sally and I and several [others] make the choices. So in a very real way Mike gives back to the world. My parents and many others have contributed generously to the foundation.

Stan: On her birthday ... we go out to the cemetery and send up balloons with a little message printed on a postcard of our faith. And there's been a lot of people who have found them, amazingly, who have been in some sort of distress and they read our message, and they write to us saying how much it meant for them to find ... (*Joy:* this message of hope) our balloon.... So we feel that her life is still going on through this, and she's still making an impact.

Kelly: We get a toy for her every year, and we donate it to the hospital. We donate ... a newborn dress [too].... She has a poster over at [one hospital] outside the NICU.... It's a picture of her taking a bath, and there's one more inside the unit, of her smiling. So she's seen as a guardian angel over there. There's equipment over at [one hospital] in honor of the family, and there's equipment over at [another, also in her honor]. She has a tile over at [one hospital] on the wall, in her memory.

Some parent narratives made clear that as part of maintaining the connection and keeping the child in the awareness of others, the memorial chosen was a symbol of an especially salient characteristic of the child who died.

Wayne: There's a big [community] arena ... for ... youth hockey.... I contributed a trophy case in Will's honor.... And he has a real good picture and tribute with the words and dedication.... You kind of want to do that ... for him to live on....

Louise: At the school, because our three girls are all still going ..., we wanted them to be able to do something that they could be part of, and so we donated ... books, 'cause I remember when he would go to the library and check out books, he loved sporting books, and he would always complain there just weren't enough up there, and so we ... chose like five or six hundred dollars worth of sporting books, and ... had the book plates put in all of them.... It's got like hockey sticks and a baseball thing and a music note.... And had a real nice plaque for the media center, and then on his birthday, for several years afterwards, the kids would ... pick a book out in his name ... and would give it to the school library.

☐ Interaction with the Child

As has been reported in other research (Edelstein, 1984, pp. 65–66; Klass, 1993, 1999; Sormanti & August, 1997), some parent narratives described the postdeath, continuing interaction of parent and child. For example, some parents felt that shortly after the death there was communication that may have been or was from the child. The way they talked about such communication seemed to speak to what was special and memorable about the child and also to say that the child continued to exist.

Chad: We buried him out in the country down here ... and, as they were doing the final thing in the casket, pine cone falls off the tree, lands in the casket. And I told the kids that were pall bearers, "You got an angel up there watching you, and he's already throwing rocks down, trying to trick you a little bit."

Erika: We have the pine cone over on the mantle. We all broke out laughing. I mean (*Chad:* Yeah), here's the saddest moment in our life

Chad: It's exactly what David would do. He'd be sitting there throwing something in along with.

Erika: And the kids knew it. One of the girls later wrote a poem about it that was published in their school magazine. And it was about him dropping that pine cone on the casket.

Across narratives that spoke of continuing contact with the child who died, the contact described was quite diverse. Sometimes communication continued; sometimes it faded. Sometimes it involved an exchange of words with the child, but sometimes it was a matter of feelings and of sense of presence.

Ken: I go to the gravesite ... two or three times a week. And at first I thought that there was this [connection], but now it's not as strong.... It was a good feeling.... When my mother died, and Glenda's mother died, I said, "... You have two grandmas now, with your two grandfathers." ... Then we'd go talk. The other day I was, "Well, what do you think of your sister?" 'cause we're not too (*Glenda:* Happy at this moment) sure (laughing) about this romance thing.... He does not [reply] ..., but I know what he'd say, "It's none of your affair." (Glenda laughs) "... Let her do what she wants to do, and if she's happy, that's all that counts."

Rosa: I *really* had a strong sense of Wendy after [she died].... We really felt her presence in the house, and there was a book that [she had] that when you opened it, it would play music. And after Wendy died, we just shut the door on her bedroom. We didn't go in it. It was just shut. But every now and then, the music would play, with nobody in it. And for a while it was sort of freaking us out, and then we said, "No, there's something there," and you could feel a presence. You could still smell her in that house.... I don't know if there's some way the spirit stays, but there's enough for me to realize to question that I really don't know what happens after you die.... I wanted a baby, and I would have done anything to have it.... But I, at that point, had a really strong sense that Wendy's presence was in the house and that if I got pregnant again that it would be Wendy, and that wouldn't look like Wendy, but it would be Wendy, and I would know it's Wendy and she would know it's Wendy. (Whispering:) ... If nobody else would know. It would be sort of my little secret. It was my way of bringing her back, 'cause you could feel her. You could just feel her presence in the house.

Tina: In the last couple of years I've ... come to a different sort of spirituality about the whole thing. I know she's here now, but she's just not visible, but she sends us signals (laughs).... I've ... come to a point in *my* spirituality where now I believe she's with me all the time.

In one family, a parent and the surviving siblings were afraid of the ghost of the child who died.

Elaine: I can remember laying in bed with [our youngest child] at night and nobody would sleep. How many nights did everybody sleep down there on the floor? The kids would not go upstairs ... to sleep.... That was real scary for them, and I remember them saying, and I even had that fear, that you were going to look out a window and he was going to be looking in at you.... That was their biggest fear.... It's real interesting how you become afraid of somebody that never hurt you before but you just do, the spook aspect of it.

A number of parents talked about continuing to say things to the child who died. Some parents talked about having mental conversations with the child (cf. Riches & Dawson, 1998; Rosenblatt & Meyer, 1986). Some parents talked with the child through prayer. The interactions might occur frequently, perhaps as part of a daily routine. Some parents found it easier to interact with the child in proximity to the child's cemetery plot or the child's room; some used a photo to help make the connection.

Denny: I'll go [to the cemetery].... Sometimes I'll go a few days in a row. Sometimes I won't go for two or three weeks, but it gives me ... comfort to go there, and if I want to talk, even though I can sit in my house and talk to them, there's something about going there and seeing their name or seeing their marker ... that gives you some kind of a touching ..., closeness and bond.

Angela: We talk to Blake all the time. When my brother died, I told Blake ..., "You have never seen your uncle, and now you get to play with him." And then when that mother murdered her two little boys, I stood in front of Blake's picture for almost a half an hour ... to tell him to take care of those two little boys, because they were up there because their mom was mean.... "Their mom deliberately killed those kids. And you gotta show them that there are good people in life, and there are better people where you are."

☐ Continuing to Be the Child's Parent

Some parent narratives were clear that the parents continued to be the child's parent (cf. Brice, 1989, 1991a, 1991b; Klass, 1996, 1997, 1999). The parents had not lost their relationship with the child.

Kathy: When I picture my kids I picture all five of them. Whenever I say to someone I [have] ... kids ..., I always think of them ... [in] order, but [the ones who died] are still babies. And that's all I know of them.... I always get an image in my head of their heads doing something. I take a deep breath, but I (sighs) always think of five. So I guess in that sense they are always with me. It's not like I had one and then the space and then two, three. It's one, two, three, four, five.

Although a child death that leaves a parent childless means that there is a dual loss (Talbot, 1996–97, 1998–99), of child (or children) and of parental role, some parents who were childless after the child death continued to think of themselves as parents.

Kelly: I don't feel I have to prove myself as a woman as a mom. I'm a mom. I always will be a mom.

Consistent with what Klass reported (1999, Chapter 3), another way some said that they continued to be the child's parent was that they counted the child as one of their children. Key in this regard was when they told others how many children they had.

Denny: If ... people ask, "Do you have children," I say, "Yes, but they're not with us," that we lost two. But I'm not gonna say we don't, because we do.

Some parents talked about continuing to take care of the child in the sense of praying to God on the child's behalf.

Earl: I say a prayer every night for them.

Jay: We pray a lot for her. I say a prayer every night.

Alice: Now that's another thing, Penny's pastor ... has asked him, "Why do you pray for her? She doesn't need your prayers." But we do it anyway.

Grieving the death of the child is also a way to continue to be the child's parent (Brice, 1991a, 1991b; Lauterbach, 1994). It is a way for the parent to stay connected to the child. The child is still important; feelings of love, responsibility, and parental connection continue. From that perspective, others who try to silence parental grieving can be experienced by the parents as trying to break the parent connection with the child (Brice, 1991a, 1991b; Lauterbach, 1994), which is not what any of the parents wanted. From another perspective, the death does not end the parent's inner representation of the child (Klass, 1999; Klass & Marwit, 1988–89), and the parent can continue to interact with that inner representation.

☐ Continuing the Child's Timeline

Another way parents continue to be in contact with the child who died is that they keep track of the timeline the child would be on (Klass, 1988, pp. 13–14; Rando, 1985). In their narratives they might note when the child would have started school, begun dating, or taken driving lessons. That means, in a sense, that parents recurrently reach new losses; each event and achievement that the child does not reach is a new loss for the parents. Another way to understand it is that parent and child are still connected in the present. Continuing to keep track of the child's timeline is a way of saying, "I have not given up on you; I still know what and who you would have been."

Louise: The year that Will would have graduated I remember calling [a friend from our support group], and said, "How did you handle graduations?" Because he would have graduated; all of his friends were graduating. We were getting announcements from all these people to go to their parties. I wanted to leave town. . . .

Wayne: I went to the parties. (Louise gives a small laugh) I went. She didn't.

Louise: I didn't. Yeah. I said, "How did you handle this? I can't, I just can't do this." And she [the support group friend] said . . . she couldn't either. So she sent cards out with a letter of explanation. So that's what I did.

☐ Future Reunion with the Child

Some parents said that they expected to reunite with the child. Consistent with findings reported by others (Cook & Wimberley, 1983; Klass, 1993; Knapp, 1986, pp. 34–35; Schwab, 1990) and with patterns that were well established in 19th century North America (Rosenblatt, 1983a), many said that they hoped or expected that after their own death they would meet the child in heaven.

Denny: When we get up in heaven . . . they'll be waiting for us. We'll be 80 years old and we'll have babies up there waiting for us. . . . That's the only thing that gives us any kind of . . . solace . . . , because I can't imagine anything else.

Vince: I know that when I die I'm gonna go to heaven, and see Randy. So I figure, "Well, I know I'm gonna to see him, so why not just take this time that I have and just live and pay attention to my wife and kids and be a support to them."

Some parents made major religious changes in order to increase the chances that they would reunite in heaven with the child.

Stan: We believe that there's an afterlife and that Jenny is in heaven now and, boy, we want to see her, so we had to know how to get there. . . . We became much stronger religiously. And that's one of the reasons why we changed churches, because we . . . didn't feel that the church we had been going to was teaching in the right direction. . . . You find comfort in knowing that there's a God who cares for you and we're going to spend eternity together, and we'll have Jenny for eternity. . . . I know that God has given me the promise of seeing her again if I believe on Him, which has led me to dig deeper. I'm probably not as soul-searching that way as Joy is. But it has made me search as to reading, especially parts in the Bible . . . , knowing that I have a chance to get to Heaven and . . . be with all of them again.

A few parents told of talking with dying relatives about caring for the child who died when they reached heaven.

Elaine: My sister, she's only 46 years old and she's dying of cancer, and had been sick for 9 years. . . . She was [the] godmother [of Kyle] and she ended up dying on Kyle's birthday. . . . [We] made a deal. . . . I would take care of her sons and she would take care of Kyle when she got to Heaven. . . . I went up to be with her one night. . . . For . . . 15 or 20 minutes she sat on the side of the bed and she just kept saying "I'm coming, Kyle. I'm coming, Kyle. I'm coming."

One could take the belief that the child is in heaven in many different ways—for example, a truth based on religious teaching and religious feeling, a way of feeling comfort about the situation of the child, or an affirmation of the child's goodness. Another way of taking the belief is that it is a language of location. If people are to continue to have some sort of relationship with the child it is easier if they know where the child is. If the child who died is thought of as being no place in particular, it could be harder for parents to continue to feel connected to the child or to know where to direct communications to the child. If the child is thought of only as a decaying corpse or ashes in a container, that also may make feelings of connection and attempts to communicate difficult for many parents. Thus, whatever else a belief that the child is in heaven signifies, it may also represent part of the process of maintaining connection with the child.

Brice (1989, 1991a, 1991b) analyzed the paradoxes in wanting to have continued contact with a child who died. Wanting the contact as though the child were like she or he was when alive, the parent can fear a loss of sanity. Wanting the contact in a way that relates to the child as dead can be extremely distressing because it denies what the child is like when alive. It seems to me, however, that some parents found a way out of the paradoxes by thinking of the child as real and as when alive but in heaven. They thought of heaven as a location from which the child could communicate and a place that they might eventually reach and then reunite with the child. However, no parent talked of reunion with the child in heaven as a time for a conversation, let alone for conversation about specific matters (for example, about whether the parent was in any way responsible for the death, why a child who was killed while risk-taking took such risks, or what it meant to parent and child to be separated by the death). So despite the sense that reunion in heaven was possible, there was not a sense of a continuing interactive, I-thou relationship. It was more a sense of reuniting entities that belong together.

When parents talked about a reunion with a child in heaven and gave some indication of what the child was now like, the child always seemed to be the age the child was at the time of death. One way to understand that is that parents imagine reuniting with the child as they remember the child. Another way to understand it is that in the belief in immortality that goes with a belief in reunion in heaven, the child cannot age, because continuing to age does not fit comfortably with the idea of immortality. People cannot imagine 100 or 1000 or million year old children. Also, an aging child might undermine what the parent imagines to be essential in the parenting relationship with the child—a child who needs something like the parenting the child was receiving at around the time of death.

☐ Summary

The child who died remains in the lives of parents. Parents want the child to be remembered by and counted by others and feel stung when friends and family do not acknowledge the ways the child continues to exist for the parents. Parents say they do not forget or want to forget a child who died. Parent memories emphasize connections between child and parent. It seemed to some parents that others wanted not to remember the child. For the parents, not remembering the child was unacceptable, like a death or a further death for the child.

As aids to memory and to maintain continuing connections with the child who died, parents talked about keeping reminders of the child who died. Often the reminders were central and important in day-to-day life and on special occasions like Christmas. Many parents also talked about finding new ways to remember the child and to keep the memory of the child alive for others—for example, identifying symbols that were linked to the child or creating memorials for the child.

Some parents spoke of continuing to interact with the child after the death. Sometimes communication continued; sometimes it faded. Sometimes it involved an exchange of words with the child; sometimes it was a matter of feelings and of sense of presence. The continuing communication meant that the child was still alive somewhere and that the parent-child relationship could, in some sense, continue.

Many parents spoke of the ways that they continued to parent the child—for example, through prayer, through continuing to include the child when they told others how many children they had, and, for couples who had no living child, through continuing to define themselves as parents. Grieving for the child is, in a sense, another way to continue to parent the child. From that perspective, an end to grief would be an end to the child.

Some parents continued to keep track of the child's timeline, noting, for example, when the child would have entered school or begun dating. Keeping track of the timeline may set off recurrent bouts of grief as new losses are encountered, but it is also a way of maintaining continuing contact with the child.

Parents talked about reuniting with the child in heaven, and a few made changes in their lives to maximize the chances of such reunion. Some parents told of arranging with dying relatives to look after the child when they reached heaven.

One could take the belief that the child is in heaven in many different ways—for example, a truth based on religious teaching and religious feeling, a way of feeling comfort about the situation of the child, or an affirmation of the child's goodness. Another way of taking the belief is that it is a language of location. If parents are to continue to have some sort of relationship with the child it is easier if they know where the child is.

From narratives about the parents' relationship with the child, is seems appropriate to turn to narratives of the parent relationship with the other parent. The couple relationship is the focus of the next chapter.

Narratives about the Couple Relationship

☐ Talk about Divorce and Emotional Distance from Spouse

All couples who were interviewed were still married and living together at the time of the child's death. The parent narratives were about the child death, but they were also about the marital relationship (cf. Klass, 1988, p. 41). One way the narratives were about marriage is that most narratives referred to a "fact" that marital relationships are very difficult following a child's death and that many couples who have experienced the death of a child divorce.

Amy: [Somebody] said "I think you should get in touch with so and so out in Georgia. He does work with families that have had ... incidents similar to this." I called him.... He was one of the most supportive people that I had throughout that ordeal. He scared the living daylights out of me. He said, "How are you and Ted communicating?" And I said, "Oh, we're doing all right." And he goes, "You gotta do better than that, 'cause do you realize the divorce rate?" I said, "What?" ... He told me, and I couldn't believe it. And he says, "You've got to work on it.... I know I'm shaking you up. But I'm shaking you up for a purpose, because you've got to react. This is your time right now."

Glenda: We talked sort of right away ... about the statistics are not good for (*Ken:* staying together. No.).

Louise: Almost every book said that 95% of all cases who lose a child through death end in divorce.

Words about divorce were used by many parents to underscore the difficult marital transformations they experienced following the death. Divorce seemed a realistic possibility for many parents, and words about a possible divorce were a way of saying how extremely difficult things were.

Fred: We've heard statistics and after a child's suicide it's (*Hannah:* More than 50%), more than 50%, almost 60% of all marriages end in divorce. We are having problems. There's no doubt about that (bangs on table). Whether ours is gonna go or not, we don't know.... Another six months and we might be separated. But like Hannah said, it's on the surface now; little things that were said years ago in kidding are now serious. Big things that were said in fun are now super-big things. Good things that were done are forgotten.... We used to laugh and joke.... We don't do it anymore.

Jack: When I say we fight, we don't fight-fight in the sense of like throwing stuff across the room or swinging at each other. It's never a ... physical fight, but there have been ... times that I think had it not been for that bond, one side or the other would have walked. So in that sense it has definitely heightened certain tensions; maybe certain expectations simply haven't been met.... I just want to be left alone sometimes, and it's not happening.... It's probably the one thing that has kept us together, yet at the same time it's the one thing that has caused the fights ... that would have separated us.... The bonds [are] of Blake being our son, and what we had together is probably what has kept us together. On the other hand, the fact that we lost him and have gone ... our own different ways has probably caused the conflicts that would have led to a break up had he simply been a normal, healthy kid.

When couples did not use language about divorce to talk about their marital relationship following the death, they usually used metaphors of an increased interpersonal distance.

Karl: I think it's truly had an effect on our relationship. I think that the first time, [when our daughter died], we withdrew from everyone else, and it was like the second time [when our son died] we almost withdrew from each other.... It was that little bit deeper, and I love Kathy as much now as I did then, but sometimes I find (crying) that (she's crying too) I just back away. I just, we both go our separate lives. . . . I've often thought whether it's, do I blame her? Does she blame me? . . . I don't know. . . . I haven't really resolved that. . . .

Kathy: I remember getting into my car everyday, crying all the way to work, then getting to work and working, getting in my car and crying all the way home, and taking care of [our surviving child], and when I was alone crying again for I don't know how long. And I don't remember Karl in the picture at all. . . .

Karl: And that was obvious. (*Kathy:* Yeah) That's the way I felt.

Paul: That you weren't in the picture.

Karl: That I wasn't in the picture. . . . We really couldn't even come home to each other, because we'd kind of withdrawn from each other too. And so we were like in different worlds for a long, long . . . time. (*Kathy:* Yeah.)

Paula: I think (very loud), there's times I feel like there's a wall between us since then, maybe partly because we have not sat down and really talked about it and let our feelings out on certain things, you know, the accident, because we really have not, the two of us. So it's (long pause), it, to me it has put up a wall between us, but not to the point where we'd leave each other. It's just there.

Developing a narrative about divorce or emotional distance might be a route to divorce, but it seemed almost always a precursor to deciding that, whatever the changes that were necessary in the marital relationship, the marriage would not end in divorce. Talking about couples who had experienced the death of a child being likely to divorce or talking about their great distance from each other, many couples made the commitment not to divorce, to do whatever was necessary in order to stay together.

Louise: Almost every book said that 95% of all cases who lose a child through death end in divorce. . . . I thought, "Oh, good, . . . we've already totally disrupted our family. Now we're gonna split up," and maybe that was a positive thing to read that, because I think both of us decided this is not gonna happen. We're just not gonna let it happen. . . . I think it would have been real easy just to say, "If splitting up really made things better, easier, I don't have to look at his pan; he's gonna be out of here." I think that being conscious of the fact that . . . this was a real thing that happens a lot with couples, just not using that as an excuse if things weren't going well.

Wayne: ... It's very easy to do that though ..., because you can get your own life, you can get *out* of the house, you can ... get away from all this environment....

Louise: Yeah. I think that would have been the easy way out, probably, just (*Wayne:* It's like suicide. That's an easy way out, too), yeah. You have ... other children that you're caring for. You ... look at them, thinking they've had enough trauma in their lives. For their sake you need to try to make this work.

Elaine: I can remember that night ..., him and I laying there and just making a vow to each other that it would not tear us apart, because so many people, their family cannot survive.... We held on tight, and just decided that we can't, we just can't let this destroy us.

In parent narratives, the language of commitment often included words that defined the partner or the connection with the partner as unique. In line with what Klass (1988, pp. 42–43) reported, key to the uniqueness were the partner's relationship with the child who died, knowledge of the child, knowledge of the other parent's feelings about the child, and the sharing of grief over the death. The language of this uniqueness is especially powerful in making a commitment to the partner in that it implies that to lose the partner is to lose more of the child who died and, in a sense, to diminish the significance of the great pain one has gone through that no one but the partner has witnessed so fully.

Kathy: He's the only one in the world who knows really how I feel. He's the only one who knew the children as well as I did, and so in that sense we'll always be connected.

Karl: She's the only one that knows how *I* feel about things like that.... She's seen me when I've been way down. She's seen me when I've been way up and what we went through together, and she really knows how I feel.

Jane: People ... seemed to be understanding and whatnot, but *nobody* knew Adam but Rob. And *my* feeling was, and I was just more and more reinforced in that, *nobody* was gonna be able to understand about the depth of our loss except this other person who had lived with him. Not that I was ever *thinking* of leaving or becoming friendly with anyone else.... I kept thinking, "There's no one in this world that understands what we've been through except each other." And I found that as a kind of a binding thing, a commonality, that more than ever I felt we had something in common.

Not just kids and a house and a marriage and all this, but ... the fact that we really understood what we were missing.

Conceivably a couple could take all that happens to them that is associated with a child's dying as a temporary condition that is irrelevant to the underlying marital relationship; the awful things of bereavement do not erase a sense of a constant, good relationship. But no couple who was interviewed spoke that way. Grief after the child died had an impact on the marriage and could lead to what Rosa, in the quote immediately below, spoke of as a shaky and slightly battered marriage. Her language was not quite that of divorce, but it was certainly of troubles that could lead to divorce. Although she was aware that the death caused difficult things to happen, that awareness did not mean that she could shrug off the difficult things as somehow temporary and not intrinsic to the relationship. It was not like she could say, "Oh, well, that's grieving, so I won't let it bother me for the years it takes before things return to normal."

Rosa: I think in the beginning as a couple we were fairly close. It's ... afterwards that *you* got depressed, and quiet, did work. And I got gottagettagottagettagotta with my sister and my mother and [best friend].... My mum kept saying, "I don't like how Henry looks." She kept trying to hug you, and you (laughing) wouldn't even let her.... But I would say it takes you at least five years to grieve. There [were] times when things were really shaky for us as a couple, I think, just because Henry was so quiet. (*Henry:* Plus I went into a new job in the middle of that year.) Yeah.

Henry: Just was tense. It isn't [an easy] job.

Rosa: Yeah. You worked. But even after we had [our two sons], you'd go through periods of being really ... either obsessive or ... being real quiet, where we'd go some place and you'd be quite happy not to say *anything* the whole day (laughing). You still do that a little, but you never did that before Wendy. No. It changes the relationship. Feels slightly battered.

Rosa's narrative goes on to describe her struggle to find a path from where she had been (caring for an extraordinarily ill child, grieving for the child's death) to some place else. She said that finding that new path was nearly impossible because of how her husband was acting, but she also said that with the help of a marriage counselor she was able to find her way to places that she felt were good for her and that did not require her husband to come along.

Rosa: A couple of years ago went to a marriage counselor ... and that sort of helped me come to terms with, "I can't hold Henry responsible for me being happy." [The counselor] gave me the option of leaving, and it's quite clear that I shouldn't (sounding amused) feel guilty if I left you. And talked about that I couldn't change the way Henry was coping with this.... I would have to find ways to work things out, and I couldn't change him.

Kathy, like Rosa, said that she struggled to find a path to some place better and was impeded by her husband's unwillingness or inability to travel a path with her. For her, as for Rosa, divorce language helped to define what went on, and, like Rosa, she said that the way out of her difficulty was to find ways to make transitions without them having to be couple transitions.

Kathy: I finally realized I can't make [Karl] do something he doesn't want to do. And that's when I started being, I think, more independent ..., because I still wanted to live my life, and I didn't want to ... leave him when he was so ill.... I couldn't do that, but I couldn't just sit home and wait for him to get better either, 'cause that was really up to him. I finally realized all my begging and pleading wasn't going to do any good, and that was up to him, and I like to know that I can control (chuckles) certain things. I couldn't control that. So I could control what I did, and that's kind of what I've done.

Comparisons with other couples who had lost a child were common in parent narratives as the parents discussed how their grieving played out in their marital relationship. It seems that for some parents, a key to constructing their narrative about the child's death and the marital aftermath was to have a basis of evaluating their own experience against the experiences of others who have been in similar situations.

Tina: In some ways we are [closer].... One of these women I mentioned earlier, she and her husband dealt with their child's death [in a way] really different than ours. Like they *never* talk about it, and they never went to support groups.

Candy: Recently we had friends ... that their ... daughter all of a sudden her heart gave out.... Going to them and thinking about them helps, thinking about other people that are worse off than you are (weeping). Sometimes you don't have to look very far ... to find somebody that's hurting.

☐ Talk about Couple Differences

Many parents spoke of struggling with marital differences. Some talked about differences in "being there," partners differing in how supportive they were to one another, how open each was to listening to the other, how compliant each was with what the other requested, or how sensitive each was to the needs of the other.

Kathy: I've always been there, but there hasn't always been someone (laughing) there for me.

The literature on parent grief says if partners differ in mutual support it is typically the man who is less available emotionally (Farnsworth & Allen, 1996; Fish, 1986; Kavanaugh, 1997; Lewis & Liston, 1981; Rosenblatt & Burns, 1986). However, a man who may seem to his wife to be emotionally unavailable may feel that he is working hard to be there for her (Cook, 1983, 1988; Peppers & Knapp, 1980, p. 21; Schwab, 1992) in the sense of being strong, trying to help her to be less emotional, trying to maintain the family economically, trying to keep his emotionality from setting off hers, or covering for things she ordinarily would do that she is not doing so much or so well in grief. Some couple narratives dealt with the different perspectives of woman and man on "being there" for each other.

Angela: That was the hardest thing when Blake died.... I needed Jack, and he wasn't there. (*Jack:* I was here) ... But he wasn't, I mean he was shut down. He wouldn't grieve with me. He grieved alone. That was real hard for me to deal with.

Jack: I supported *your* grieving.

Angela: Yeah, but wouldn't let me support his.... You're there for me but you won't let me be there for you. So I was in a catch-22 situation. I need him for me, but I need to be there for him, and he's not letting me be there for him, but so then I shouldn't really want him to be there for me, and (breathing audibly in amused disgust) ... I felt like I was gettin' pulled every which way.

The most commonly reported findings in research on parent bereavement is that there is often a difference in how publicly, intensely, and long women and men grieve, and typically it is a woman who grieves more, grieves more openly, expresses feelings verbally, or seems less controlled (Arbuckle & de Vries, 1995; Carroll & Shaefer, 1993–94; Cook, 1983, 1988; Cordell & Thomas, 1990; Cornwell, Nurcombe, & Stevens, 1977; DeFrain, 1991; DeFrain, Martens, Stork, & Stork, 1990–91; DeFrain, Taylor, & Ernst, 1982, Chapter 5; Donnelly, 1982, Chapter 7; Dyregrov, 1990; Dyregrov & Matthiesen, 1987b; Edelstein, 1984, p. 89; Fish, 1986; Gilbert & Smart, 1992, p. 61; Hughes & Page-Lieberman, 1989; Johnson, 1987, p. 64; Kavanaugh, 1997; Lang & Gottlieb, 1993; Lister, 1991; Mandell, McAnulty,

& Reece, 1980; Miles, 1984; Peppers & Knapp, 1980, p. 21; Rosenblatt & Burns, 1986; Schwab, 1992; Shanfield, Benjamin, & Swain, 1988; Smart, 1993; Stinson, Lasker, Lohmann, & Toedter, 1992; Thomas, Striegel, Dudley, Wilkins, & Gibson, 1997). The couples who were interviewed typically seemed to know about such research findings, often through reading or through support groups like Compassionate Friends. According to many parent narratives, a goal in the support groups (and a couple goal as well) was to minimize marital trouble by acknowledging gender differences and defining them as normal and okay as they played out for a couple. So in many couples, partners spoke about their differences by acknowledging them and framing them as "normal and okay."

Todd: Some of it you just don't understand. It's just the way it is. You learn that, okay, this is the way she feels. I don't understand why, but that's the way she feels.... Sometimes it was things she said and explained to me, and maybe I still wouldn't understand, but at least I knew what she said, and it's just one of those things. It takes time ..., at least it took me time.

Iris: There's things that have come up recently that we've talked about and come to understanding of. Sometimes you almost have to agree to disagree.

Todd: Yeah. Yeah. 'Cause she's different, and I'm different. And we're wired up differently.... She's the kind that wants to be with somebody when she's feeling bad. I'm not. Just leave me alone.

Iris: I've learned not to take that personally. (*Todd:* Yeah, yeah.) I figured out that it doesn't have anything to do with me; it's just ... him (laughs).

Vince: We finally came to the realization that we ... grieve at different levels. We don't always grieve about the same thing at the same time. We're not always in the same mood ..., and once we came to that realization and came to respect each other's level of needing, like if I was having a particularly bad day or grieving about this box that was closed that now came undone, she respected me enough to let me go on about it and comfort me about that, as opposed to saying, "... I thought you were done.... Why don't you just go on?" ... It was nice that we recognized that we grieve at different levels and gave each other the latitude to regress.... I really think that that wasn't until we had joined (bang on table) Compassionate Friends, 'cause that was one of the big things I got out of Compassionate Friends was, "Hey, that's okay to do that."

Gail: ... We heard that happened to other people and ... that couples were at different points at different times individually. And we've heard that from them, that that was okay.

Parents commonly said that they differed in how much they went outside the marriage for talk about the death and its aftermath and how much when they talked with others they brought up emotional matters, with the woman turning to others and bringing up emotional matters more often than the man (cf. Brabant, Forsyth, & McFarlain, 1995; Carroll & Shaefer, 1993–94). Typically, in parent narratives, that difference was spoken about as a matter of gender.

Joy: There was really someone always there. I had my friend ... that we've been friends with since I was three. I could call her anytime, and she would relate as much as she could.... She loved Jenny as much as you could love someone else's child.... My mom was always there. My mom and I can still talk about Jenny. My Mom probably cries about Jenny easier than I do.

Stan: Yeah, I think Joy had a lot of people. I think ... men aren't as open ... with each other. And my friends, they came to the funeral and some sent cards.... I heard from kids that I haven't heard from in years, which made me feel really good.... [The minister] helped me a lot as being another man that I could talk with. But normal friends, they really didn't want to get too close feeling-wise. But I think Joy did have more people she could really get.

Joy: ... I ... feel like, even now, I can talk about Jenny easier than Stan can.... I think it probably is easier for guys not to deal with the feeling part of it.

Judging by parent narratives (and by the scholarly literature), it is much more likely that partners will differ in important ways than that they will not (Gilbert, 1996; Rando, 1986, 1991; Raphael, 1983, p. 249).

At another level, the narrative accounts of differences seem to me to be talk about gender in U.S. society. As the differences played out, typically it was the man who felt put upon to feel, relate, and act in ways that did not fit for him, and typically it was the woman who felt emotionally abandoned and that she had to fight to have her feelings acknowledged and respected. There was also a retrospective element in this. The death opened the couple's past to examination and reemplotment, and in the process the couple relationship prior to the death was opened to question. I think this was particularly so for women, some of whom came to question how much emotional understanding and support they had prior to the death. That may have been a part of why divorce seemed a realistic possibility to some couples. I think that fitting things into a narrative that said "we grieve differently and should accept our differences" worked to reduce couple difficulties with all this. But there are feminist perspectives that would say that the acceptance-of-difference narrative does not give some women the social support and understanding they want from the partner.

In some couples one consequence of the child's death seemed to be an empowerment of the woman partner. The dynamics surrounding how the couple came to a shared, mutually accommodating narrative were related to the woman's empowerment, fueled by her strong needs and her upsetness with her husband. In those couples, I think, the relationship dance had changed; the woman was leading and the man watching her feet and following.

☐ Talk about Conflict

In accord with what has been reported in other research (Cornwell, Nurcombe, & Stevens, 1977; Gilbert, 1989; Gilbert & Smart, 1992, p. 52; Lewis & Liston, 1981), many parents talked about marital conflict connected to their bereavement. Although sometimes there were issues of blaming, the conflict was most often framed in terms of differences—in thoughts, actions, beliefs, emotional reactions, meanings (given to the child, the death, their emotional reactions, and other things), support, and relationships with others. Some of the language they used when saying they felt strongly about the conflict was the language of divorce, but many parents who had used that language could, months or years after the peak of intense conflict, look back at those relationship difficulties with amusement.

Tina: Initially we were very close emotionally and sexually. As we moved a little bit further out from it, and . . . there was talk of being pregnant, then it was like *he* thought the only reason I wanted to have sex was so I could get pregnant. And there . . . was a lot of tension about that, a lot of fights. . . . If he thought that we were gonna be close to being sexual, it was like he'd do everything in his power not to do anything. And I can remember this one night just sitting up here just sobbing and being so sad because we had *both* agreed we were gonna have another child. But then I didn't think he was playin' his part in it. And I remember, goin' through my mind, "That's it! We're done! I'm divorced! I'm leavin' him!"

Scott: . . . Normally, our sexuality, I've always been the aggressor and my desire level is, let's say there's a significant gap between mine and hers. So . . . [after] Gina's death, . . . once we were . . . able to . . . conceive . . . , it was like the shoe was on the other foot. So . . . I did avoid it. I mean the shoe was *really* on the other foot. Not to say that Tina always avoids it . . . , but . . . I did feel pressured, and because of that pressure I was indifferent, and in some cases would try to avoid the situation. . . . In retrospect, it's kind of humorous . . . , but it was very real at that point. . . . It caused a tremendous amount of stress in our relationship.

Sometimes there was still pain or anger in talk about marital conflict. Here, for example, is a couple talking about how they came to be so separate. Notice Kathy's "beat a dead horse" statement, which I think says something about how she saw Karl or their relationship (dead) and also about what she did with her anger about Karl and their relationship. She would have liked to beat him or it, but saw no point to it.

Karl: I feel . . . a freedom from her. . . . She makes it very clear, it's like she doesn't need me anymore. I sometimes feel that way, like she doesn't need me.

Kathy: Well, I never say *that.*

Karl: No, no. No, you don't.

Kathy: I'm not, (*Karl:* No, you never say that.) I'm not dependent on him, but there's a difference. I think we all have needs, and when I've expressed those things to you and you turn me away, there's only so many times, you know, I've told you. I hear you when you say, "I can't do it," or, "No, I'm not going to," and I don't care to hear that over and over again. I don't care to beat a dead horse, and so I just move on. And I think for me that's been better than feeling bad that you won't meet me half way or you won't do things that I tell you I would like you to do to help. And so . . . I've gone off. And I tried (slight laughter) to take you with, a lot of times, but you really weren't interested.

As couples talked about their relationship in bereavement, not infrequently they talked about a pattern of distancing and pursuit, with one wanting to be more alone, to grieve privately, or not to talk about certain things, and the other wanting to be more in contact, to share grief, to be heard and supported.

Angela: Jack grieves by himself, and I know that. . . . It's like I used to bang my head against the wall.

Jack: . . . At the top of our lungs and the heat of anger? . . . We've (laughing) discussed it that way. . . . (*Angela:* Tell me to leave you alone) . . . I finally get to the point where I say, "Get off my back." . . . To a certain degree I want to be left alone. I know internally how I work. I know what is going to get me through the day. And I would appreciate it that people would let me get through the *day.*

Angela: "You are just to leave me alone." ... That's kind of how you say it too. (speaking slowly and distinctly:) "Leave me alone."

Jack: (laughing) No, that's not what I say. I do not say, "Leave me alone." I say, "Get off my back."

Angela: I interpret it as, "Leave you alone."

Jack: It just means don't nag me, don't *press* for things that aren't coming.

Angela: And I do. I push him. 'Cause I want him to be able to open up to me. If you can open to anybody it should be your wife. But he can't, he can't open up.

Jack: And you do push.

Angela: I do. I do, but I never win. But I do push. And I don't quit either. If I want him, I push and push and push. Then, of course, that just pisses him off (laughing). But I *try* real hard. I don't ever get what I want, 'cause he's stubborn. He just sucks it all in.

There are many ways to understand what happened to the couple who divorced and to the couple who was very close to divorcing. One element of the narratives of both couples was that things had occurred between the partners that could not be forgiven.

Earl: Molly asked me, I don't know how many times, if I blamed her. And I told her, "No." And things just kinda worked their way into a (pause) unrelationship type thing.... Molly didn't understand why I did not cry at first. And I told her that I had to be there for her. I said "I'll cry, and I do cry, but I'm here to support you." And I've never been forgiven for that, for not crying at the time.

Having divorced or almost divorced, a person could feel that in a sense the spouse had died. Bill used that metaphor inadvertently. He had experienced grinding anger from his wife since their son's death, and she was divorcing him. At one point while telling the story of their son's death, Bill talked about "her" death.

Bill: The pastor would stop by ... I think probably the first three or four years of the anniversary of her death, and having it come out, because of the way Becky felt, presented it as a problem. It wasn't a consoling type of thing. It was bringing up *conflict* ... to discuss it at that time.

☐ **Becoming a Stronger Couple**

In narratives about the marital relationship following the death, there is a sense of the death creating a new bond in the couple at the same time that it pushes them apart (cf. Dijkstra & Stroebe, 1998; Klass, 1986–87). Thus, couples not only talked about being pushed apart, but as has been reported in other research (DeFrain, Martens, Stork, & Stork, 1990–91; Edelstein, 1984, p. 90; Klass, 1986–87; Lehman, Lang, Wortman, & Sorenson, 1989; Peppers & Knapp, 1980, p. 75; Rosenblatt & Burns, 1986), many talked about how they had become strengthened as a couple by the death.

Denny: I hear ... some people get torn apart by it or have problems, and we have the best relationship I know of. And it only made us stronger....

Marsha: You think you're close to your spouse, but I think when you have a loss like that, ... it brings your souls closer together. He is my soul mate....

Denny: There's no other word for it (*Marsha:* Yeah). Souls or hearts or closeness, but ... when you've lost your baby and then you lose another one ..., it's ... all that down the tubes.... After you pour your heart [out] with going through this stuff, and like I say I broke down ... tons of times, hard, and she's there for me, and when she does, I'm there. And once in a while, be at the same time.... There's a connection, yeah, a different side.

Marsha: And you see a different side of the emotions of your spouse, that—

Denny: Parental side. I don't know what you call it.... She's not just Marsha and a wife; she's a mom.... I got more respect and love for her than I ever had before, and I didn't think that [could] become more, but she's unbelievable.... We have bad days, but we're not gonna get divorced or anything close to that.

Sometimes, as with Denny, narratives about strengthening were partly about seeing good things that had not been seen before in the spouse.

Brett: I admired her, 'cause I always thought she was, well, not weak, but not as strong emotionally. And it made me realize that my wife was strong, and that was something that I admired, and I didn't know that she had.

Some narratives about strengthening highlighted sharing the experience of the child's death and the grieving. Some narratives of strengthening said that the death pushed the partners to talk with each other more and reveal more to each other.

Stan: It probably brought us closer together. I guess a lot of people it ... tears them apart, but I think for us it probably brought us closer together ... emotion-wise. Just being really able to dig down deep in your soul and ... let everything out. I think men have a tendency not to do that (laughs). And that time period it was very easy for me to do it.

Greater closeness might not be permanent (or desired), but it was what a number of couples said they experienced. Although the language of close-ness in marriage is a positive language in the U.S., it seems that some parents did not see the positive in the closeness of a married couple grieving a child who died. For them, the language of closeness was not about a higher level of love, communication, and understanding so much as it was about des-perate, hurting, needy people who would be much better off and happier if their child were still alive and they were not so close as a couple.

Vince: I think it brought us closer together, (4 second pause) for that period of time. . . .

Gail: I think we [grew] closer because of survival. Don't you think we hung on to each other? Maybe until we felt stronger and then branched out to talk to [others] and go to group (*Vince:* umhm). . . . I think it *forced* us together. (*Vince:* Yes.) Yes, it did bring us together, but it forced us. It wasn't by choice. We chose to cling to each other, because each other was there. . . . We had to cling to each other. And I'm sure if . . . other people had been that supportive to us . . . , we would have clung to them as well. . . . I don't think we got strength from it. . . .

Vince: . . . We got forced closer together. . . . I don't know if that's a strength either (laughs). . . . I'd rather be further apart and have Randy here.

☐ Speaking about Sexuality

Talk about sexuality can be a way of talking about the future (should we try to have another child), about grief (I hurt so much that we shouldn't do this or we should do this), about the couple relationship (why are we together if we are not sexual partners), and about healing. It is about healing partly because many couples went through a time after the child's death of not having sexual intercourse or of having a lower level of sexual intimacy (Gottlieb, Lang, & Amsel, 1996; Hagemeister & Rosenblatt, 1997; Johnson, 1984–85; Peppers & Knapp, 1980, Chapter 9; Schwab, 1992), so talk about intercourse can be talk about moving along the path of grieving. It is also about difference, because partners often differed in what sexual contact meant to them and what they needed and wanted (Fish, 1986; Hagemeister & Rosenblatt, 1997; Peppers & Knapp, 1980, Chapter 9; Schwab, 1992).

Gail: As far as (laughter) having sex, I can remember wanting to throw up, because I thought it was just horrible and how could you ... possibly think of that.... I do remember you saying that that made you feel close, and that was comforting for you. But I know that we felt opposite that way.

Talk about sexuality is also about meanings (Hagemeister & Rosenblatt, 1997), with couples understanding the break in their sexual relationship and the resumption of sexual contact in terms of the meanings sexual contact had for them. Some narratives spoke of a break in sexual intercourse because of depression, emotional fragility, emotional emptiness, emotional distancing related to the loss and grieving, or a low level of physical or emotional energy. Some said it was emotionally difficult to have intercourse because intercourse was how the child was made. For some, the pleasuring of sexual intercourse was inconsistent with grief. Some feared another pregnancy, feeling they were not ready for pregnancy or new child care responsibilities. On the other hand, some were eager to resume intercourse because they wanted to make another child, and then their intercourse was saturated with that meaning. For some, resuming intercourse was an affirmation of life, of returning to couple togetherness (perhaps after being engulfed for months by concerns about a child who was extremely ill), and of moving forward in trying to live life. For some, particularly men, intercourse was comforting.

A resumption of sexual intercourse was not, in some narratives, a resumption of intercourse as they had known it in the past. It might, at least at first, include crying and emotional release or a bittersweet sense of shared loss.

Jane: One thing I've noticed, any time we were intimate ..., almost always, even though I wasn't sobbing or anything like this, just the emotion. Almost every time one or the other of us would say, and it just really didn't exactly relate, and yet we just really missed Adam. You just were emotional, and that was the biggest emotion in our lives. We just missed Adam and so frequently we, I would get tears in my eyes, or Rob would, and we would just say to each other, "I sure still miss him."

Sexual meanings do not inhere only in intercourse. Some parents defined touching and holding as sexual and felt that in their bereavement they may have moved to an even higher level of touching and holding than they had experienced with each other in the past. However, there were also couple narratives in which part of the pain of grieving was that one partner could not or would not provide the hugging and holding that the other wanted.

☐ Summary

Parent narratives dealt extensively with the marital relationship. Most narratives referred to a "fact" that marital relationships are very difficult following a child's death and that many couples who have experienced the death of a child divorce. Words about divorce or about increased marital distance were used by many parents to underscore the difficult marital transformations they experienced following the death. Having recognized how much their marriage was at risk, many couples said that they made the commitment not to divorce, to do whatever was necessary in order to stay together. Among the reasons for that commitment, many couples cited the partner as uniquely important because the partner knew best the child who died and what the spouse had gone through in connection with the child's death.

In the narratives, valuable ingredients for getting along and staying together included an acceptance of partner differences and a willingness to do things without the spouse that would help in dealing with the loss. Often comparisons with other couples who had experienced the death of a child were said to be helpful. Couples learned from their own experiences and from comparisons with other couples that partners grieve differently, and the differences usually can be framed in ways that are congruent with standard ways of thinking about gender in U.S. society. However, the differences were not necessarily easy to accept. Many couples talked about marital conflicts connected to these differences and about patterns of distancing and pursuit that were frustrating to both partners.

In many narratives there was a sense of the death creating a new bond in the couple at the same time that it pushed them apart. Many couples talked about how they had become strengthened as a couple by the death. Included in that strengthening might be a greater closeness. Although closeness might be what some people in the U.S. think of as ideal in marriage, the closeness the couples experienced arose out of their pain and neediness following the loss and was a closeness they might have gladly foregone in exchange for the child continuing to live.

Most parents talked about a gap or decline in marital sexuality following the child's death. The gap or decline was explained in various ways but primarily in terms of decreased energy and motivation and of the meanings sexual contact had for one or both partners. When couples eventually moved to greater sexual activity, it often continued in the shadow of the child's death, with a different character and different meanings than it had before the child's death.

Most parents in the study had the experience of parenting other children following the death. In some ways, the issues were the same in the parent-child relationship as in the marital relationship, with the parent grieving, the continuing presence of the child who died, and the prominence of meanings that arose because of the child's death. The next chapter focuses on narratives of parenting following the death of a child.

10
CHAPTER

Narratives about Parenting
Other Children

☐ Grieving and Distance from Surviving Children

In the narratives of many parents who had children who survived the
death of their sibling, there were stories of increased distance from the
surviving children after the death. Many of those parents talked about the
death preoccupying and demoralizing them in ways that led to the greater
distance. An observer might speak of parents whose depression, decreased
energy, inward gaze, and preoccupation produced neglect, and some parents
spoke that way, but there was more to it than that. Some parents seemed to
feel that they were protecting their children by being distant, that by keeping
their most intense grief out of the sight and hearing of surviving children
they were protecting the children from frightening levels of parental pain
and irritability. (The surviving children may "neglect" their parents for the
same reason.)

Glenda: I don't think [our children] ever really saw us cry.... We tried to
protect them from emotion ..., by not showing enough of it. I don't know
that they know how hurt we've been ..., but then they don't tell us, 'cause
they probably didn't want to (*Ken:* Yeah) add to it, so we don't know how
hurt (*Ken:* how hurt they are) they are.... I have apologized to them a
couple of times for ... neglecting ... them.... They didn't say it, but I think
we did it, that we were so consumed that we let them [go off on their own].

☐ "Replacement" Children

As reported in other studies (Cornwell, Nurcombe, & Stevens, 1977; Johnson, 1984–85; Klass, 1988, p. 33), many parents who were in their twenties, thirties, or even forties at the time of the death told about considering having another child. Most parents who had no living child reported a sharp urge to get on with a life that included parenting a living child. In fact, as reported in research by Powell (1995), quite a few grieving parents did have a subsequent child.

Parents expressed concern about what their wanting to have another child after a child died might do to a subsequent child. They spoke of concern about a next child becoming a replacement for the one who died (cf. Cornwell, Nurcombe, & Stevens, 1977; Powell, 1995).

Amy: We were a little bit warned about that, be cautioned as far as a replacement baby.

Brett: I was afraid that [our next child] might be replacin' Alex.

Despite parent concerns about a subsequent child being a replacement for the one who died, many parents who had a subsequent child said that in some sense the next child was a replacement. A next child allows parents to do the nurturing that they could not continue with the child who died, may allow them to have a story of parenting with a happy ending, and may let them use the room, clothing, toys, furniture, and other things they had for the child who died.

Rosa: Wendy died May 6th; [her brother] was born the following year May 8th. So that was a big thing, 'cause I didn't want [him] to be born on the anniversary of Wendy's death. It was hard having [him] that close. I can remember, after he was born, thinking I was betraying Wendy. But we were only having her sense that it was okay. And probably when [he] was born, I lost that close feeling to Wendy, but he was so big and so healthy (*Henry:* Umhm). Wendy had been tiny and delicate. [He] came out ... nine pounds, cheeks ... rosy.... I wanted a baby, and I would have done anything to have it.... I, at that point, had a really strong sense that Wendy's presence was in the house and that if I got pregnant again that it would be [her].... And then it wasn't, it was *obviously* not Wendy. No.

Scott: We had another child.... To a certain degree, the need for another child to replace the child that you had lost had kinda been fulfilled.

What does it mean that parents say they do not want a next child to be a "replacement" for the child who died? I think it means that they want to define the next child as a different person, an autonomous person with the right to differ from the child who died. In this regard, parents who had a next child often emphasized, as did Rosa in the quote above, how the next child was different from the one who died.

Another aspect of not making a child a replacement child was, as some parents talked about it, not "spoiling" the child who was born after the sibling death.

Amy: I don't see [our son].... as a replacement baby.... partly because I ..., back to my mom, when she lost [her baby]. Then she had my brother.... I heard so much about replacement baby, be careful,... that that kicked up things in [me] to think about how I can't *stand* my brother.... He was *incredibly* spoiled.

So it was clear that some parents were comfortable with replacing a child who died (in terms of having a baby to nurture and having a "happy ending" to some stories) as long as the new child had the freedom to be her or his own person and was not overindulged.

☐ Parenting a Child Who is Grieving

Rosen (1984–85) suggested that for all sorts of reasons, siblings of a child who died are blocked from fully mourning. No parent in this study talked directly about the matter, but some implied that a child or children held back grieving and that parental neglect could have been a factor in that.

PR: Did you think [your oldest son] was affected?

Paula: He was. At the time, he just wanted to be left alone....

Pete: It was a long time before he opened up about it.

Paula: He finally opened up because I caught him [in town] skipping school. And he said he was there with the class, and I said, "Where's your teacher?" He says, "Well, over in [the mall]." ... I said, "Go get in the truck. I'm going to take you back to school." ... I took him back to school, and we talked to the counselor. And it seemed like it wasn't just Jerry's [death] that was working on him. It was a lot of things.... Once we talked with the counselor that afternoon and then the next morning, and he got everything out in the open, that seemed to help a lot, because we didn't have any trouble with him after that.... He was having ... trouble with some kids picking on him on the bus. . . . That was the big thing that was bothering him, and he was really hurt because he [had] been looking forward to teaching Jerry how to play ball.

Perhaps it's only a guess, but I think one can read Paula's story as saying that her son holding back his grieving was related to his having big troubles about which his parents did not know.

☐ Making the Child Who Died Real for the Child's Siblings

Most parents said that they talked to their other children about the child who died. For these parents, such talk was a way of keeping the child who died in the memory of the other children, creating and maintaining a set of family memories and perspectives about the child who died, and helping the other children to maintain connection with the dead sibling. For some parents, this was an important part of parenting other children.

Joy: I related a story to [our younger children]. I said Jenny was getting out of the car at my mom's one day and it was spring and it was real slushy and there was nowhere for her to step besides the icky slush. And she said, "Sometimes you have to walk in the icky slush." And it's like we've sort of used that . . . when we're doing something we don't really like to do, but there's no other path to take, . . . we'll say, "Sometimes you have to walk in the icky slush." . . . Maybe sometimes they'll say, "Where did that come from? Why do we say that?" And then we'll tell them the story about Jenny walking through the icky slush.

From a social constructionist perspective, keeping memories and talk about the child who died alive for other children provides a social environment for the parent to construct and maintain memories of the child who died (Shotter, 1990). Thus, the parents who worked at helping living children to remember the child who died were helping themselves to remember as well.

☐ Protective Parenting

Parenting after a child dies is often a matter of anxiety (Dyregrov & Matthiesen, 1987b; Powell, 1995), and parents who have experienced the death of a child often are more protective in their parenting than they otherwise would have been (Cornwell, Nurcombe, & Stevens, 1977). A parent is more aware than before of the fragility of child life and of the vulnerability of self and partner to a child death. Small wonder then that many parent narratives described how the parents were extremely protective of their other children (Rosenblatt, 2000). They talked about the protectiveness being a consequence of what they had experienced and learned and also a way of communicating that experience and learning to their children. It was also a way, in a sense, of honoring the child who died by marking the magnitude of the child's death.

Louise: I became very protective of them at first. I remember . . . calling the school saying, and I don't know what I was afraid of, they were gonna get (*Wayne:* their crossing the street or something). . . . I was afraid of everything. And I remember calling the school saying, "Don't let them go home with anybody. Don't let anybody take them out regardless of what these people say to you." I'm sure the school thought I was real loony. . . .

Wayne: And sleepovers.

Louise: Yeah, I didn't let them sleep over.

As discussed in more detail in Rosenblatt (2000), parent protection took many forms. Louise, in the quote above, talked about greater vigilance. Other parents talked about being protective through more rapid response to any sign of trouble, concealing parent grief, or subordinating personal needs in order to benefit the child. In some ways, the greater protectiveness seemed to me that bereaved parents with surviving or subsequently born children lived a more child-focused life and a less marriage-focused life.

Protection seemed typically to occur in a system in which children collaborated in their own protection. That is, there were few stories about children resisting parent protection and a number of stories of children accepting and going along with parent efforts to be protective. Protectiveness can also become part of an intergenerational family system. Erin and Gene, for example, said that the accidental death of their son 35 years before the interview continued to have an impact on the family in that they are much more cautious in their grandparenting than they would have been had the accidental death not happened. Erin also said that their daughter, who is now a mother, is always very concerned about her children when they visit the farm, and Erin thinks it's because of the accidental death.

☐ Summary

Many parents told of increased distance from surviving children after the death, partly because the death preoccupied and demoralized them. Parents might speak of neglecting their other children, but they also might feel that they were protecting their children by being distant in ways that kept the children away from parental pain and irritability.

Many parents told about considering having another child, and most parents who had no living child reported a sharp urge to get on with a life that included parenting a living child. In fact, quite a few couples did have a subsequent child. With a subsequent child, many were concerned about the child becoming a replacement for the one who died, but in some ways parents who talked about the matter were glad to have a replacement. Parents might be glad to have a child be a replacement in the sense of meeting parent emotional and role needs as long as the new child would not have her or his individuality submerged in some kind of confusion with the child who died and would not be "spoiled" by parents who were too affected by the death of the child's sibling.

Parents generally said that they tried to keep the child who died real and present for the child's siblings. This was consistent with parent concerns that others not forget the child who died, and at the same time the parents were creating a social environment for themselves that would support their own memories and determination to remain connected to the child who died.

Parents talked about protecting other children following the death. The protection arose from an increased awareness of the fragility of child life and of parent vulnerability to a child death. It was also a way of honoring the child who died by marking the magnitude of the child's death. The protection took a number of forms, including increased vigilance, and children generally complied with parent protectiveness.

From focusing on relationships within the family, the next chapter turns to parent narratives about seeking, failing to find, and finding support outside of the immediate family.

CHAPTER

Finding Support

The grief of parents does not occur in a social vacuum. Parent narratives about the death and its aftermath refer repeatedly to family, friends, and others. This chapter focuses on common aspects of bereaved parent narratives as they referred to support from family, friends, and others. Most parents who were interviewed, but not all, said that they found valuable support of their grieving from at least one other person. Some talked about finding valuable support from many people.

☐ Who Was There

Almost all parents talked about people who bridged the chasm reported in chapter 6, people who were there for the parents following the death and who provided support (cf. Klass, 1996, 1997). In talking about who was there for them, the parents painted a picture of the kinds of support they valued. At the core of support, parents seemed most to value good, nonjudgmental listening (Brice, 1991a, 1991b; DeFrain, Martens, Stork, & Stork, 1990-91; Schwab, 1990); constancy; asking questions that helped the bereaved parent to come to understandings about what was going on; and witnessing (the dying, the funeral, and what came after that).

Hannah: My best friend, we've been friends since 1980, and I think that's probably the person that I've leaned on the most. She's probably the most nonjudgmental (*Fred:* Psych nurse (laughs)), she's the best listener I've ever; she's a friend. She's really, truly a friend.

Brett: My little brother, it made me and him closer, 'cause he's the only one that ... would ask me all the dumb questions everyone else was afraid to ask me. So it made us closer.

Iris: [Todd's father] scolded us for upsetting Todd's mom, and we weren't supposed to call and tell 'em such awful (chuckling) things (*Todd:* Yeah). So after that we called and told them only the good news.... But the rest of the family was fine. They were really good; they were supportive. (*Todd:* Yeah....) Nobody came out to see Jeff at the hospital, but everybody was in touch all the time.

Todd: ... When somebody's in intensive care, you wonder how much you can do coming out to the hospital.... They came out sometimes, and ... a couple of people from work came down one time.... People at work would ask, "How's he doing?" ... I'd give 'em an update. Certain people in particular would ask, maybe half a dozen people.

Some people who were there for them also helped by giving them words about how the child was special.

Stan: Our friends were constantly there. It really helped just to have people. And even people just sending cards.... We really looked forward to getting mail 'cause we'd get cards....

Joy: And they'd talk about Jenny and tell what Jenny meant to them. And then I had a friend who, we'd been friends since I was 3 years old, and I think the first year she sent me a card every day.... She had us over for dinner a lot. And our families were real supportive.

The support most often described in parent narratives showed the parents that they were not alone. Also, many parents talked about a catharsis of grief, saying that for them (or for the partner) there was a need to talk to someone else in order to have a catharsis of feelings (Schwab, 1990).

Hannah: One thing that people need to know ... when it was a child that suicided is that they need to encourage the ... parents and ... relatives to talk about it, because a lot of people avoid the topic of [my son's suicide].... My daughter will not talk about. As a matter of fact, we found out she threw away all his letters and stuff that he brought her.... Her way of saying, "Okay, I don't have to deal with this now." And I think that people need to talk about it, and I talk about him a lot more than [my husband] does.

And maybe it's just because I needed it more, but I really think that people should talk about it, because ... it's a catharsis for one thing. But I think that if you avoid talking about what happened, you just bury it deeper and deeper, and I think it's harder to deal with it.

I think the catharsis is also a catharsis of thought in the sense of getting rid of confusion and unclarity. The feelings that go with what could be called a catharsis of thought are feelings of finally figuring some things out or finally deciding what to believe. Many parents spoke about the importance of having listeners, I think partly because the listeners helped them to get clear what their narrative was and in the process to figure out what happened and to come to terms with it.

Elaine: I don't think we spent a day alone for what? Five weeks? Six weeks after [the death]? Someone always was here with us. Some people said they didn't think they could handle ... all those people. But ... you need somebody to tell that story over and over and over.... You need people that are willing to listen to it over and over, and I don't mean for months. I mean for years.... *You* never get sick of telling it. And that's how you get through that is to tell the story over and over and over.

Many parents talked about how supportive it was that others acknowledged their reality that the child was a living human, was important, and was worthwhile remembering.

Joy: We ... have friends that still send us cards on [her] birthday or the day she died. And just to know that, and the first year we just had a flood on the anniversary of her death.... People that you wouldn't even think are thinking about [her] just ... call us ... and [say], "I wanted you to know we're thinking about you today and we haven't forgotten." ... I think that's maybe one thing when parents lose a child they still want to know their child's life has meaning. And that it's still impacting others.

In the process of talking about who was there for them, some parents also talked about who was not there for them (Farnsworth & Allen, 1996; Klass, 1996, 1997; Lauterbach, 1994), people who remained on the other side of the chasm from bereaved parents.

Sally: My parents are really into denial. I think they think it's a good thing that he died. They just feel like, "Okay, it's over, get on with having another baby." That is so disrespectful. We were really misunderstood by lots of people. Everybody wanted our grief to go away. That was an erosion of support. His parents were much more supportive, but they were out of town. With my family, it was like we had a hamster that died, or a goldfish. Luckily we had taken photos of Mike.... I put a picture of Mike on my parents' refrigerator. After a few months (*Bruce:* no, it was much less), yes, after 3 weeks (*Bruce:* a week) my dad took the picture down. I was devastated. I told my dad, it's like taking my picture down.

Bruce: Her dad said, "I can't have pictures of dead people in my house. I don't even have pictures of my parents up." It hurt me because it showed such a lack of respect for Sally.

Both the support and the nonsupport parents received were ingredients for their narratives about what they would do for others who experienced loss.

Todd: You pretty much came to the conclusion after it was all over that we weren't ever gonna tell anybody that we knew how they felt, 'cause they don't know how you feel, really they don't. And the best thing at least for us was just people tellin' us that they care, and offer any help that they could, and the ones that came up and said, "Oh, I know just how you feel. My poor Billy got a sliver in his toe once, had to go to the hospital." (Iris laughs) Well, (*Iris:* laughing hard) Sorry.) (Todd laughs) It wasn't quite that mundane, but

Iris: Well, it was, yeah

Todd: In some cases they obviously just had no clue.

Iris: One friend thought she knew how I felt because her child almost died once. And I tried to tell her, "Almost dying isn't the same as dying." (laughs) ... She can't understand that, but it's okay.... I don't want her to find out (laughing).

Todd: They meant well (*Iris:* Yeah), but it was just really not well thought out.... They were kinda pathetic tries at making us feel good. But ... I guess we've benefitted from that. We've been able to help some people, I think, who ... had ... serious problems with sick kids. And I think that they appreciate it (*Iris:* Umhm), our approach as compared with some others who have a more superficial, "That's too bad for you, and I know how you feel."

☐ The Support of People Who Have Had Similar Losses

The narratives of many parents spoke of the value of support from people who had similar losses. This is consistent with the findings of other research studies (DeFrain, Martens, Stork, & Stork, 1990–91; Gilbert & Smart, 1992, p. 38; Lauterbach, 1994; Schwab, 1990, 1995). The knowledge and experience of those who have had similar losses enables them to give strong validation to the things a bereaved parent says, a kind of expert validation about such things as continuing pain and the continuing bond to the child (Klass, 1996, 1997, 1999).

Some parents talked about turning to others who had similar experiences because of discomfort telling their story to parents who had not had a child die. Partly it was a matter of parents who were not bereaved being uncomfortable reminders of the child's death.

Joy: To be able to talk about it in a group with people who could really relate to our loss.... If you talk about this with your friends ..., they could still go home to all their kids and tuck 'em in bed.... People who understood what the empty bed and the empty place at the table [mean] could relate to all those things. It really was good to talk with people like that. And then we did see a Christian counselor who had also lost a daughter. He lost her to cancer, and she was quite a bit older than Jenny was, but he could really relate to what we were going through, and that really helped us a lot.

Some parents spoke of enormous benefit received from a support group of others who had experienced a child death, for example, Compassionate Friends. Such a group could provide a safe place to air feelings and could help a couple learn to be tolerant of their couple differences in grieving (Klass, 1986–87). A support group could give a couple a vocabulary for talking about their individual grieving and couple relationship, a sense of how they are like other bereaved parents (Klass, 1986–87), a place to honor the child, a place to get experience-based understanding, a way to find solutions to practical problems related to the death (Klass, 1988, p. 111), and contact with people who are comfortable with a bereaved parent.

Vince: We ... came to the realization that we do grieve at different levels. We don't always grieve about the same thing at the same time. We're not always in the same mood ..., and once we came to that realization [we] came to respect each other's level of needing.... It was nice that we recognized that we grieve at different levels and gave each other the latitude to regress.... I really think that that wasn't until we had joined (bang on table) Compassionate Friends, 'cause that was one of the big things I got out of Compassionate Friends was, "Hey, that's okay to do that."

Gail: ... We heard ... that couples were at different points at different times individually and ... that that was okay.... We found that we just hurted differently. It seemed like, at first, we were just very tight and very close, and we just moved re-e-al slow ahead together, and not without each other. We wouldn't move until ... one of us moved a little bit.... And it was pointed *out* to us after we went to group and heard it talked about.

Louise: One of my oldest daughter's soccer coaches ... noticed that ... we were having a real hard time. And they had lost a child ... in a car accident.... This mom herself, because there was never anything available ... took a lot of classes and ... grief counseling.... She said she and her husband were interested in starting a grief group for parents who lost children,... so that's what we did.... There were ... four, five of us [couples] that kind of stuck it out.... She would get in counselors to speak ... and get some videos and a lot of handouts and really tried to help us.... We've met quite a bit for a year or two.... They've been a real good group.

A support group can help with meaning-making, because every practical issue, every issue of working out couple differences, and all the other matters that come up in a support group are in part meaning issues. For example, issues of how to answer the question of how many children a couple has or what to do with photos of the child are issues of meaning (Klass, 1988, pp. 114–115). In a support group a parent also acquires meanings for feelings, thoughts, and experiences—for example, that the parent is normal in the sense of being like other bereaved parents (Klass, 1988, p. 112).

Support from others who have lost a child may also go on with very little said. Erin, for example, talked about developing a close friendship with a woman who had also experienced the death of a child. She said the woman had been a good friend and support in dealing with her son's death, but that they don't talk much about the deaths. They understood each other's feelings without having to say much about it. Also, Erin was one of a number of parents, more women than men, who talked about how supportive a hug and touching could be.

☐ Sorting

Many parents spoke of a process of sorting relatives, friends, and acquaintances. Consistent with what was said in chapter 6 about the chasm between bereaved parents and the rest of the world, other studies of bereaved parents indicate that bereaved parents report that quite a few people in their life drift away, disappear, or are simply not there for them (Brabant, Forsyth, & McFarlain, 1995; Klass, 1996, 1997; Knapp, 1986, pp. 154–156; Lauterbach, 1994; Lewis & Liston, 1981; Peppers & Knapp, 1980, Chapter 6). Although Brice (1991b) suggested that bereaved parents may sometimes understate how much others are there for them, a number of narratives included vivid accounts of people pulling away from the parents. There seems to be a shortage of people who are willing to bridge the chasm, who are comfortable and willing to be with those who are grieving (Attig, 1990).

Karl: I recall a period of time where ... you almost got the impression that people felt that whatever was wrong was catching in some way.

Kathy: After both of them had died, it was that way. Even in the neighborhood.

Karl: It was like nobody wanted to associate with us then.

Kathy: Like there was something really wrong with us, and I think some friends who were having babies at the time were kind of afraid to be near us, or to be near me. That was particularly hurtful. . . .

Karl: There was definitely a feeling that whatever we had, if we touched anybody, they'd get it and they'd have problems. . . . So we hid. I mean in a sense, we did.

Kathy: That was really our way of surviving.

Karl: We had each other, and we just could back away from the world. . . . (*Kathy:* Yeah.) Unfortunately, it was a very long while.

Steph: People don't want to see you.

George: Like all of a sudden you're HIV positive. . . . They're out of your lives . . . , forever gone. (*Steph:* They don't know what to say to you.) . . . You could have a thousand friends and then you lose a child, you can almost bet within probably 60 days you won't have any left, outside of just a few, very, very few.

Even when others were willing to remain in contact with bereaved parents, the kind of interaction they provided could be too aversive to the parents. Some narratives spoke of dropping acquaintances who were not good listeners, seemed to try to silence parent talk about bereavement, were not supportive, said offensive things, offered unsupportive religious judgments or formulas, or were too uncomfortable with the bereaved parents (cf. Brabant, Forsyth, & McFarlain, 1995; Farnsworth & Allen, 1996; Lauterbach, 1994).

Some parents spoke of new people who entered their lives being sorted. Some—for example, clergy who said hurtful or angering things (Gilbert, 1992)—would be sorted into a "reject" category. But others might become valued associates.

Joy: There's been people that we've met that never knew Jenny that have been drawn to us, just because of Jenny. I'm thinking of one family at our little church.... That's what drew us together was us telling them about Jenny.

Relationship sorting is an n-way process in that everyone is sorting everyone else. Each party may back away or come forward (Brabant, Forsyth, & McFarlain, 1995; Lauterbach, 1994). Sometimes it is unclear who sorted whom.

Brett: I lost some friends at work.... I don't know how I lost 'em, but ... they and my relationship has deteriorated.... Some cases that I think it was a decision on my part, but these relationships were somewhat phoney, and I want something different. So if you can't give it to me. But in other cases I think I did things that, I don't know if I hurt or made people dislike me, but I know that some of my relationships changed.

From another perspective, what I have labeled the sorting process may reflect what Attig (1996) calls relearning the world after a death. Following the death, a bereaved person will learn to travel new paths and to be a different person. That guarantees that some past relationships no longer work as well and that the bereaved person may seek new relationships that are more satisfying.

☐ Talking to Others about the Death

Although many parents spoke as though they were rather passive in whether they talked with others about the child's death, some said they tried very aggressively to engage others in talking about the child.

Brett: We also opened up our friends and families. We told them that this is the way it's gonna be, because ... a lot of time they were lookin' for direction from us, even when he was in the hospital.... We said that Alex is going to be part of our life. He's going to be part of our family forever. And never be afraid to ask us any questions or include him.... So ... they all do it.... We invite people to talk about it. You're not gonna hurt our feelings by talking about it.

Joan: We were trying [to] open other people, because of the way society is when there's a death. People just ... don't talk about it, and I think to us it's better and easier and nicer if people do talk about it.

Chad: The first week school was back in, ... we brought in a grief counselor to the school for explanations.... We had to shove it down their throats to get it done....

Erika: Sat in the front row. They were going to tell how [he] died, and then they were going to deal with the children and their grief....

Chad: Erika went to the school that day with our daughter, 'cause she's gonna be sittin' there. And so the principal went through his spiel, what he was going to say, in front of Erika [and our daughter]. Erika just ... looked at [our daughter] ..., "You understand what he said?" She said, "Nothing. Absolutely nothing." (*Erika:* Gobbledygook, gobbledygook) (Chad laughs) So it got revised, and some additional people came in. But we just had to jam it right down their throats. They just kind of wanted ... [to] forget he was ever there.

Erika and Chad and a few other parents said that they spent considerable time and effort trying to educate others about matters relating to their child's death and found in their words to others a healing for themselves.

☐ Summary

This chapter focuses on the support most parents said they found when the chasm between them and the rest of the world was bridged. Most parents talked about people who were there for them, and what they valued from those people. What they valued constitutes a substantial list. At the top of the list were good, nonjudgmental listening, constancy, asking good questions, witnessing important events related to the child's death, witnessing the parent grieving, and acknowledging the parent realities. Some parents said it was especially valuable to them to interact with parents who had similar experiences of child loss.

Some parents talked about a process of sorting people they knew and people newly met, hanging on to those who could be supportive and distancing those who could not be. Many also talked about the ways in which others sorted them, often into a category of people who made these others uncomfortable and who might best be distanced or avoided.

Although this chapter focuses a great deal on emotional support and support through listening and acknowledging, informational support was touched on at a few places. Information can help parents to understand what has happened and what is happening and can help them to develop a satisfying narrative and to deal with the wide range of practical problems that arise in bereavement. Information comes from many different sources. The next chapter focuses on parent narratives of the search for information about the death and its aftermath.

Learning What There Is to Say

Parent narratives of grief are in part narratives of the search for answers to questions (cf. Braun & Berg, 1994; Cornwell, Nurcombe, & Stevens, 1977; DeFrain, 1991; Gilbert & Smart, 1992, p. 37; Hogan, Morse, & Tasón, 1996; Klass, 1988, pp. 23–24). The search might include trying to learn more about the human body, how an accident happened, what the parent could have done to prevent the death, God's intentions, the proper way to feel, whether life is worth continuing to live, justice, what to tell people about the death, or who or what the child is now.

Erika: We didn't know how widespread the practice [of autoerotic asphyxia] was.... I never heard of it before. I had to have them explain it to us several times, how it could be accidental. I had assumed it was a suicide....

Chad: We studied and worked hard to find out why this happened or how this happened, and what can you do about it.

Angela: Nobody knows why he died. And that *still* bothers me. It's like I want to know why I lost my son.

Wayne: The frustrating part when I start talking about this is ... where you look at ... this really kind of a neat kid, and you wonder why he is dead, and there's other kids out there ... who are not such nice kids, and they're out there running around. And you just [wonder], how does this happen?

The answers parents find to their questions shape their grieving and what they say about the death. Parent narrative evolves as more is learned. Parents also, to some extent, choose the likely path for that evolution, because they choose what questions to ask and where to seek answers.

From another perspective, it is the narrative that drives the quest for additional learning. Holes and inconsistencies in the narrative, plus questions that listeners ask and the parent cannot answer, demand that more be learned. From that perspective, narratives have their own dynamics. Once a parent enters into narrative related to a child's death—for example a story about how it came to be that the child died—the parent is likely to feel pressed to make it a good story, one in which all reasonable questions are addressed. Of course the parent may choose to stay away from certain lines of learning—for example, information that may lead the parent to feel guilt. Still, I have the sense that some parents were pulled along in the development of their narrative to places in which they were quite uncomfortable.

☐ Learning the Language of Medicine

Consistent with findings reported by others (Cornwell, Nurcombe, & Stevens, 1977; DeFrain, 1991; Dunn, Goldbach, Lasker, & Toedter, 1991; Gilbert & Smart, 1992, p. 37), many parents sought medical information in their quest to learn what there was to say about the death. Autopsy information was important to some in determining what to say and feel about the death. Although some parents had negative or mixed feelings about having the child's body autopsied, they might also value the autopsy information.

Iris: At first they approached it that we did not have to have an autopsy. And I was kind of glad. But then he said that the cardiologist really wanted to take a look and see if they'd been doing the right things, so we agreed. We got a lot of really good information from them, so we were really glad that we [agreed to it].

Vince: I just felt very insulted that [they] required . . . an autopsy. . . . I wasn't insulted about the autopsy itself, because *I* wanted to find out why he died, but it was like . . . , "Do you think I did something? . . . How can you even think of that about Gail because she (laughing) was here?"

Gail: . . . [But] we owe a lot . . . to [the doctor] who was . . . head of the Minnesota SIDS department. . . . He sat down with us for an hour or two (*Vince:* A long time) and went through the autopsy. Some of it wasn't [what you would] want to hear (crying). He said that he did skip over some of that, but he did go through it with us, and it said . . . he was a healthy baby boy, and all the different things that they had checked and did not find ... wrong. And he explained to us that's how they come up with the conclusion that it is SIDS, 'cause there was nothing else wrong. And he explained to us what his personal theory was and what happens to the babies that died of SIDS.

One couple concluded from the autopsy information that their decision not to have their daughter start a series of major surgeries was correct.

Lance: [It] would require three surgeries and would not have corrected what was [really] wrong with her.... They were concerned [that any] time she would go into cardiac arrest. We later found out, after the autopsy, that any surgery or any heart-lung procedure would have proved fatal.

Some parents whose child had not been autopsied had regrets about that, because they did not know as much as they could have about how the death came about.

Bonnie: The [woman] that she had lived with mentioned to me that they had approached her about an autopsy. And that was never brought up again, and now I really wish that I would've thought of it or somebody would have asked me.... I would have really liked to have known where the primary cancer site was.... I can't imagine somebody just having a lump in their breast and dying from breast cancer, even though ... what it says on the death certificate was metastatic breast cancer.... If they would have asked me, maybe I would have given it more thought.... They did take some fluid from around her heart ..., and that had ... cancer cells, so it's pretty invasive.

A couple's detective work about a death might also include medical studies of themselves to explore possible genetic factors in the death.

Todd: We had some tests done afterwards, (*Iris:* Chromosome studies on us) chromosome studies, and the cardiologist office wanted to do some typing.... We got some family history stuff together. They wanted to determine if there was a likelihood that this would happen again (*Iris:* Umhm), 'cause a lot of heart defects are family type things. And this one, they said, the odds of you having this happen again are the same as they were before, which is

Iris: One in a hundred thousand (laughs).

PR: Did you get any genetic counseling?

Tina: Yeah (*Scott:* Oh yeah)....

Scott: On this particular abnormality, we saw everything from one in 2000 births to one in 10,000 births, but they were *all* pretty concrete when it came to our chances of it happening a second time. And they put it at one in a 100.

Tina: Well, they called it a fluke. It wasn't a genetic thing (*Scott:* Right) that we were carrying. They called it a packaging error. (*Scott:* Yeah) Either the sperm or the egg had one extra chromosome. (*Scott:* Right . . . and there was no way for them to tell.)

Sometimes physicians could not determine with certainty, what caused a death. They might not, however, reveal that uncertainty. Some parents were angry with physicians who pretended to know what they did not and grateful for those who were honest about their uncertainty, even though that meant that what the parents learned was conjecture. One couple who had a second child who died of the same thing as a first talked about their feelings about physicians.

Karl: I personally won't trust doctors very much, because I feel that if they don't know what it is, rather than tell me, "I'm sorry. I don't know what it is," they just tell me anything they want. And I'm supposed to believe it, whether or not that's actually true. . . . I would've been happier if they would've just said they didn't know, if they really didn't know.

Kathy: Well, and some did. We came across so many, and some, like the geneticist. She was really neat, and she was probably the one that worked the hardest for us, and she said, "If it has a name, I'll find it." . . . She wrote to doctors all over the country. She went above and beyond . . . , and that's why she said, "This is what I think, and there's no way of proving it. . . ." It wasn't anything you could find out by doing any sort of test, and that's the closest she could come.

This couple chose not to have their children autopsied, feeling that it would not provide useful information and that it would be an insult to the bodies of the two childrens.

Kathy: They didn't do autopsies on either one of them. I asked that they not, and our doctors said that they should respect [that]. They said that given the circumstances of . . . their births . . . there was no way to explain anything anyway. . . . That would've been just the ultimate cruelty. We *knew* that they weren't healthy, and that was enough to know. We knew that everything was done for them that could have been done. They died on their own. There was no trauma. There was no neglect. . . . It was just a complete shutdown.

Physician unwillingness to give them an answer did not necessarily stop a couple from coming up with their own medical explanations (cf. Gilbert & Smart, 1992, p. 37).

Brett: I know that we talked with the doctor about [Alex's premature birth].

Joan: Yeah. [The doctor said it] was just a fluke thing. I always thought it was because I had a yeast infection at the time. And I have talked to a couple of other ladies that have had premature babies ..., and a yeast infection seemed to be kind of a thing that we all had experienced while we were pregnant. So I always attributed it to that.

John: Stress seems to predispose to cancer, and I just think of her as being so young, and yet the stress she went through was just more than I could handle.

☐ Learning Through Comparing

Comparisons can be important in coming to terms with a death (Nadeau, 1998, pp. 118–125). Some parents talked about developing a frame of reference for evaluating a child's medical treatment, the death, and their reaction to the death by comparing their experiences with the experiences of other grieving parents (cf. Gilbert & Smart, 1992, p. 36). The frame of reference provided a basis for coming to meanings and feelings. Parents who made comparisons might refer to them, for example, as a basis for saying that they were not alone and that others wrestle with the same issues.

To make comparisons requires a parent to deny personal uniqueness. Comparability is not obvious. Every death, every child, and every bereaved parent is unique. It would be easy to think and speak about the death and one's personal feelings as unlike anyone else's. But nobody who was interviewed did that. Perhaps that is in part because when people do not have a basis of comparison or a frame of reference, there is too much anxiety and uncertainty. Or perhaps comparison is a fundamental kind of thinking, so (whether by nature or by learning that everyone experiences) people value comparison and ignore uniqueness in order to compare. Whatever the reasons, comparative statements like the following were common.

Elaine: [It was] comforting when people came that had experienced the same thing that I had, because I kept thinking, "Well, they survive. They're living a functional, happy life now."

Ken: Mark was then basically comatose for—I couldn't understand how the Butchers did it for 17 years, 'cause we had it for almost the four.

The Butchers were a family whose son lived in a persistent vegetative state for 17 years, until they obtained a court order to remove his life supports. Ken and Glenda did not say that in contrast to the Butchers they had it easy, but said that given their own ordeal, how the Butchers were able to handle the situation was courageous, perhaps even saintly.

Some comparisons with other parents who had lost a child made the parent's own loss seem in some ways worse. One woman, for example, talked about her relationship with a neighbor who experienced the death of an older child.

Paula: It was hard, because they have more memories, he was 18, than we do of Jerry.

Some parents found consolation in comparing their child's death with some other deaths.

Erika: He's a lot more fortunate than most of us would be. He died in a way that he wasn't scared. He didn't know he was dying. It must be awful to watch a child of yours suffer, and know they're going to die, and have to tell them they're going to die. So he died painlessly and without any fear. . . . You want him back, but that's given me some consolation.

———————————

Joy: I really got help from [a Christian counselor] because he came from a biblical perspective. He we could relate to, plus he had also lost a daughter, so he could especially identify with what we were going through. It wasn't an accident, she was sick, which I think would almost be worse.

Joy and Stan compared their relationship following the death of their daughter in a car accident in which relatives were driving with what it would have been had the child died with Joy or Stan driving.

Stan: I thank God that neither of us were . . . involved in it, because that could be just completely different, like if Joy . . . or if I would have been driving, . . . it could have been really guilt, laying guilt on someone else. . . . The one couple that we made friends with, their son drowned while they were all around swimming in a pool.

Joy: And the dad was supposed to be watching them, and the mom was in the hotel room with the baby, and I know [the mom] went through a lot of blaming, and I'm sure [the dad] went through a lot of guilt, and . . . we don't have that. . . . We weren't even involved in the accident.

Many parents who had lost a parent as well as a child compared the two losses as a way of saying how much the child's death hurt.

Jane: My dad was important to us and . . . I was sad that my dad had died, but it was like *nothing* compared to the loss of my son. I just hardly felt it at all.

George: I lost my dad . . . , and that was real tough, and by comparison it was a walk in the park compared to losing my kid. Until it happens a person just can't even fathom just how horrible, how terrifying, how devastating, how numbing it is.

Louise: When my father died, I loved my father a great deal, I miss him a great deal. It hasn't affected my life. I miss him. I feel sorry for my mom, because she's left alone, but my kids had a lot of good years with my dad. I had a lot of good years with my dad, and . . . he didn't live with us. It really doesn't affect my daily life any, except . . . I have to run a lot more errands for my mom. . . . I feel bad for her that she's lost her companion, but I can go on with my life. . . .

Wayne: The funerals were a whole lot different . . . and the wake. . . . There wasn't a lot of crying (*Louise:* No, umhm), whereas with [our son's] situation, there was [a] tremendous, tremendous amount of crying.

Elaine, who had experienced quite a few deaths of people close to her, used those experiences to help other family members anticipate what would happen as a result of her son's death.

Elaine: You remember the night we sat the kids down . . . and told them that if they expected their life to go back to perfectly normal, then they were never going to be able to heal from this, because our life could never be the same . . . ? He was gone, and he was a very big part of it, so it can't be the same. Yes, we will be happy. Yes, we will laugh. Yes, we will have fun together, but it will always be different, because a very important part of our family is gone. So I said, "If you expect it to go back to normal, then you're kidding yourself because that can't be. It's going to be different. . . . "

TK: How did you know to say that?

Elaine: I think because of all the disruption in my own . . . family. And I can remember when my brother died. See, I lost my brother and my mother and my dad in less than six years, and I always wanted . . . everything to be the way it was before, and . . . it can't be.

Some parents compared their marital situation with the situation of couples dealing with very sick children or children who had died.

Amy: Just this last weekend, when I was with [a friend] (*Ted:* Yeah), they were talking about [a couple we know].... Their little girl had leukemia, and she made it. But their marriage didn't.... The wife ... blamed a lot of her ex-husband's alleged style on the cause of leukemia. And it became a big issue; it got ugly, and they're divorcing.... She just got really angry at him. And I thought, "My gosh, we never felt that." (*Ted:* No, we didn't.) And I feel *really* thankful for that (*Ted:* umhm).

Gail: When we get together with people from Compassionate Friends, we talk about when this first happens to you, you feel that you have a very large hole in the middle of your chest, and the wind blows through that. Everybody can see it.... [If] you go to a meeting, and there's new people there, ... you know those new people have that hole in their heart, in their chest, and as time goes on, a lot of that closes up. Part of it out of self-defense. You have to; you can't be that vulnerable.... Part of it because time's going on and you [have dealt] with some of it, and gone through some of the healing process and actually have healed some of that hole.... New people come to the group and we'll have the meeting and they'll leave, and there'll be some of us standing around talking, and we'll say (whispering in a kind of awe) "Boy, they've just got that big hole." ... We look at each other and go, "We hurt too. (whispering) We don't hurt like them. We're *so* glad we don't hurt like them."

Some comparisons involved observing and speculating, but a great deal came from interaction with others who had similar experiences.

George: I found out that [a coworker] lost two of his kids in a fire, ... and I introduced myself, and I said, "... If you have a few minutes I'd like to talk to you about something kind of personal." And two days later we sat down and [I] said, "I just want to compare notes with you. I lost a kid about a half a year ago. I'd heard that you lost kids and it was some time ago. [If] you don't mind my asking, what's your life been like? How did you handle it?"

In some parent narratives there was talk of resisting comparison. Most commonly, the comparisons that were resisted were those made by others that seemed to diminish the loss—for example, if someone seemed to a couple to say that the death of their child was not as bad as an older child's death would have been.

Brett: Sometimes I feel like I have to justify myself that my son was only seven months old and had never came home.... Sometimes it seems like you have to have a 10 year old or a ... 23 year old son before you can have such a hard time about a death.... I respect and understand women that have miscarriages or stillbirths ... a lot more now than I did before.... A loss is a loss is a loss is a loss. But ... I did get the real strong message that, "Your son was only seven months and never came home. You shouldn't be behaving this way. It shouldn't have this effect on you."

☐ Learning from Reading and Song

As has been reported by others (Attig, 1996, p. 8; Schwab, 1990), many parents, perhaps women more—or more ambitiously—than men, said that they read in searching for things to help them deal with the loss. Reading could be frustrating or provide little, but it could enable a parent to find rules of thumb, ideas to bring to interactions, "facts," and perspectives. Reading could also help by providing a narrative framing for experience. For example, some parents gained from their reading a language for dealing with the distancing they experienced from others.

AH: Did the reactions from family and friends, like showing up at first and then suddenly being gone, surprise you?

Wayne: It didn't.... It says in the books you read (*Louise:* Yeah, it tells about that). It tells that you will most likely lose the friends that you have, and you'll get other friends because the first friends.... will avoid you, or you aren't going to be going in the same circles anymore.

Some parents said that they learned from reading (or from other bereaved parents who cited their own reading) that bereaved parents are at high risk for divorce. The research literature actually does not give clear support to that view (Dijkstra & Stroebe, 1998; Schwab, 1998), but the erroneous assertion can be found various places in the self-help literature and in writings for professionals (Schwab, 1998). It would be best for the things bereaved parents read about grief to be as accurate as possible, but, as was said in Chapter 9, the ways they used the "fact" that they were at risk for divorce may have benefitted some couples.

Couples sometimes disagreed about reading, with the partner who read more wanting the partner who read less to join in the reading, I think partly as a way of developing shared language and perspectives.

George: After I lost Nils ... I bought every book I could find on the subject of a child loss.

Steph: Yeah, you did. You kept wanting me to read 'em, and I didn't want to.

George: ... It was very good to read the stuff, but it was also very painful. But I think that's how I was able to work through it, to come up with some answers, whereas [she]—

Steph: 'Cause they do say that you can't (exhales) sympathize with the other parent. You don't have enough inside of you. You're hurting too much to sympathize with your spouse; ... you can't help them through it.

George: ... This one book they said no matter how strong a relationship, they ... say about 99% of those relationships are in immediate (*Steph:* 89) [danger], and that's, well, I read that, and that was very significant.

A number of parents, particularly women, found verses from the bible, condolence card messages, the writings of other bereaved parents, or songs so significant that they not only noted them but saved them, often in a scrap book or a box of memorabilia.

Joy: [I have been] collecting little poems that ... remind me of Jenny. In fact, we were at the cemetery on her birthday, and there was a stone ... that we hadn't noticed ... before, and it had been there for two years, and I can't believe we never noticed it, but it was a young girl, like 21, and the family had written a big long poem on it. She had two markers, there was so much that they wrote. And it's like I have to stop right now and copy this down.... I collect poems and stories and articles that remind me of Jenny.

Bonnie: I was just going to mention the song that has been so neat: "If You Could See Me Now." ... The words are just beautiful, and you can just imagine her up in heaven.... A [coworker] taped it, just the one song for me, and I've played it many times. The first few times I played it I just cried and cried and cried. It was such a release to me.

With songs, one additional element is a sense of having shared the language and feelings of loss with many others, not only others in the audience (if a parent is at a concert) but all others who have heard the song and were touched by it.

Joy: We went to a ... Twyla Paris concert, and she sang a song called "Visitor from Heaven." ... One of the verses was, "It broke our hearts to let you go, but we sure are glad you came." ... The way we feel about Jenny is God gave her to us. What did we ever do to deserve having her? We were blessed to have known her for the five and a half years that we had her, and to let that wreck our lives would really destroy the memory of Jenny.... When

Twyla Paris was singing the song . . . , we were both . . . sobbing. We couldn't have wrote a nicer song for Jenny.

Angela: Bette Midler's song, "The Wind Beneath My Wings," that's Blake's song. That was played at his memorial service, and I've yet to hear that song and not shed a tear (breathes out audibly). I paid $75 a ticket for Jack and I to go to see her this past August, just so I could hear that song so I could cry (she is crying). . . . I even stood in line the day after I miscarried my . . . last baby. . . . to get those tickets, so I could have the semi-decent ticket to see her, just to have her sing that song so I could cry. And I did (cries). And I knew I would. There's hymns at church, "Amazing Grace," "The Battle Hymn of the Republic," every song that was at his memorial service, anytime it is played during church, I just lean on Jack. And of course he knows why all of a sudden I'm cryin'. People around me just like, "Oh, look at the woman." . . . They don't understand, but Jack knows.

☐ Limiting Learning—Not Wanting to Learn More

Some parents reached a place where they did not want to learn more about the cause of the death; they accepted that the death had happened and wanted to go on from there. Some parents avoided learning certain things related to the death and thus limited what they could talk about. Some avoided learning what might be hurtful to them, might increase their feelings of guilt, or might lead to difficulty with others. All of these possibilities may have been involved in the following instance.

Ken: So who's responsible? I don't know. I think that's the big thing I think we have avoided. . . . Who is responsible for the accident. Was it the driver? Or was it the fact that other people were egging the driver on? Or were there other complications happening at the time in the car?

Glenda: We don't know. It wasn't alcohol. They'd had some beers, but—

Ken: And we have avoided that. I think we have avoided it. I don't know if I want to know the answer.

Glenda: . . . I guess that that part I've never thought too much about.

In some couples one partner continued to question and to hope to learn more, while the other accepted the death and wanted to go on.

Rob: Medicine isn't an exact science. There was one child that had the same thing Adam did, and it was a much more sickly child. And she's still alive.... You don't know the reason why. They did an autopsy but ... the cancer was gone. Could less chemotherapy have been sufficient and not ... damaged the lungs so much? Was it the radiation?... Was it that time of year? Because he was more susceptible in December. Maybe got some sort of viral infection that damaged the lungs. You don't know. Could we've just taken him down to Arizona and get him away for a while, while he was being treated? So there's always questions....

Jane: I don't really think on that. I just cope with the reality, I guess. I don't really think why ... did it happen.... I don't have any questions about what happened.

☐ Limits to Learning—When There is no Language

Despite their best efforts, and the real learning that occurred, there was for some parents the realization that ultimate questions of "why?" could not be answered. Why this person rather than that? Why now rather than later? For some, the acknowledgment of the limits to what could be learned and the frustration associated with those limits was couched in religious language.

Todd: As far as fairness, unfairness, who are we to judge what's fair or not? God has a plan for it, a reason for it. Just 'cause we don't know doesn't mean that it was wrong.... It was hard, but life isn't always fair....

Iris: Why not, (*Todd:* Yeah.) why not us?

   Suicides produce their own variety of unanswerable "why" questions. Even with a lifetime of knowledge about a child who committed suicide, even with a suicide note that offers answers to "why" questions, and even with years of searching, "why" questions can remain unanswered.

Fred: It'd be a tragedy [if I died], but you'd get over it. My sister was a quick, "Okay, what?" We've had friends die. Yeah, it's quick.... Mom died of cancer. It takes a while, but you get over it. My cousin ... died. It was quick. I missed her, because we were so close. But it's over. You don't even think about it.... But a sui—, I don't care who it is, if it's friend, your kid especially that commits suicide, you wonder why. In the end, the "why?" is never answered. "Why?" can never be answered. And it's like if ... my cousin had committed suicide, I'd want to know, "Why did it happen?" Well, there is no answer. And I'll wonder why ... [until] the day I die.

With accidental deaths, too, there could be a sense of never being sure why things happened the way they did.

Al: We had talked this over ... a lot of times, why that kid didn't say anything when I put the machine in gear. That's the thing I could never figure out. He's a bigger guy than I am, than I was by far, and he could have let out a holler, "Hey Dad! Hold it!" ... He's allergic to corn like I was. We were just wondering, we had wondered about it many times if ... being in that silo in the corn, didn't ... make him so that he wasn't really aware of what the hell was going on!... And we just have been over, tried to figure out why the devil this happened.

Barb: Well, he had his leg broke also. And we just kind of think that as long as he didn't holler maybe he heard it and thought he could get out. And maybe it caught his leg and he couldn't make it.

Al: He was a very strong kid, a pretty athletic kid, so we just figured maybe, I don't know, you can't, you know you can't figure. You sit and wonder for years.

Some parents felt that they had to stop wondering what happened, that to heal they must end their questioning.

Red: You gotta just quit second guessing it. Otherwise you will drive yourself nuts.

Elaine: You would. I mean, you were, you were.

Ending the questioning does not mean that the questions have been answered, but perhaps only that a parent realizes that crucial questions can never be answered. In a sense, there may be a realization that no reason for the child's death is an adequate reason (Brice, 1989, 1991a).

☐ Summary

Parent narratives of grief are in part narratives of the search for answers to questions. The answers parents find shape their grieving and their narratives. From another perspective, it is the narrative that drives the quest for additional learning. Holes and inconsistencies in the narrative, plus questions that listeners ask that the parent cannot answer, demand that more be learned.

Many parents sought medical information (including autopsy and genetics information) in their quest to learn what there was to say about the death. Some parents talked about developing a frame of reference for evaluating a child's medical treatment, the death, and their reaction to the death by comparing their experiences with the experiences of other grieving parents or using other standards of comparison (for example, comparing their experience of a parent's death with their experience of the child's death). Some parents also found a frame of reference or solace in reading or song.

Some parents reached a place where they did not want to learn more about the cause of the death; they accepted that the death had happened and wanted to go on from there. Some parents avoided learning certain things related to the death—for example, what might be hurtful to them, might increase their feelings of guilt, or might lead to difficulty with others. In the end, some parents came up against the limits of learning, or decided they had learned enough, and gave up the search for additional information.

In a sense, the search for additional knowledge is about meaning-making. Parent narratives are meaning-making, so this entire book can be seen as about meaning-making. To make explicit what has been implicit so far in this book, the next chapter focuses explicitly on the dynamics of bereaved parent meaning-making.

Meaning and Meaning-Making

☐ Grieving as a Process of Finding Meaning

The death of a child opens all parent meanings to question (Rubin, 1993). A child's death may set off a crisis regarding the meaning of the parent's life and of the parent's past, present, and future (Braun & Berg, 1994; Miles, 1984; Wheeler, 1993–94). Grieving parents may question their relationship with each other and with God, the meaning of their work, the meaning of their everyday activities, and whether their life has enough meaning to be worth continuing. As with other bereavement narratives (Cochran & Claspell, 1987, pp. 64–65), the parent narratives speak of the effect of the death on meanings. The death is not encapsulated; life does not go on as though nothing happened; things are not seen in the same way as they were before the death. A death infects all of life with meaninglessness (Cochran & Claspell, 1987, p. 66).

Glenda: As time goes on, I find that this pain truly doesn't go away. One can mask it with work, food, drink, feverish activity, but the bottom line is a meaningless existence that is bittersweet at best. [In a letter to Paul; at this point her son had been dead seven years]

Meaninglessness cannot be ignored. People think in terms of meanings and organize their lives in terms of meanings. They want to, perhaps even have to, live a life in which things make sense. The child's life and death demand not to be meaningless. Without meanings to account for the child's life and death, a parent has an unpleasant and unnervingly indefinite sense of where she or he is in the world and no confident sense of purpose and direction (Attig, 1990, 1996).

With the child's life and death both demanding not to be meaningless and challenging meanings in all areas of life, grieving necessarily involves the search for and creation of meaning (Nadeau, 1998). Meanings are demanded by questions that arise with a child's death (Edelstein, 1984, pp. 42–44)—Why my child? Why any child? Why that kind of death? Why me? Why now? How can such a bad thing happen when I/we have been good? Could the death have been prevented? So it is not surprising that, in accord with what others have noted about parental grief (Brabant, Forsyth, & McFarlain, 1997; Brice, 1989; Gilbert & Smart, 1992; pp. 37–42; Knapp, 1988, p. 34; Moss, Lesher, & Moss, 1986–87; Rando, 1986), every parent narrative dealt with meaning-making related to the death.

☐ Parent Meaning-Making

As Nadeau (1998) has shown, the things bereaved people have to say about a death and their grieving are saturated with meaning. Every interview quote in this book and every discussion is in part about meanings and the processes of making meaning. This chapter extends the analysis of meaning-making by exploring parent narratives in five areas.

What Is Real and Natural and What Is Not

In making meaning out of things related to the death, every parent narrative spoke in terms of a "real" reality. For every parent, the death was real. Believing in the reality of the death not only challenges all life meanings but also is the start of meaning making. The death is a fact that all other meanings must take into account.

As has been reported by others (Braun & Berg, 1994; Edelstein, 1984, p. 43; Rando, 1986, 1991; Raphael, 1983, p. 234; Ruiz & Atwood, 1996; Stevenson, 1988), in many parent narratives the child's death was said to be unnatural. It was unnatural because the child died while the parents were alive.

Bonnie: It just seems *so* wrong. . . . We're supposed to go before the kids. It's just out of sequence. You expect to lose your parents sometime, but to lose a daughter is just—

John: Yeah. The senior pastor was out here one time. He says, "Children are supposed to bury their parents, not the parents bury their children." Well, it's not the way (chuckles) it's supposed to work, but it happens.

Some parents said that the unnatural quality of the death shook their faith in nature, in the orderliness of life, and in the expected happening. The death attacked the meaningfulness of living life as though all is natural, in sequence, and as expected. The unnaturalness of the death was something that parent meaning-making had to take into account.

Finding Meaning by Knowing What Has Been Lost

Every parent said that with the child's death came many losses. One can take that as a way of saying how much has been lost, a way of explaining pain, and a truthful accounting of how much was linked to the child. It is also a foundation to meaning-making. It is a way of delineating areas in which meaning-making must occur and a way of giving meaning to the death and to feelings about it. Consider, for example, a loss that almost every parent narrative addressed, the loss of the future. Consistent with the findings of a number of other accounts of parent grief (Cornwell, Nurcombe, & Stevens, 1977; Edelstein, 1984, pp. 40–42; Hogan, Morse, & Tasón, 1996; Klass, 1988, p. 14; Knapp, 1986, p. 19; Leon, 1990, pp. 33–36; Moss, Lesher, & Moss, 1986–87; Schiff, 1978, p. 23), many parents talked about the loss of the future. The loss of a future is not only about the loss of the child in the future, but also the loss of the future in terms of parental role, identity, and activities, parent-child companionship, and parent-child love. Some parents symbolized all those losses by talking about the loss of specific aspects of their future relationship with the child (cf. Brice, 1991a, 1991b).

Vince: When a child dies … you're grieving the loss of opportunity to see the kid go to kindergarten and stuff.... From a child to an adult, to see them graduate from school and college and get married and have grandchildren. It seems to me that a lot of the grief is grieving the lost opportunity.... I'll never see him hit a ball in the batting cage with his two brothers. A big thing for me was golf. I remember, after [he] (chuckles) was born, it's like, "Yes! Now I can have a foursome. The boys and I can go out golfin'."

I see such talk as an essential part of the cognitive and feeling processes of meaning-making. Until one can name what has been lost, one cannot make meanings. And naming what has been lost gives meaning to the death.

Searching for Positive Meanings

People do not necessary find positive meanings in a death (Nadeau, 1998, Chapter 7), but many parents spoke of efforts to find positive meanings in the death. A search for positives is part of a process of moving out of the depths of grief and of deciding life is worth living. It is also a way to make the loss less of a loss, not to erase or forget how terrible and enormous the loss was and is, but to say that it was not all negative.

Vince: I think the kids *definitely* are very compassionate [and] very sensitive.... This is one good thing that I think that came from Randy's death. I'm sure there's many others.

Gail: It's just the property that emerged now.

Vince: That's right.... I guess I credit it for all the good that has come from his death. There must be a good.

   Some parents talked about the search for positives not as an automatic thing, but as a choice.

Rosa: I think that the only control you have when you lose a child is how you decide to handle the grief. You can't bring him back. You can't save him. You can't protect him. You can't change how your partner grieves. You can only decide that you're going to somehow make something positive out of this.

Molly: I think about the kids a lot and think that I'm going to be a better person because of them. The death was such a negative thing that I have to do something positive to survive it. And I think that's why I'm probably in school, working with the homeless, street people, the elderly, and poor.... I've always had the mentality [to] love the elderly anyway, being raised with grandparents.... I think since I've lost the kids, that's probably 10 times, 100 times stronger than what it was before.

It Could Have Been Worse

Some parents framed the death and their grief by saying things could have been worse. In comparison to something else, this terrible event was not so terrible.

Elaine: That fall he had went out ... squirrel hunting and he didn't come home and didn't come home. Starting to get a little ... nervous, just kinda a little on edge. I'd think, "God, I wish he'd come home." I'd keep lookin' ... and he didn't come ... and I thought, "Oh God, what if something happened to him?" ... Pretty soon I saw the orange tassel hat coming through the weeds, and you kinda breathe a sigh of relief. He came in ... and he said, "Boy, I decided I was comin' home instead. Huntin's too dangerous. I tripped on a" What was it? A log or something, and he said, "I thought that gun'd discharge, and I could get killed. I decided I was comin' home." ... I kept thinking, "Thank God he didn't die that way." If he had to die, thank God it wasn't on that day, because then you'd never know, did he take his own life?

Joy: There's times when I feel ... joy about where she is and that nothing of this world can ever hurt her again. I feel a lot better that she's in heaven than if she would have been kidnapped.... She had a little tiny bruise on her hand, and for being in such a serious car accident, she could have been totally mangled, and the last look at her could have been horror. But she looked exactly how she looked. She looked just like a little sleeping angel. That's how I always remember her. And I think that was God's mercy.... We didn't have to ... have her laying in the hospital in a vegetative state. We didn't have to decide whether to pull a plug.... It would have been a lot worse to go through a long, lingering illness watching her deteriorate and getting ... in debt.... If you have to lose a child, this was probably the easiest way.... She didn't disappear. We didn't wonder where she was. We weren't searching for her and then find her little mutilated ... body somewhere.

Quite a few parents said, as did Joy, that the death was better than having the child in a persistent vegetative state.

Nick: They told us even if there was something you could do, he would never pull out to be normal.... There're so many blood vessels right there, critical ones, that he'd have been a vegetable. (*Lisa:* Yeah) Thank God that that didn't happen.

A key phrase in many parent assertions that things could have been worse is "at least." When people said "at least" about a death, they were making a comparison that said things could have been worse.

Louise: At least, in Will's case, he left on a happy note (she's crying).

With death following premature birth, some parents found meaning in comparing the child's death with what might have been had the child lived.

Denny: We didn't want her rushed to NICU, that if she was gonna make [it], she was gonna make it, and if she wasn't, she wasn't. Luckily ... we didn't have a choice to make. She was stillborn, and that helped a lot, because that's a very tough decision to ... make. Do you want to let this baby that's two weeks earlier than Matt and smaller than Matt ..., and you know the chances of survival are terrible and that if they do make it they're gonna have brain damage or all these different terrible problems their whole life, and be walking around not even knowing what day it is, slobberin' on themself? ... My heart goes out to anybody that can deal with that.

The Child Has Been Freed from Terrible Things

Many parents whose child had gone through persistent intense pain, surgeries, and prolonged hospitalization spoke of the death as meaning the child was freed from all that.

Denny: I was trying to look at it as, "He's okay and he's in heaven. He's not getting poked or prodded or cut open anymore. And going through pain...." The stuff he dealt with in 10 weeks is more than people deal with in a lifetime as far as surgeries and just everything they have to do, being hooked up to everything.

Some parents found positives in their child being freed from living with the dangers of modern society.

Angela: People say that parents worry about their kids, and I will always worry about [my daughter]. I will always worry about [our younger son], but I won't ever worry about Blake, 'cause he's in the safest place there is. I just wish he wasn't there yet, but at least I know I won't have to worry about him getting shot....

Jack: There's a difference between worrying and grieving.

Angela: Yeah, because I fear for my daughter gettin' raped. I fear for [our young son] having some kid wanting his skateboard or something and pulling out a gun and shootin' him.

Jack: We fear the trauma of this world. (*Angela:* Yeah) But I don't worry at all about the next world.

I/We Have Changed for the Better

Many parents talked about the painful lessons learned and the ways they had changed for the better as a result of the death (cf. Brabant, Forsyth,

& McFarlain, 1997; Farnsworth & Allen, 1996; Klass, 1999; Knapp, 1986, p. 39).

Ted: Any experience like that is going to make you appreciate life that much more. . . . I don't want it to be a cliche about . . . making the most of every day, and yet I think there's a lot of things that you tend to get trapped in that make you forget that. But an experience like that . . . for us it was a big hit about we've got to live for each moment, and that's a consistent theme . . . as a result of Noah's death. . . . We talk about . . . ownership of kids . . . , realizing that they're their own being. . . . I think it's helped me . . . with these kids. . . . And I think just in life in general, that it's very precious, and that it helps to keep things in perspective at times when things maybe are going haywire.

_____

Rob: I think we become more perceptive with . . . people in similar circumstances, just because it is a scenario that you *don't* really understand unless you have been through it.

_____

Iris: We were pretty self-sufficient and maybe self-centered before. And we've become a little more (*Todd:* Yeah) sensitive to others. . . . People were giving us help and food and things. . . . We learned how to accept things . . . , which was maybe a little humbling (small laugh). . . . It was good for us.

Todd: One time we got a chance to . . . talk to a woman's group about what to do for people in a crisis. And a lot of 'em learned a few things, I think. . . . I feel like I need to look for some of those good things. It's real easy to dwell on the negatives, 'cause . . . it's a big disappointment to us to lose a son. But certainly there's some positives too. There is to everything, and so while I can't take away any of the loss, at least I can focus . . . on the positives. . . . If I focus on the disappointments . . . , I could just make myself into quite a mental wreck. . . .

Iris: I've kinda looked for ways to make it better for somebody else. And that makes it better for me.

Notice how Todd and Iris not only had the positives come to them in a kind of passive way as a result of their son's dying but also sought them out and saw them as necessary in order to ward off feeling depressed and devastated.

Some parents said that from the death they gained precious religious insights. For example, as was reported by Brabant, Forsyth, and McFarlain (1997), some parents talked about no longer fearing death.

Nick: From Craig now there's a whole new different thing I've learned.... I know ... it's *not* the end.... It's a new beginning, which us humans right now can't see or nobody can see beyond this.... There's gonna be some day when, I have to be patient and just live my life to the fullest ... and just wait for, 'cause life is very fast. We're gonna be old and gone before you know it.... That's not sayin' that I'm scared of it anymore; ... I'm not. I'm just hopin' about it. Before I *was* scared, before Craig died I didn't know what the heck's, so this is a ... learnin' experience.... I've learned ... a *lot* about it.

Tina: Because of Gina's [death] I'm not afraid to die, to go through the actual physical act of it. But what I am afraid of is if I die and my kids are here.... That scares me. And I don't want any of them to die, but on the other hand, there's kind of this part of me that thinks, "Well, it's not really that bad" (chuckles). It's not. You go to a different place, and it's ... nice.

Some parents talked about their marriage being a lot stronger as a result of dealing with the death and its aftermath.

Amy: I think it cemented [our relationship] ... a lot stronger....

Ted: You have another common bind together. (*Amy:* Yeah) You're going through all these things and nobody else understands, nobody else experiences.... It takes you to a different level of knowing that person....

Amy: That made us closer (*Ted:* Yeah), made the marriage closer....

Ted: ... Noah was a common cause for us.... The worst thing is to see your child in pain and going through something, so I think we were able to derive some mutual togetherness by being able to comfort that as much as we could.... He gave back to both of us.... I also am very grateful to Amy for ... when he got sick, just slapping me into the realization ... [of] what was going on and to spend the time with him. 'Cause I think that I would be crazy if that hadn't happened. I'd have a lot of regrets.

Brett: It actually strengthened our marriage.... I know it made me a better dad, losing a child. More involved, and I know that I know what's more important as far as money and career and stuff like that.... This whole thing strengthened our marriage.... My family's probably a lot more important than if I hadn't gone through that....

Joan: I think it made our marriage stronger. It was like I had a bond with Brett, 'cause no one else had gone through exactly the same thing as I had, except for him, being the parent and then the child died.... I thought about our marriage harder ..., wanting to keep that bond there, knowing that if something happened, if we split up, that if he wasn't there, I didn't have that.

As has been reported in other research on bereaved parents (Brabant, Forsyth, & McFarlain, 1997; Klass, 1999; Knapp, 1986, pp. 36–37), many said that they had a new perspective on life, on what was important and what was not.

Henry: I think [we've changed to] sort of live life to the fullest, really enjoy things. We're probably more day-to-day people than we were before. (*Rosa:* Before, yeah).... The thing that we got, which we think is important,... it's ... just enjoy the intensity of life.

Sally: I am a far better parent because of losing that child. You realize how precious and fragile life is. You enjoy the moment, because who knows how long it can last?

Elaine: Things that were so important the week before [Kyle died] were not important at all anymore.... Our oldest daughter ended up getting pregnant the year before she was married, and I think at one point in my life that would have probably been the most devastating thing that could have ever happened.... But it was like, what is that in comparison to losing, I'd rather have her that way than not have her at all. So it was just like things just were not that important anymore. They're still here.

Some parents said that the new perspective gave them a resiliency in dealing with other adversity, because there was nothing worse than losing a child.

Rosa: I always had the sense that losing Wendy and grieving her would be the hardest thing I've ever had to do in my life, and so if you look at it that way, the rest of my life's gotta be easy. (*Henry:* That's right) And it was sort of like, leaving my career, leaving my family, moving to [this state], all of the changes that's involved. Basically having to restart in terms of any sort of profession.... And it's sort of like, "Well, I handled Wendy. So like what am I complaining about? It's not as bad as that." I think it helps put a lot of things in life in perspective.

Some parents said that the death had made them better able to deal with matters related to death.

Scott: When I was growing up and had family members or friends of my parents who died,... they were always very, very uncomfortable experiences for me. . . . Now, after having my daughter die in my arms, they're not a big deal anymore. So I go to funerals much more upbeat. And it just is something that's much easier to do. . . . When I was young, going to an open casket, forget it; I hated that. I remember seeing my grandmother in a casket when I was . . . eight, . . . and to me that was a traumatic experience. Even when I was a young adult, that was something that was unpleasant. . . . But now, "Pfft!" It's not that big of a deal. . . . Having gone through that experience, it's helped me mature and have a different reaction . . . and understanding.

Good Has Come from the Death

As has been reported by others (Brabant, Forsyth, & McFarlain, 1997; Klass, 1999; Schwab, 1990), some parents talked about the good they had done as a result of the death.

Kelly: We joined Parent for Parent. . . . We tried to make Leanne's passing a positive legacy, because we felt to make her life worthwhile we had to continue teaching, because that's what we felt she had come to do is teach. And I got involved with [a support organization], in that they could call me when they would have parents who had lost older infants. Then I'd be willing to talk to people.

Chad: We studied and worked hard to find out why this happened, or how this happened, and what can you do about it. . . . We talked to schools; we were in the . . . paper; we . . . fought with the legislature to just get this in the sex education programs in the schools. They mandate AIDS. Two kids have died of AIDS in Minnesota in five years in that age and probably 15 (bang on table) have of this. . . .

Erika: I guess we're doers too, so that has helped. . . . When people would ask us for anything, I tried to give them one of everything we had. . . . I'd try and hit media. I'd try and go medical. I'd try and go educational; I'd try and go legislature. And just keep on plugging along. The more people that know about it the better; we just can't allow it to happen again.

Angela: Jack reads the obituaries every single day. Anytime there's . . . a child in there that dies, . . . Jack sends them a little letter and a check. Let them know that we know what they're goin' through 'cause we've been through it.

Several parents talked about how they had become more "there" for other people as a result of the death and the support they received from others.

Sally: You just become more sensitive to people's problems ... surgery, breast cancer, a child with a tracheotomy. One of my friends has a child who had a tracheotomy. The child was a few months old. I was much more able to understand and be empathic and supportive. I'm more able to help people, even if it's just to send a card or to listen empathically.

Elaine: I think the one thing that I have tried to do is, there has got to be since Kyle died what? at least six people in the ... area that have had children that have been killed. And that's the one thing I have tried to do is I try to reach out to those people.

One child had been a subject in an experiment on a new medication to keep children like him alive. His father spoke about that as a good that came out of his dying.

Brett: If Alex was born today with the same kind of problem, chances are he probably would have survived because of the surfactin. And when he was born, because he was part of a study, I don't know if he got surfactin or if got, what do you call, the (*Joan:* Placebo). Yeah.... I was always ... curious if he got the placebo, or if he got ... surfactin. But it doesn't really make that big of a difference to me, because it's not gonna bring him back.... I'm pleased that the kids are living today with that problem, that Alex helped with that.

Joy talked about the death of her daughter as motivating some family members to strengthen their religious faith.

Joy: We see how God has used her life even in her death to bring people to Him. Both my brothers have become Christians since the accident.... I've always said if one person from my family can be saved because Jenny died, to me it would be worth it.

Making Meanings with Things

Most parent narratives referred to the potent meaning of certain things associated with the child. One sign of that potency was how determinedly most parents hung on to certain things that had belonged to the child or been used by the child. As other researchers have reported (Davies, 1987; Klass, 1993; Wheeler, 1998–99), there was a range in when and how parents dealt with things of the child, but most parents spoke of keeping and cherishing some things. Things that were especially connected to the child when alive—for example, an infant's pacifier—and things that were reminders of the child at the very end of life often spoke intensely to parents about the child and were cherished. The cherishing and the meaning may be strongly related to the way the objects link the parent to the child (Klass, 1993, 1999; Volkan, 1981).

Wayne: [We've] got all his little elves and stuff like that,... [a] trumpet player and (*Louise:* Yeah) ... a little baseball ... that used to be his (*Louise:* Yeah) and a hockey puck.... When he died, people got together and made a ... sign.... That's downstairs with a picture on it of a few of his trophies.... It's not a shrine. We ... seldom look, but it's there. His presence is still there....

Louise: Yeah, like up here too, we have ... a shelf with his things.

Wayne: ... Some of the little stuff we saved, the memento stuff.... All his toys and athletic equipment ... are still down there.... They're away, but they're marked. (*Louise:* Yeah.) And there's no hurry to get rid of 'em.

Bonnie: I just feel her presence.... You look around and see so many things that were hers or that she brought from [her trip overseas] or sent us or little notes.

John: Everywhere you look there's something. That was something on the refrigerator there that she did. She made it.... Always making ... sketches and ... little things that probably, at the time, didn't mean anything.

Pete: I still got his toy tractor underneath the bed....

Paula: He had two of 'em, (*Pete:* Yeah.) because one—

Pete: Yeah, the smaller one we (Paula clears her throat) put in the casket with him (his voice is shaky).

The special things seemed to link parents to two kinds of meanings. One kind of meaning was about the past. "This hockey puck, sketch, or toy tractor has meaning because it links me to the child as the child was before death." The other kind of meaning was about life since the death. "This sign reminds us of how strongly people felt after he died; this tractor reminds us of a loving thing we did at the time of his funeral; all these things remind us of our continuing love for this child who died."

Dealing with things associated with the child could be extremely painful because of prior meanings connected to the things. A few parents talked about an almost desperate need to put things that were reminders of the child out of sight soon after the death.

George: The most painful thing I'd ever done in my whole life was to box up everything.... This went on for a couple of days.... Boxing up everything carefully, and labeling it, and repainted the walls, and cleaned the carpet and the windows. And it was absolutely devastating.... I *had* to box that stuff up so I wouldn't be confronted with [it]. It's like ... if I was involved with a real *bad* accident out here on the corner with my best friend, my first thought was get that mess; I don't want to see that anymore.... The pictures and the crayons and the shoes, to me I just had to, the only way I could regain my perspective is by (6 second pause), it was my way of moving forward.... The way I was looking at it, that was one chapter in my life, and then we had to sell the house, in my mind. I had to get that house ready.... It's just a way of moving forward.

Several parents told of the pain of washing, organizing, and packing up the clothing and toys of the child. A few parents told of being coerced into sorting and packing up things by a family member who thought it would help move the grieving process along.

Molly: When it came to toys, when it came to clothes, when it came to washing things, that was my job.... [My mother] made me fold the clothes. And she said, "You're going to go in there by yourself. You're going to fold the clothes and put them in boxes and suitcases. And as you fold them you are going to say, "They're dead and they're not coming back." ... You're going to deal with that this is permanent. You're not living in a fantasy world because we're going to do this. You're going to face reality." So she helped me more than probably a counselor ever would. And I can remember being just hysterical,... screaming, and throwing things. And my sisters, it was just tearing them apart. They said, "We're going to pack for her." And my mother stood by the door and ... made me do it.

George: Steph and I got in a big to-do because (*Steph:* Yeah) when Nils died ...

Steph: He cleaned up his room, or *we both* did. He said, "Okay, let's clean out his room. We've got to go through all his clothes," and get rid of all his pictures. Well, not get rid of them, but put 'em away. And I learned later that a *woman* does not like to grieve that way. She'd rather *have* everything of that person ... close to her, so she can look at it, to remember, "Yes, he *was* actually there." Where he was typically male. He wanted to get rid of it.

George: Not so much get rid of it, but ...

Steph: (sounding irritated) No, but put it out of sight.... I'd never gotten rid of any of it. It's still down in the basement. That's why we've got so darn many boxes down there. But I think for me it would've been better ... to clean it the other way.

Because of prior meanings, things associated with the child can be both painful reminders and cherished reminders. However, it is likely that over time the meanings change. Some of the prior meanings may drop away—for example, the hockey puck is no longer a memory link to a specific sporting goods store or to hours of the parent bored, cold, and irritated waiting at the ice rink for hockey practice to end. At the same time, a thing may acquire new meanings and perhaps, in a sense, new memories. Now the hockey puck reminds the parent of the child's grace on ice, a grace the parent might not even have been conscious of while the child was playing hockey, and of the way that all that waiting for the child's hockey practice to end was loving.

Documents (for example, legal documents, school records, or medical records) can have special meanings because their official nature gives them extra credibility. Angela talked about hanging on to written records that were saturated with meaning as official acknowledgments of her son's existence and what happened to him. They could be taken as an objective, outsider statement about him. They also contained mysteries, perhaps not yet defined let alone solved, about what happened to him.

Angela: We have his birth certificate. We have his death certificate; we have his cremation certificate; we have the autopsy report; we have the 911 report. We have [the hospital] report.... I have three boxes in the bedroom, that has nothing but Blake's things in it. And I have people that tell me I have a shrine for him. It's like, "I don't give [a] fuck what you say." This is all I have left of my baby. And think what you want, but he ain't goin' nowhere. And those things aren't goin' anywhere either.

Some parents said that they did not know at first what would have meaning to them and what would not and decided not to get rid of anything until they knew. There was a kind of potential meaning in things, and until it emerged parents were reluctant to get rid of anything. Meaning has to be made of things; it is not automatically a property of them (Radley, 1990).

Jane: Rather than make any instantaneous decisions about [his things] and regret getting rid of something later, since there wasn't all that much, I kept everything.... About the one year anniversary of his death, I went through his dresser drawers and put his things away.... Rob made cedar shelves in Adam's closet, so that we could just bag everything up and put it in there. So it's all there (chuckles). Everything's still there (chuckles), pretty much.

For months or even years, some parents did not want to move anything that was the child's. There was too much meaning in the things as they were, too much pain in moving and disposing of them, too much risk of undermining meaning-making yet to be done, and perhaps a fear that moving or putting them away would cross a boundary into a territory that was still the child's private and personal space.

Bonnie: [We] still haven't gotten into her cedar chest. That's (small laugh) going to be tough. She's got this cedar chest stuffed full, and that just seems so personal. I never could go in it, even though she left it at home all those years. To me it's like a purse (small laugh). It's so personal.

Eventually many parents came to a point where they sorted the child's things, storing some things and giving away or discarding other things. In their stories of sorting a child's things, some parents spoke about how powerfully the things (even things that others might define as garbage) spoke to them about their child and their loss.

Louise: After Will died, all three [of our daughters] slept in this . . . very small room . . . for a couple of years. . . . That bothered my mother; it bothered my neighbors. And they kept saying, "You got to clean that stuff out." I said, ". . . I'll do it when I'm ready." And I wasn't ready. And neighbors said, . . . and my sister-in-law, too, . . . "If it bothers you, we'll come and do it," and I said, "No." . . . My biggest fear was that I would come home . . . someday and find that these people, meaning well, my mother probably in charge of the group, would have cleaned all of his possessions out. And I told Wayne and the kids, " . . . If anyone ever (bangs on table) comes in and does that, I'll kill him. . . . You just tell 'em I will do this when I'm ready. Just don't touch it!"

Wayne: . . . It was hard. . . . Like the floor, we cleaned the floor, little sun-flower seeds on it. (*Louise:* Yeah) He loved to eat sunflower seeds. . . . So when you're cleaning up and walking through all these sunflower seeds, now this is a couple of years later, and Louise and I were cleaning his room, we're just *sobbing.*

Some parents talked about using things associated with the child to help them grieve when they wanted to grieve.

Joan: If I felt like I needed to cry . . . , it was more like when I was alone. I wanted to grieve alone more. . . . If I was feeling bad and I wanted to get through . . . , instead of just thinking about it, I would grab something that had a particular memory of Alex. I'd grab a baby blanket, or I'd play the tape that we played the night he died. Or go look through his pictures or his cards.

_____

Kathy: This summer when I'm not working I have a box for each of them, and I have stuff that was theirs. I go through it. I can't do it when I'm working, 'cause it kinda sets me off for a time, but I'll take an afternoon.... I didn't keep much, but (sniffles) just to kind of keep in touch.

There was, for some parents, an essence of the child in some things. To dispose of those things would be like disposing of the child.

Alice: We took all her clothes, ... which I haven't done anything with. And that's another thing that makes me feel guilty in a way, because I know there's people that could use those clothes, and yet I'm not ready to give them up. It's been over a year, and I'm still not ready to give them up.... I just feel that if I give them away I'm giving her away.

When parents talked about the meanings of things, sometimes they were talking about the meanings the things had to the parents and sometimes they were talking about the meanings the things had to the child. Occasionally the difference in the two meanings made it difficult to decide what to do with things. For example, for something the child treasured but in itself had little meaning to the parents, the parents might agonize about whether to save it or to dispose of it.

Things were instrumental in the child's death were usually abhorrent to parents. Their meaning was that this is what killed the child.

Pete: After the ambulance left, ... I went into the garage and I got a crow bar, and I was going to go out and beat that bull to death.... I got into the pen and I said, "What are you doing out here with a crow bar? If you're going to kill the bull you get a gun," and I met one of the neighbor ladies in the yard then. And that's when I told her, just get the animal out of here.

Paula: In fact the couple that came and got the bull ... took him back to their place, and they loaded up their bull and shipped both of them.

Making Meanings with Places

Like things, places can have and reinforce meaning. Several women talked about reluctance to move from the house where they had lived with the child, because the house was so filled with meanings of the child.

Joy: We needed a bigger house. And it was actually kind of hard for us to leave her only house. . . . When we were there we could picture her still like in the window looking out. It's like . . . the memories we have of her in this house, are we still going to have them when we don't have the house to look at?

Rosa: We stayed in the little . . . house . . . a long time . . . 'cause it was our tie in to Wendy.

As Davies (1987) found, some parents kept the child's room much as it was when the child died. Some were fearful of accidentally destroying something that would be important to them later on and some experienced the room as an important tie to the child and a cherished source of reminders.

Erika: We basically have everything. . . . [But] we gave away some of his things to his friends. We asked them if they wanted things. But we didn't pack up things. His room is pretty much the way he left it. . . . Chad said we had the room; we'll keep his things. They (*Chad:* Yes) belong to the family. They weren't just David's personal belongings. There were shirts that [our daughter wore] to school. Or a friend would come over and borrow a book. Or, "Can I have the rocket launcher?" . . . One of his friends said, "It's . . . like he's still here." If they would've come over and seen his room all packed up and bare, "What were you going to use it for?" Where I know that's happened in some households. Some of David's friends' parents offered . . . to come over and help me pack up [his] room, and I said, "Why?"

There were also parents who spoke of wanting to flee the house in which they had lived with the child or to get rid of the house. The house brought up memories and feelings that were extremely painful.

Louise: I wanted to move out like that day. I wanted out of here. And people have said you shouldn't do anything major for a year. So we waited like a year, and it was probably that following April we put it on the market. But houses just weren't selling at all. And financially we really couldn't afford it.

Wayne: To get into what we were gonna get into.

Louise: Yeah. . . . We . . . picked a lot out and picked a house out that we were gonna build. It just didn't work out, but I'd move tomorrow if somebody let me. I still feel that. . . . It's not . . . the memories as much anymore, . . . but I'll still sometimes in the front hall have visions of that (voice cracking) policeman.

Wayne: And they keep coming back. . . . I think it's helpful just to get into a different place. It would just be good.

Al: Another thing, you got to do, you got to get out. You got to get the hell away from the house.... We did. We got a mobile home here before. We got rid of that (*Barb:* Changed houses) and bought this one. This is a new one.... That was a rough sucker, to come in the house and walk down the ... hallway, and go by his bedroom every day. So we got rid of that, put this one in here, which made a hell of a difference.

The specific place where the death occurred was an especially painful place for some parents.

Elaine: We had thought about moving.... We were going to sell the place. I mean, when it's right out your front door [that he was killed], that's a little hard to drive by.... I don't think you can ever drive by there that you don't think of that.

For some parents the burial site was a particularly meaningful place.

Kathy: I went to the cemetery a *lot* ... this year. I'd never ... been able to go by myself before ... 'cause I felt ... too much. I just would lay down. I ... wanted to be with them. If someone would have dug a hole, I would have ... jumped in.... I was just drawn to them. I just wanted to be there and take care of them. [Our three living] kids are off to a good start. They're fine; they're healthy (sniffles). I need to take care of these two. I always feel that when I go, and I was able to go this summer. I started cleaning up around them. It was just not well kept, and I didn't have anything with me. I just had my hands, and I was (sniffles) cleaning everything up and making it nice and trying to get all the dirt out of that. That kept me busy, trying to get the dirt out of the letters and stuff. And that helped me.

☐ Summary

The death of a child opens all parent meanings to question. Grieving parents may question the meaningfulness of their marital relationship or their relationship with God, the meaning of their work, the meaning of their everyday activities, and whether their life has enough meaning to be worth continuing. Until new meanings develop, a death infects all of life with meaninglessness. Meaninglessness cannot be ignored. Parents try to live a life in which things make sense. The child's life and death demand not to be meaningless.

In making meaning out of things related to the death, parents spoke in terms of a "real" reality and of what is natural—with the child's death being real but unnatural. Every parent narrative said that with the child's death came many losses, and in the process the narrative delineated areas in which meaning making was necessary in order to give meaning to the death. In describing the search for meanings, many parents talked about finding positive meanings in the child's death—for example, "it could have been worse," or "the child has been freed from terrible things."

Parents talked about the use, in meaning-making, of things associated with the child. The meaning potential of things was so great that some parents found it agonizing to sort through, clean up, store, or give away things, and some parents held off for years making decisions about what to with anything associated with the child. Some parents used things as a link into emotional contact with the child and a link to memories of the child. Spouse differences in the meaning of things or in what they were most comfortable doing with things was a source of great difficulty in some couples.

Places also could be powerful bearers of meaning. A child's room, the house the family was living in when the child died, the place where the child died, and the burial place all had potent meaning for some parents. These meanings strongly influenced some couples for years—for example, in the ways they used the room that had been the child's or in their desire to move or never to move from the house they occupied with the child.

Although this chapter has touched on some of the aspects of meaning and meaning-making linked with religious beliefs, the next chapter deals much more extensively with religious meanings associated with the death and with the meaning-filled spiritual situation of the child following the death.

God and Religion

Religion was central in the narratives of many bereaved parents. It is not only because religion and a religious community are important in the lives of many of the parents, but also because religion is a major area of discourse in the culture for dealing with death, life-meaning, morality, and fairness. Religion is also drawn into the lives of bereaved parents through death rituals. And religion offers a conceptual and behavioral path for remaining in contact with the child, for thinking of the child as still alive, for possible reunion with the child, and for finding meaning in the child's death.

When people use a religious way of talking about a death, they also use religious language when addressing problems concerning the death (Cook & Wimberley, 1983). Like any language, a religious language comes with a set of riders, things that fit it and make sense in it. When a narrative uses a specific kind of language, things that do not fit that language and do not make sense in terms of it are less likely to be brought into the narrative. Thus, the choice of language constrains and shapes problem-solving. What's more, each language brings with it a set of problems. Once one chooses a language, there is a set of dilemmas to deal with. The dilemmas might overlap from language to language, but the language choice crystallizes what the dilemmas are and how they are to be expressed. For example, in the following quote, Joy talked about her feelings of devastation and grief in religious terms, about the dilemma of grieving in a way that honors the child who died without becoming a "tool of the devil", and about the religious grounds for becoming committed to getting on with life.

Joy: I remember reading a book called *When Bad Things Happen to Good People,* and although I didn't agree with a lot of the theology in that book, I gleaned something from [it] that really ... helped me, sort of a handle for me to hang on to. And it was, the life of that person, it was so beautiful to you, that in some way if you let it destroy you, then that person becomes the devil's martyr and in a certain sense the devil wins. And it's like, "Oh no, Jenny's life was too beautiful." ... I made up my mind right then for the devil not to have any part of it. And that was really a handle for me.... I think that was one thing that really sort of pulled me out of it.

Her thinking in terms of religious language also defined a problem in her husband's grieving and shaped her concern about his grieving.

Joy: When [my husband] was angry I understood why he was angry, although reading that book I didn't want anger to destroy him and in that way have him letting the devil [have] a victory.

This chapter lays out areas of religion that were common in parent narratives. When speaking within these domains, parents were crystallizing issues around the death in religious terms, solving problems (some of which arose from religious language) raised by the death in religious terms, and using religious language and ideas to find meanings in the death and a sense of the path to take in grieving. They were also working on the ways they might continue to have a relationship with the child and to have the child continue to have identity and activities. They used these narratives to talk about the death and their grieving (not only with other people but with God and with the child) and to figure out what to do with the challenge of the child's death to their religious beliefs and activities.

Why Did God Do It? Why Didn't God Help?

The Death as a Challenge to Religious Belief

Many parents' narratives dealt at length with the death being a challenge to their religious beliefs, because they believed in a God who is just, wise, caring, compassionate, and all powerful. They could not understand why such a God would take the child's life or allow the child to die (cf. Cook & Wimberley, 1983; DeFrain, 1991; Gilbert, 1992).

Hannah: We were both born a Catholic, and ... being brought up with Catholicism, good things happen to good people and bad things happen to bad people. So I spent the first six months after Tyler died trying to figure out what I had done that was so bad.... When I was sitting in the church during the funeral,... I kept thinking, it's a feeling of punishment (starting to cry).... The Guy that I was always taught about doesn't punish.... But I really felt like we were being punished.... I went and talked to a priest; he told me that this happened because of original sin. And I said, "But I was taught that Christ died on the cross to pay for original sin. So why are we still paying for original sin?" ... Another priest ... said the same thing. And I thought, "Then all these years I've been lied to."

Vince: God took him away from us, which pisses me off and ... when I die and I go to heaven, that's one question that I know He's gonna answer. I (bang on table) got to ...; it's an unresolved issue between me and God. He knows I'm pissed at Him, and that's okay (he laughs). He's got broad shoulders, and I know that when I get to heaven, He knows I'm gonna ask the question. He knows I'm gonna be mad, and I know that whatever answer He gives me is gonna be right. And then I can finally be at peace....

Gail: It's changed the way that I think about God. And for a while it was very uncomfortable to be in church, and I found myself going only to see the other people, and for the friendship and support ..., not because of my religious beliefs. And I used to believe that God was ... controlling of everything, and that He was the one that made every circumstance be the way that it was. And I no longer believe that. I believe that He has the power to control things, but He chooses not to. So *my* point of view has changed, but not ... my basic belief, that I believe in Him....

Vince: It's funny how we have different justifications (*Gail:* We do). Yeah. I still believe God has control over everything, and I still believe to this day that He took Randy away from us.

Tina: My mom said ..., "God doesn't give you more than you can handle." I just wanted to like choke the life out of her. That really bugged me. And then people said that it was God's way, and then I'd blow a gasket.... (Imitating an indignant voice:) "You can't tell me that God is taking a baby away from me for a reason." I just couldn't handle that.... I do have religious beliefs. And I've always prayed every single night. In fact every night I pray that Gina is at peace.... When it happened,... whatever I believed in, my spirituality, I felt a sense of loss of it for a while. And I really struggled with how people could feel closer to God when one of their kids had died. Like this was some great thing this Guy had done to them, "Oh, thanks God for taking my kid. That was wonderful." I couldn't relate to that, and I still can't.... For a while I stopped praying too. I was really mad at God.

Elaine: I did in the beginning think, "If God is so all-loving and so all-caring how could he take this child who had done nothing?" What could he have ever done in his life that would have been so wro—, you know what I mean?. . . At one point [my religious beliefs] kinda faltered. Never that I . . . quit . . . participating in mass . . . , but . . . I felt kind of let down by all that. Like why have I been expected to give up so much and some people never have to give up anything? I felt that I was being treated very unfairly. And if He's all-loving and all this, how could He deal all of this to one person? I felt very cheated by that. And then the person that could've really helped me the most would have been my mother, and she had been taken also.

These four quotes are representative of religious concerns in the narratives of many parents. The narratives include questioning of and about God; struggling with matters of faith, fairness, justice, and the validity of religious teachings; coming to terms with the limitations of clergy to help; concerns and questions about the death as a punishment; channeling of anger spiritually; the undermining (at least temporarily) of religious practices; spousal differences in religious thinking and feeling about the death; and feelings of having been betrayed by One who had been totally trusted.

Questions about what God was up to when a child died are also community issues. Not only do parents deal with religious questions when a child dies, people around them also struggle with such questions. It is an area parents may have to come to terms with in part because others want answers. Small wonder, with others raising religious questions and offering their own answers, that many couples had a well-developed religious narrative for talking about the death. Moreover, bereaved parents may be on the defensive in addressing religious questions. In the thinking of some people, including some parents, God punishes sinners. To accept that belief is to accept the designation that the child who died or a parent had sinned. To the extent that nobody wants to think of a child or one's self as a sinner, the parental approach to framing the child death religiously necessitates asserting that the child and the parents were not sinners. Some parents spoke of how much others tried to drag them into unacceptable religious interpretations of the death.

Molly: People tried to make me feel it happened for a reason. They're in a better place. One of my children . . . ended up getting a staph infection on her face, so it would heal and then it would open and drain; and it would get bigger; it wouldn't totally heal. And someone said to me "Now that she's gone, maybe it's better 'cause this could have probably eaten her face away." The logic people use on you, it's unreal. I very much believe in God, very religious. . . . I didn't fall away in my faith; I went to church. . . . I don't feel that I was punished by God or I was chosen for any reason. I think it was a human accident, a fluke of fate. People have said, "People don't get chosen unless they've done something wrong." Crap, I don't buy that.

Parent Responsibility and the Power of Prayer

The question of what God wants when a child dies is complicated by the belief in the power of prayer. If prayer is a petitioning to an all-powerful Decider, the Decider has the ultimate power. But the prayer is a request that, if honored, represents human responsibility for what happens. Thus, for some parents the question of why God allowed a child to die or made a child die is entangled in what the parents prayed for. Some parents with a child who was extremely ill, with no sign that recovery was possible, prayed neither for recovery nor for continuing life for the child. After the child died, some of those parents felt deep regret at having not prayed for life for the child.

Ken: I was lifting weights, and ... I asked God ..., "What can be done? What can happen here?" I was asking for help. And all of sudden says, "Hey, don't worry. Everything will be fine. I'll take care of it." Like, it came out of the blue.... Then I felt guilty, because I didn't ask for enough (he laughs). Then I said ..., "I want him *back*!!" I wanted Mark back (crying), because God said "take care of him." (*Glenda:* (crying) Which He did) Which He did (still crying). I felt guilty later on.

Denny: We prayed the day he died, and then I had to curse myself for that, because I said, "Hey, if you're gonna take him—"

Marsha: "Take him."

Denny: "Take him," cause this roller coaster we've been on for 10 weeks is just terrible. One day, "Oh, his numbers are great. He's fine." The next day, "Better get him here...." I said that the day it happened. I'll never forget it.... Should I [have] said that or not ...?

Marsha: When you start thinking as a parent, you start thinking about not just the life of your child but the quality of life (*Denny:* Yeah). Wearing a bag is one thing, but you wonder, our son was so tiny that there's things like cerebral palsy (*Denny:* Many, many things that can go wrong), mental retardation, seizures. There's a lot of things that can go wrong.

A parent's feeling of having responsibility, through prayer, for the child's death may have colored the parent's perception of God, but it did not seem to eliminate the challenge to religious belief. God was still seen as all-powerful, so questions about why God did it remained even for these parents. They may feel guilt, but they still have searching questions about God.

Resolving the Challenge to Religious Belief

The child's death challenged the religious beliefs of many parents. There were seven distinct ways parents dealt, in their narratives, with the challenge.

God Did Good, But I Still Have Questions

The narrative of some parents included language that affirmed their religious belief while raising questions. Similar to what was reported by Cook and Wimberly (1983), they accomplished this by saying that although they may not know and may puzzle about why God took the child, they remained sure God exists and is wise and benevolent, and they could even see good in the child's death.

Todd: He's in heaven. I think that's clear from what the Bible says. I don't have a question about that. God is a holy ... and ... just God. God can't stand sin, because He is a holy God, but He's also a just God, and ... He's not unfair. And so He doesn't hold [little children] accountable, so Jeff is in heaven.

Iris: But we weren't mad at God for doing it.

Todd: No. As far as fairness, unfairness, who are we to judge what's fair or not? God has a ... reason for it. Just 'cause we don't know doesn't mean that it was wrong. I think there's been some positives that have come out of it. It was hard, but life isn't always fair.... I don't think it *should* be.... As far as why God did this I don't know. I'll find out someday, I guess.

Iris: Why not (*Todd:* Yeah), why not us?

Todd: Yeah. Why not us? ... We feel like Jeff needed a lot of loving, and we were able to do that. He needed a lot of care, and the insurance that my company provided enabled him to have (*Iris:* Everything) everything that the doctors could think of that they could possibly do. And so there's one answer for you. God knew we'd need a lot of that, and He provided that.... Sure there's lots of questions.... (*Iris:* The disappointment.) Yeah, but they aren't questions about the fairness ... or the rightness of it all. That's not a matter of fairness or rightness. It's just, I wonder why; a curiosity more than anything.

God Didn't Do It, and the Child is with Him

Other parents dealt with the challenge to religious belief by saying that the death was not a result of God's action, but that God claimed the child's soul after the child died.

Nick: [God] ain't tryin' to get my attention or nothing. I just know that He doesn't kill. He ain't a God that goes out and kills people. He's the one saves people, loves people, and that's why people when they come to me and say, well, "God took him" and blah, blah. God didn't. He took him after the fact. He didn't come and kill him.

God Did It after the Child Completed Her or His Mission

Other parents talked about the death as part of God's plan, with the child having served a mission on earth.

Joy: We feel like she almost knew that she didn't have much time, so she had to learn all she could while she was here. She never wasted time. She never sat around and complained about being bored or "What can I do, Mommy?" She was just always, always busy.... In a lot of ways we feel like she was our teacher. We really feel like we would rather have had her and lost her than to never have had her at all. We feel like just to have had her was a real gift. Not that our other children aren't. Just their mission isn't as short as Jenny's was.... She had a short mission and she was lucky, really, that she got her job done so quick.

God Didn't Do It, But He Could Have Intervened

Some parents felt that God did not make the death happen but could have intervened and chose not to. That it is a subtle distinction is indicated in the following narrative, where Joy first said it was God's will and then corrected herself and said He allowed it.

Joy: The ... grief group said there's always the "ifs," and it's not like you can go back and do it over again, so why beat yourself up with the "ifs." ... This is the way it happened and all the "ifs" in the world aren't going to change [it]. But ... you still keep thinking about it. I guess until I came to the resolution that in fact it was easier for me to accept that this was God's will, and I don't mean He willed this, but obviously if He allowed it He is sovereign, then there was nothing I could do to change it. God's in control.

This Only Makes Sense if There is a God

As reported by others (Cook & Wimberley, 1983; Gilbert, 1992; Knapp, 1986, pp. 34–35), some parents said a child's death strengthened their faith. They said the death forced them to examine their faith, and the outcome was a sense that the world only makes sense and is comfortable if there is a just God, a heaven, and everlasting life for the child.

Elaine: I realize that He is an all-loving God but that He's also just, and if you really believe that, then how could He have taken this child from us? Because it was not a just act, and it certainly was not ... loving.... So that's why I kind of had come to the thing that it's an accident, it happened, it's unfortunate.

Red: Yeah, but then you can look at it the other way. If He's a loving God, all the suffering Kyle went through with his allergies and sores in his mouth and stuff, that really relieved his pain....

Elaine: I do think that my religion got me through that though, because if I wouldn't have believed that there was ... anything everlasting, how could you accept ... what happened?

Also, consistent with findings reported by Gilbert (1992), some parents said that they gained a renewed or strengthened faith as a result of their sense that the only way they could have survived the loss was through the action of God.

Kathy: It's nice to know that there's still some good days that we had after that.... Somehow we made it through. And Somebody was watching us, I think, to help us. I probably think that more than him, but we had to get the strength from somewhere.

These Things Just Happen

Some parents rejected religious language in addressing questions of why the death happened (Cook & Wimberley, 1983), and some even saw reasons as arbitrary.

Brett: People will say that ... there's a reason for somebody dying.... I don't think that way. I think that things happen; there's a chain of events, and things happen, and people die. And the reason comes afterwards. You can make your reason for it ..., but I think the reason is afterwards.... Like I was talkin' to ... a friend of ours. She had a niece ... that had.... too many chromosomes.... She was supposed to die and she lived, and [the friend] was saying, "It was a miracle," and then she asked me, "Do you believe it was a miracle?" And I said, "Yeah, just as much of a miracle as it was that [my son] died."

Brett's rejection of a religious language seemed to be accompanied by a sense that God is not controlled by human prayer and that God is not an arbitrary punisher. Thus, his belief that God was not responsible for his son's death was accompanied by a sense of God as unknowably and unreachably powerful.

Brett: Prayer kind of confuses me.... You see people in the news, "We prayed, and it came out okay...." I don't believe God selectively chooses who prays the hardest.... I don't believe that God punishes people. He didn't take our son from us because of something I did when I was 17 years old or anything like that. And that God didn't sit and decide this friend of ours little girl ... should live and our son should die. They were gonna live and die anyways.

After This I Can't Believe There's a God

A few parents said that they could not believe in God after the death of their child. That might not stop them from some forms of religious participation, but it moved them to talk as though God does not exist.

Sally: It blew us out of the water religiously, losing a baby. It really shakes up your religious belief. I never was very religious. I was a cultural Jew. I never had to put it to a test whether there was a God or not. I don't get why a baby has to die. How could God do that? ... We are doing observant things like lighting shabbos candles now. But for me, I just can't believe there's a God after all this.

When the Challenge Remains Unresolved

The challenge to religious beliefs was not resolved for all parents. Some said that they remained, even years after the child's death, angry at God, shaken in their beliefs, and sure that the death was unjust or unfair. For them, religious language was about their strong feelings of having been betrayed, strong feelings of confusion, grieving not only the loss of the child but the loss of faith or of a God who could be trusted to be just and fair.

Hannah: I tried going back to church. But when I'd walk in ... I feel all this resentment and I'm still really angry with God. When Tyler's very best friend was killed in a car accident, and [Tyler] was talking to [us] about it, ... he said, "What I don't understand ... is why, if there's a God, ... good people die and the bad people who rape and murder and rob ... are ... allowed to walk on the earth. And the people that haven't done anything wrong are the ones who are dying. It doesn't make any sense to me." And that came back to me a thousand times after ... Tyler died. And Tyler wasn't perfect, but he was a good kid (bangs on table). And all three of our kids, we never had the cops at our door; we never had drug problems; we didn't have alcohol problems.... We worked really hard.... Maybe I'm looking for justice.

Jay: I've been to church once since the accident.

TK: Is that a difference for you?

Alice: Oh, very much.

TK: So you used to go to church—

Alice: Very much more. Oh, yeah. Every Sunday, unless it's sickness....

Jay: You can still keep your faith, but you can still be angry at God for taking her life. Now, she didn't get into anybody's hair. She was a good person. She kept her nose clean. She was no drug addict or booze-cide. And yet He took her away, and look at all these people ..., they're on drugs, they drink, and they are permitted to live. Now to me that's very hard to understand.... I told them to my preacher, but he can't even come up with the answer.... I read, and I read, and I read, and I read. You can read the Bible. They don't come up with an answer. So it's very hard for me to understand why she got taken away so young.

☐ Interacting with God about the Death

Some parents felt that they interacted with God about the death, that God listened to them and answered their questions. Similar to findings reported by Gilbert (1992), some parents felt that God communicated with them in ways that helped them to find peace, meaning, and perspective.

Joy: The night of the accident [my husband] went out to the car.... It was two in the morning. [Our son] was in the hospital so we were [there], and he went out to the car and there was a little bird, a baby robin chirping at him, and it's like, how often do you hear baby robins at two in the morning? Birds are sleeping then. And he felt like that was sort of a message of hope ..., so baby robins have become a symbol of hope for us. And last [year on the anniversary of her death] ... this little baby robin comes hopping right up. We're eating supper, and it comes hopping right up on the back stairs and sits there and chirps at us and then hops back down and hops away. And it's like I really feel like God does use nature to give us hope. It's His creation; He obviously orchestrates it. And I believe He can give us hope through things like that. And stuff like that does comfort us.

Some parents yearned for a sign, felt upset when for a long time none came, and then felt at peace when one finally came.

Louise: [A] neighbor had taken the girls to buy flowers for the funeral, and [our youngest] ... was looking for a specific flower.... The florist said, "... What color do you want?" And she said, "... His favorite color is yellow." Now that just came out of the blue, because [his school] colors are orange and black. Yellow certainly wasn't a color Will had anything to do with. And ... it was a specific yellow. She looked and looked and looked till she found a specific yellow flower that she needed to have in her brother's funeral.... A couple of days after that, when she was walking ... with her day care provider, she bolted off and ran quite a ways into the woods, and came out with a bouquet of yellow flowers, the same color, bright, bright yellow flower, and said, "These are Will's flowers," and proceeded to put them in his bedroom. And we didn't think too much of any of that, but it was like a month after Will died, ... I was about as low as I got. I just thought, "If I could just die today I'd be happy." (crying) But ... I had these kids I have to take care of, and so I just thought that, "I gotta get through this." And I remember praying to God and just saying, "Please help me. I need some kind of a sign to tell me Will is okay, or I can't go on." And so I went for a walk.... I walked out in front (still crying), we had these purple iris around the mail box, that we've had for many years. And they were in full bloom. And as I walked by, (*Wayne:* Purebred) yeah, ... I just kinda glanced at the flowers, and I noticed there were some yellow flowers in there.... Got about half a mile from the house, and all of a sudden it just dawned in my mind. I came running home.... Here were these flowers, and we had these purple and white purebred iris that a neighbor gave me.... They'd been there for, oh, six, seven, eight years.... Here are these two beautiful yellow iris, bright, bright yellow, ... the *exact* color that [our daughter] was insistent was Will's favorite color, and they were tall.... They hadn't been there a couple of days before, ... and now here they are.... bigger than the rest, like they'd been growing before. And we took it as a true sign from God.

Marsha: I was looking for a sign.... It bothered me that I never ever dreamt about Matt.... I remember sitting up in bed one night, and I was real teary, and I said I hope for a sign that he's okay. And we have a picture of Matt that we had in a frame at the funeral, and it's of him laying on [my husband's] chest, and there's a yellow blanket behind him. And way across the room, in the light, when I looked at him it looks like a perfect halo around his head.... I said [to my husband], "Come up here, come up here! You have to see this!... Look at that picture and tell me what you see," and he said, "My God, he's got a halo on his head." And it was then I knew ... "It's okay now. Don't you worry." And I know it's a blanket.

Some parents found a sign from God in spiritual messages that were available at or just before the time of the death.

Alice: We have a booklet of Bible verses sitting on our table, and on ... the day she was killed the Bible verse read (she cries), "Let God have your life; He can do more with it than you can (sobbing)."

Other parents experienced spiritual messages from God at turning points in their grieving.

Joy: I know that we, at least I know for myself, I was physically carried by the Lord.... I don't know if you've ever seen that poem called "Footprints," and that is exactly what I felt like. I knew I was not moving on my own strength.... In fact, I remember the date the Lord put me down, and I was sort of like, "No! No! I'm (laughing) not ready." ... It was like He was reassuring me, saying, "I'll still be here, but you need to walk on your own."

Brett: I was wondering when did I decide that I didn't kill Alex and when I let him go. And I remember it happened at night when I was sleeping.... I woke up and I knew that I'd made the right decision. And to me that was somethin' between me and God.

☐ The Child is with God in Heaven

Consistent with what Klass reported (1999, Chapter 4), most parents said that they thought of the child as in heaven. Many of those parents said that they continued to have faith and could find solace in the belief that the child was safe with God.

John: If it wasn't knowing that there was a supreme being, I don't think I could handle this very easily at all. I just know that she's someplace she's supposed to be....

Bonnie: I just look at it ... that she's in *heaven* and happy and healed and just sitting at Jesus's feet.

Even for those who questioned God or were angry with God there could be solace in the belief that the child was safe with God.

Marsha: I think we know in our hearts that they're okay, and they *are* with God, and that they are (*Denny:* Safe from violence). I think that's been kind of our solace is that we know that they're okay. I think in our hearts, even though we've been angry ... and bitter at times, and resentful.... I guess we know in our hearts that they are okay and they are with God.... (*Denny:* Yeah, that's the only thing that keeps you going.)

Consistent with what Cook and Wimberley (1983) reported, some parents talked about the death strengthening their faith and said that a part of that strengthening was that the faith brings with it a possibility of seeing the child in heaven.

Joy: I think Heaven becomes much more of a reality when your child is there. You do absolutely want to be sure of seeing that child again.... I do wonder how much we'd be thinking about God if Jenny were here.... I definitely think it's made me more serious about spiritual things and making sure I'm right with God.

Stan: Yeah, and when things are going well and you're going along your merry way, you really don't, (*Joy:* What do you need?) most people don't think of spiritual things.

Joy: ... Although I was a Christian before the accident, I [was] ... maybe not as serious as I should have been.

Stan: Yeah, we weren't as serious as we should have been or as we are now....

Joy: We believe what the Bible says. We believe that the way to eternal life is faith in Christ. That when you turn your life over to Him, He gives you a new life and you are born again. That is the way to eternal life. And I guess before the accident I knew that, but had I really surrendered (*Stan:* Did you practice it?) had I really surrendered everything to Him? Had I wholeheartedly turned my will over for His?

Even many parents who felt angry with God, doubted the existence of God, or wanted nothing to do with a God who could kill a child or allow the child to die, spoke of faith and religious commitment as the only route toward a possible reunion with the child. To think that there was no God and no heaven, that the child's death was a meaningless, random event and that the death was an end to the existence of the child in every way was intolerable for most parents. That, too, pushed them toward continued, renewed, or strengthened faith.

Louise: If I did not believe in a hereafter, heaven, for instance, I could not *believe* where my mind would've gone, that if Will would've been killed and gone just into this hole, and that's all he was gonna be, I'd 've been so depressed I'd commit suicide.

☐ Realities for the Child in Heaven

Consistent with the finding of other research (Edelstein, 1984, pp. 64–65; Klass, 1988, p. 64, 1993, 1999; Schwab, 1990) that almost all bereaved parents feel that a child who died is in heaven, every parent who talked about heaven said that they believed or knew that their child was in heaven. Some parents who talked about a child being in heaven talked about what the child was doing, who the child was with, and what life there was like for the child.

Louise: We kind of figured he's up there, and we've known a couple of young boys who have died since.... Just 10 months later one of his good friend's older brother was killed in a automobile accident. And whenever something like that has happened, we've just kind of said, "Well Will's got this team up in heaven now" (*Wayne:* It's a very good team now (laughs)).... After my father passed away, he and my dad were so close, (crying) I think that really helped that he died. (*Wayne:* Yeah. And he's up there too.) Which is maybe why it was (*Wayne:* Umhm) really easy for me to accept father's death (still crying).

Wayne: He's obviously going to get there with Will.

Louise: Because Will is not by himself (still crying).

Denny: My aunt ... died at 42.... My ma's ... very religious, and she swears to God that the day before Matt's funeral that her dream was [her sister] was sitting there waiting with her arms open, that she would keep Matt till we get there.... Here I'm mad at God, yet I'm sittin' there believin' in all this.... You try to find some comfort, and the only comfort I had was thinkin' that they're both up there now. [My aunt] has one [of our children] in each hand.

One thing the quotes immediately above say about children in heaven is what many bereaved parents said, in heaven there is nurturance for the child (Layne, 1992), especially from relatives and friends who have died. Parents also found support in people they did not know well talking about visiting the child in heaven. Erin talked about feeling grateful for the support of a local politician who visited her a week after her son's death. She said that he said:

> I didn't come to the funeral.... I am 80 years old and am going to die soon. I want you to know how nice it will be to see young faces like [your son's] in heaven.

In a society where so many people believe in the continuation of the spirit beyond death, it is not surprising that parents would try to communicate with the child's spirit, would have a sense of the child as a spirit, would have a sense of location of the child's spirit, and would have a sense of who the child is in the spirit world.

A few parents moved outside the language of conventional religion and into that of an alternative spirituality in order to find their spiritual connection with the child who died.

Ted: We went to a, I don't how you classify this guy.... He was heavy into astrology.... He went through this whole physical change ... connecting with the spirit world.... Basically he said Noah was helping people get to the other side. That was his role right now.... He said things like it took him a while to cross over, which was true.... Blew our minds listening to that. But I think we felt good that he was in a good place, so that was comforting.

Tina: When [our daughter who was born after Jenny died] started dance, ... there were two other women ... that had daughters there. One day one of them said, there's ... a bar and restaurant across the street, "Hey, anyone want to go have a beer while the girls are in dance?" So we started talking and within about 15 minutes, all three of us, in the past three to five years had had children that had died. And it was just weird. We're all like, "Wow! This was meant to be." And one of the women, about a year after that, ... told me about a book ..., *We Don't Really Die.* And it was written by a ... psychic.... *I* don't normally believe stuff like that. But when I read that, and read the stories and the things that he says, that he's communicated with people that have died, ... I believed it.... He says that you get signals from people that have died, and that something will happen ... and you just kind of brush it off like you don't even think about it. And it's really a sign from this person, showing you that they're still ... in your life. For example, this fall ... I flew to Phoenix to visit a friend. ... This guy is sitting next to me in the plane, and he starts talking to me, and he's got this book. ... about near death experiences. So, I'm thinking, "Wow! This is a sign from Gina. She's here! She's with me. She's going to Arizona!" (laughs) ... Or like around her birthday, *several* times, there's been like a talk show on about death. And one year, the day of her birthday, the Minneapolis paper did a big article on near death experiences.

☐ Summary

Religion was central in the narratives of many bereaved parents. Using a religious way of talking about the death was associated with a religious language when addressing problems concerning the death. A religious perspective also created a number of dilemmas for parents, the most salient of which was why God had taken the child's life or allowed the child to die. For a number of parents, the child's death led to a crisis of religious belief. For a few, the death was associated with great personal guilt about what they had and had not prayed for.

There were seven distinct ways parents dealt with the religious questions the child's death raised. Some, for example, came to believe that God did good in allowing the child to die or taking the child's life, but the parents still had questions (which they might believe would be resolved when they joined the child in heaven). Other parents came to believe that the child was on a mission on earth and returned to heaven when the mission was complete. There were also parents who decided that the death just did not make sense or who decided that they could no longer believe in God. In trying to resolve their spiritual questions, some parents said that they had received communications from God that were helpful.

Every parent who talked about heaven said that the child who died was in heaven and that there was solace for them in knowing the child was there. For some parents, believing the child was in heaven led to life changes that they believed would maximize the chances that they would be able to join the child in heaven. Some parents who talked about a child being in heaven talked about what the child was doing, who the child was with, and what life there was like for the child. Central in this regard was the idea that relatives and age peers of the child who had died were with the child in heaven, as nurturers or companions. Some parents also said that they communicated with the child in heaven or experienced signs from heaven about the child.

15
CHAPTER

Perspectives on Parent Narratives and Society

☐ Parent Narratives

This book is my narrative about the narratives of bereaved parents. What is offered in this book are my truths about what the parents thought were their truths. This book is not the only legitimate representation of the experience of grieving parents, nor can it be claimed to be more accurate than some other approach. But hopefully it offers ways of thinking about and knowing bereaved parents that will be helpful to those who want to understand the experience of those parents.

The book describes and analyzes parent narratives in the areas where the parents who were interviewed had the most to say—areas where problems arose and were solved and where language and culture took the parents. These were the locations they focused on when trying to find meaning for the child's death and the locations they went to when figuring out their feelings, working out their relationship with the child, making sense of funeral rituals, figuring out what to make of their marriage following the death, deciding where they stood religiously, and making sense of their relationships with the people around them.

Parent narratives are also, in a sense, about what it takes to make stories of a child's death and the aftermath of the death. Among other things, it requires a characterization of who the child was for the parents—a child with certain feelings, abilities, and character, and always a child who had a relationship with the parents. For children who died young or from problems present at birth, the parent story was also about the pregnancy and even about issues in conceiving the child.

The parent narratives always deal with the child's dying and death. The parents provide the facts that explain why there is a story to tell and why the parents had to deal with all they had to deal with. They are often about the parental process of learning that the child is dying and about efforts to save the child or prolong the child's life. They are usually about the details of the last day, hours, and minutes of the child's life. And they are always, in great detail, about the child's death.

The parent narratives always deal with rituals following the death—rituals that acknowledge the death and in some sense establish the relationship of the parents with the child, the community, and perhaps God. The rituals often are important in giving reality and meaning to the death and the parents' grief.

Parent narratives always deal with the continuing relationship between parent and child. The child continues in the parents' lives. Frequently parents experience the child's presence or continue to interact with the child. Many parents made special efforts to insure the continuation of the child in their lives and worked at making the child a presence in the lives of others, especially in the lives of their other children. Some parents continued to parent the child, through mental conversation or prayer. Some parents felt the child had become more parental of the parents, for example, as a protecting force. As part of maintaining their relationship with the child, parents held on to possessions, spaces, and other things associated with the child.

Parent narratives must be selective. The parents cannot tell the whole story, because the whole story would take years to tell. In their selectivity the parents omit the ingredients for many alternative stories, and they omit what they do not want to say, including their secrets, and what does not seem to them to fit within their narrative. With all these things left out, it is easy to imagine how individuals or couples could come to other narratives with other audiences or in other times, places, and situations (Rosenblatt & Wright, 1984).

Much of this book is about couple reality in the sense that the narratives were gathered in a couple situation and often were a jointly told couple story. Usually the couples talked as though they were telling stories they knew well and had told before, but that does not mean they were not constructing on the spot—for example, using details that had been left out of previous tellings, changing emphases from previous tellings, individually or jointly addressing an issue for the very first time, recalling things that they seemingly had not recalled ever before, or telling about new realizations.

Narratives are so much about words that sometimes we may overlook emotions. Yet the parent stories were never consistently low key and matter-of-fact. It was clear that for every parent the child's death was one of the most significant, difficult, life-dominating, heart-wrenching, disruptive, upsetting, and life changing events of the parent's life.

☐ What Parent Narratives Say about U.S. Society

Parent narratives say a lot about the society in which the parents live. As parents talked about their child's death and what has happened as a consequence of the death, they said a lot about U.S. society, both by the words they said and by the gaps in what they said.

Their narratives are about what is important and meaningful in U.S. culture(s). These are the issues that count. There are the ways to think about relationships. These are the issues and ideas people in the U.S. think about when dealing with dying and death. These are the categories for generating meanings and the important areas for meaning in U.S. culture(s).

The narratives are told, I think, on the assumption that all or almost all of what the narratives deal with will make sense to most people, including visiting interviewers. In fact, I think one reason the narratives were delivered with such strong conviction, as they were, is that they make sense in the parent culture(s) and that the parents think that they can count on them making sense to interviewers who seem to be from the same culture(s).

Money-Earning Work Comes First

Parent narratives make crystal clear the primacy of money-earning work in U.S. society. Money-earning work limits, controls, organizes, suppresses, and shapes the grief process. Grieving parents who have money-earning jobs seem almost always to have to return to work soon, almost always in a week or less. They seem not to have other possibilities offered to them and, in many cases, do not include in their narratives an account of serious thoughts, immediately following the child death, about quitting the job or demanding long term leave in which to grieve. The U.S. seems to be a society where workers must work and in which employers, the community, the government, the church community, health insurers, and other institutions and collectivities express no interest in excusing from work a person who is deeply bereaved or in providing a time for the strong feelings, confusion, and so on of early bereavement to be carried out without the requirement of wage-earning work. These constraints and forces in bereavement are underlined by the occasional parent who is grateful for the few extra days of sick leave or family leave that are granted after the child's death.

Having arrived at work, bereaved parents are expected to do their jobs. Not only are they supposed to be there, but they are supposed to be doing the work. One man lost his sales job because, with grief so dominant in his thinking and feelings, he could not do the work well enough. Another who was having difficulty at work after the child death was forced by his boss to enter counseling along with his wife. So not every bereaved parent can do the job well. But some talked about walling off their feelings while on the job—for example, the teacher who cried all the way to work, suppressed tears while at school, and then cried all the way home.

The Primacy of Social Order

Parent narratives make clear that grief is a challenge to social order, the sense that for the people around the parents life should go on as before without disruption or even inconvenience from bereaved parents. Some parents talked about their distress at seeing their neighbors, coworkers, and extended family members going on with normal, daily life following the death. Parent narratives made clear that many others distanced them, avoided them, or tried to act as though nothing had changed. Parents could take that as others not knowing what to say or not caring, but between the lines of parent narratives it is clear that the parents realized that others did not want parents to disrupt their lives; parents seemed to accept that. Parents ordinarily kept their grieving from others and colluded in others distancing the parent grief and the parents. There were a few stories of parents disrupting the social order—for example, the woman who threw a piece of chicken during the post-funeral dinner or the couple who insisted that their local school warn children and families about auto-erotic asphyxia. But even in those stories of disrupting the social order there was a sense of respect for the social order. The woman who threw a piece of chicken did not repeat the act. The couple who tried to influence the school went through channels and respected the rationality and organization of educational institutions.

The Privatization of Tragedy

Every parent narrative made clear that a child's death is not supposed to be experienced as a community loss, that it is the parents and immediate family who "own" the grief. There may be community expressions of support and of loss at the time of the funeral, but there is rarely a hint that the child's death is a community event beyond the first few days after the death. Perhaps that seems to be natural, an obvious consequence of who had the most contact with the child, whose future was most tied to the child, who had the most memories of the child, and who had the most hopes for the child. I know from my research for *Grief and Mourning in Cross-Cultural Perspective* (Rosenblatt, Walsh, & Jackson, 1976) that in many of the world's societies the deaths of young children receive relatively little ceremonial attention. But some of the children in the present study were adults, and in many societies around the world, the whole community will engage in a long series of funeral rituals, perhaps extending several years, following adult deaths and will collectively express a sense of loss on a number of occasions (Rosenblatt, Walsh, & Jackson, 1976, Chapter 5). However, in the narratives of parents who lost an adult child there is a sense that the loss is theirs, not the community's.

Most parent narratives talked about others distancing the grieving parents and also about the grieving parents distancing others. Parent narratives seemed to offer a psychological view of the segregation—for example, a view of others avoiding discomfort or not knowing what to say, and of parents feeling distress at being with others. But one can also see the narratives as being about societal factors in the isolation of bereaved parents. No doubt the situation of bereaved parents in relationship to others has unique qualities, but in the U.S. other kinds of families dealing with difficulty also tend to be isolated. For example, families dealing with mental illness, losing a farm (Wright & Rosenblatt, 1987), or the aftermath of a natural disaster. So one could understand the isolation bereaved parents talk about as in part the action of general mechanisms in the society for dealing with others who are burdened. Perhaps the message is that each family is more or less on its own or that there are winners and losers, and the winners owe little or nothing to the losers. Perhaps the message is that misfortune can be contagious, so people experiencing misfortune should be avoided or that people dealing with adversity are so overburdened that they lack the resources to engage others in trying to find help. Perhaps, as the next section of this chapter suggests, the problem is that there is little community empathy for bereaved parents.

The Failure of Communal Empathy

Every bereaved parent talked about finding empathy somewhere, most often, in the long run, from the spouse and from other parents who had experienced the death of the child. Some parents experienced continuing empathy and support from one or a few neighbors, friends, or relatives. Some parents purchased empathy from a counselor or sought out a support group of bereaved parents whose life experience made it easier for them to empathize. But no parent talked about being surrounded by an empathic community, a community of people who felt caring concern for the grieving parents and whose empathy continued on beyond the first days of bereavement. Although the U.S. is a society where, through watching television dramas and television news and through other sources, many people have considerable exposure to the expressions of feelings from grieving parents, most people around the grieving parents did not allow that knowledge to become a basis of empathic contact with the grieving parents, let alone sustained empathic contact. Nor did their own experiences of loss or their own imagination of what it would be like for themselves to experience a similar loss become a basis of empathic contact with the grieving parents. I think it is not obvious that the community would be so unempathic. I can understand the failure of empathy in terms of other things discussed in this chapter—the demands to keep on with wage-earning work, the primacy of social order, and the privatization of tragedy. But what is not obvious, even when we say wage-earning work has primacy, social order continues, and so on, is that so many people would seem to block off empathic feelings. It is not merely that social relationships are arranged in certain ways, but that feelings are arranged to fit the social arrangements.

The Array of Frames for Dealing with Tragedy

Parent narratives make clear that every parent has an array of frameworks for understanding the child's death and its consequences. The parents offer religious, legal, medical, psychological, social, and technological understandings of things. At one level, that means they have a lot of resources for meaning-making. At another level, it may mean that they have their work cut out for them, because even when they come to some clarity about how to understand things in one framework, they have many other frameworks that still call for them to work out things. For example, a parent may understand what happened mechanically when a fatal accident with a tractor occurred, but the parent may still have to struggle with why God allowed the accident to happen or with what the legal implications of the accident are.

Despite the array of frames parents used for dealing with their child's death, there are frames that most or all parents excluded. For example, nobody talked about the death as evolution in action. Nobody talked about the ways U.S. capitalism might have been involved in a death (for example, every farmer has to own tractors, though sharing of resources might mean each could afford to use safer equipment). Nobody talked about the ways U.S. capitalism might have been responsible for the community providing so little support. These are among the big picture views of events that parent narratives stay away from. Perhaps there are many reasons for staying away from those big pictures, but I think one is that it has become "un-American" to raise certain questions. More parents were angry with God or even came to doubt the existence of God than questioned U.S. capitalism or the ways social relationships have become so fragmented.

Parent narratives say a lot about the parents and their experiences, and they also say a lot about the society in which the parents live. As was discussed in Chapter 1, the narratives of bereaved parents are concentrated in certain domains and stay away from others. Parent narratives did not enter domains that questioned capitalism, the absence of community grieving, or the lack of community empathy. The parent narratives fit the society they are in. Even parents who were very upset about the chasm that formed between themselves and the rest of society or about the number of people who dropped out of their lives following the death did not frame what upset them as a critique of society. Even as they were bruised and deprived by the way society constructs and deals with a child's death and parent grief, the parents did not challenge what seem to be the basic rules of society.

REFERENCES

Arbuckle, N. W., & de Vries, B. (1995). The long-term effects of later life spousal and parental bereavement on personal functioning. *The Gerontologist, 35,* 637–647.

Attig, T. (1990). Relearning the world: On the phenomenology of grieving. *Journal of the British Society for Phenomenology, 21,* 53–66.

Attig, T. (1991). The importance of conceiving of grief as an active process. *Death Studies, 15,* 385–393.

Attig, T. (1996). *How we grieve: Relearning the world.* New York: Oxford University Press.

Book, P. L. (1996). How does the family narrative influence the individual's ability to communicate about death? *Omega, 33,* 323–341.

Brabant, S. (1989–90). Old pain or new pain: A social psychological approach to recurrent grief. *Omega, 20,* 273–279.

Brabant, S., Forsyth, C. J., & McFarlain, G. (1994). Defining the family after the death of a child. *Death Studies, 18,* 197–206.

Brabant, S., Forsyth, C., & McFarlain, G. (1995). Life after the death of a child: Initial and long term support from others. *Omega, 31,* 67–85.

Brabant, S., Forsyth, C. J., & McFarlain, G. (1997). The impact of the death of a child on meaning and purpose in life. *Journal of Personal and Interpersonal Loss, 2,* 255–266.

Braun, M. J., & Berg, D. H. (1994). Meaning reconstruction in the experience of parental bereavement. *Death Studies, 18,* 105–129.

Brice, C. W. (1989). The relational essence of maternal mourning: An existential-psychoanalytic perspective. *Humanistic Psychologist, 17,* 22–40.

Brice, C. W. (1991a). Paradoxes of maternal mourning. *Psychiatry, 54,* 1–12.

Brice, C. W. (1991b). What forever means: An empirical existential-phenomenological investigation of maternal mourning. *Journal of Phenomenological Psychology, 22,* 16–38.

Carroll, R., & Shaefer, S. (1993–94). Similarities and differences in spouses coping with SIDS. *Omega, 28,* 273–284.

Chase, S. E. (1995). Taking narrative seriously: Consequences for methods and theory in interview studies. In R. Josselson & A. Lieblich (Eds.), *Interpreting experience: The narrative study of lives* (pp. 1–26). Thousand Oaks, CA: Sage.

Chase, S. E. (1996). Personal vulnerability and interpretive authority in narrative research. In R. Josselson (Ed.), *Ethics and process in the narrative study of lives* (pp. 45–59). Thousand Oaks, CA: Sage.

Cochran, L., & Claspell, E. (1987). *The meaning of grief: A dramaturgical approach to understanding emotion.* Westport, CT: Greenwood.

Cook, J. A. (1983). A death in the family: Parental bereavement in the first year. *Suicide and Life-Threatening Behavior, 13,* 42–61.

Cook, J. A. (1988). Dad's double binds: Rethinking fathers' bereavement from a men's studies perspective. *Journal of Contemporary Ethnography, 17,* 285–308.

Cook, J. A., & Wimberley, D. W. (1983). If I should die before I wake: Religious commitment and adjustment to the death of a child. *Journal for the Scientific Study of Religion, 22,* 222–238.

Cordell, A. S., & Thomas, N. (1990). Fathers and grieving: Coping with infant death. *Journal of Perinatology, 10,* 75–80.

Cornwell, J., Nurcombe, B., & Stevens, L. (1977) Family response to loss of a child by sudden infant death syndrome. *Medical Journal of Australia, 1,* 656–658.

Davies, B. (1987). Family responses to the death of a child: The meaning of memories. *Journal of Palliative Care, 3,* 9–15.

DeFrain, J. (1991). Learning about grief from normal families: SIDS, stillbirth, and miscarriage. *Journal of Marital and Family Therapy, 17,* 215–232.

DeFrain, J., Martens, L., Stork, J., & Stork, W. (1990–91). The psychological effects of a stillbirth on surviving family members. *Omega, 22,* 81–108.

DeFrain, J., Taylor, J., & Ernst, L. (1982). *Coping with sudden infant death.* Lexington, MA: Lexington Books.

de Vries, B., Dalla Lana, R., & Falck, V. T. (1994). Parental bereavement over the life course: A theoretical intersection and empirical review. *Omega, 29,* 47–69.

Dijkstra, I. C., & Stroebe, M. S. (1998). The impact of a child's death on parents: A myth (not yet) disproved? *Journal of Family Studies, 4,* 187–199.

Donnelly, K. F. (1982). *Recovering from the loss of a child.* New York: Macmillan.

Dunn, D. S., Goldbach, K. R. C., Lasker, J. N., & Toedter, L. J. (1991). Explaining pregnancy loss: Parents' and physicians' attributions. *Omega, 23,* 13–23.

Dyregrov, A. (1990). Parental reactions to the loss of an infant child: A review. *Scandinavian Journal of Psychology, 31,* 266–280.

Dyregrov, A., & Matthiesen, S. B. (1987b). Similarities and differences in mothers' and fathers' grief following the death of an infant. *Scandinavian Journal of Psychology, 28,* 1–15.

Dyregrov, A., & Matthiesen, S. B. (1987a). Anxiety and vulnerability in parents following the death of an infant. *Scandinavian Journal of Psychology, 28,* 16–25.

Edelstein, L. (1984). *Maternal bereavement: Coping with the unexpected death of a child.* New York: Praeger.

Farnsworth, E. B., & Allen, K. R. (1996). Mothers' bereavement: Experiences of marginalization, stories of change. *Family Relations, 45,* 360–367.

Fish, W. C. (1986). Differences of grief intensity in bereaved parents. In T. A. Rando (Ed.), *Parental loss of a child* (pp. 415–428). Champaign, IL: Research Press.

Gergen, K. J. (1982). *Toward transformation in social knowledge.* New York: Springer.

Gergen, K. J. (1994). Mind, text, and society: Self-memory in social context. In U. Neisser & R. Fivush (Eds.), *The remembering self: Construction and accuracy in the self-narrative* (pp. 78–104). New York: Cambridge University Press.

Gergen, K. J., & Gergen, M. M. (1987). Narratives of relationship. In R. Burnett, P. McGhee, & D. D. Clarke (Eds.), *Accounting for relationships* (pp. 269–288). New York: Methuen.

Gilbert, K. R. (1989). Interactive grief and coping in the marital dyad. *Death Studies, 13,* 605–626.

Gilbert, K. R. (1992). Religion as a resource for bereaved parents. *Journal of Religion and Health, 31,* 19–30.

Gilbert, K. R. (1996). "We've had the same loss, why don't we have the same grief?" Loss and differential grief in families. *Death Studies, 20,* 269–283.

Gilbert, K. R., & Smart, L. S. (1992). *Coping with infant or fetal loss: The couple's healing process.* New York: Brunner/Mazel.

Gorer, G. (1967). *Death, grief, and mourning.* New York: Doubleday Anchor.

Gottlieb, L. N., Lang, A., & Amsel, R. (1996). The long-term effects of grief on marital intimacy following an infant's death. *Omega, 33,* 1–19.

Gubrium, J. F., & Holstein, J. A., 1997). *The new language of qualitative method.* New York: Oxford.

Gubrium, J. F., & Holstein, J. A. (1998). Narrative practice and the coherence of personal stories. *Sociological Quarterly, 39,* 163–187.

Hagemeister, A. K., & Rosenblatt, P. C. (1997). Grief and the sexual relationship of couples who have experienced a child's death. *Death Studies, 21,* 231–252.

Harvey, J. H. (1996). *Embracing their memory: Loss and the social psychology of storytelling.* Needham Heights, MA: Allyn & Bacon.

Hinchman, L. P., & Hinchman, S. K. (Eds.) (1997). *Memory, identity, community: The idea of narrative in the human sciences.* Albany, NY: State University of New York Press.

Hocker, W. V. (1988). Parental loss of an adult child. In O. S. Margolis, A. H. Kutscher, E. R. Marcus, H. C. Raether, V. R. Pine, I. B. Seeland, & D. J. Cherico (Eds.), *Grief and the loss of an adult child* (pp. 37–49). New York: Praeger.

Hogan, N., Morse, J. M., & Tasón, M. C. (1996). Toward an experiential theory of bereavement. *Omega, 33,* 43–65.

Holstein, J. A., & Gubrium, J. F. (1995a). *The active interview.* Thousand Oaks, CA: Sage.

Holstein, J. A., & Gubrium, J. F. (1995b). Deprivatization and the construction of domestic life. *Journal of Marriage and the Family, 57,* 894–908.

Horacek, B. J. (1995). A heuristic model of grieving after high-grief deaths. *Death Studies, 19,* 21–31.

Hughes, C. B., & Page-Lieberman, J. (1989). Fathers experiencing a perinatal loss. *Death Studies, 13,* 537–556.

Johnson, P. A., & Rosenblatt, P. C. (1981). Grief following childhood loss of parent. *American Journal of Psychotherapy, 35,* 419–425.

Johnson, S. (1984–85). Sexual intimacy and replacement children after the death of a child. *Omega, 15,* 109–118.

Johnson, S. E. (1987). *After a child dies: Counseling bereaved families.* New York: Springer.

Kavanaugh, K. (1997). Gender differences among parents who experience the death of an infant weighing less than 500 grams at birth. *Omega, 35,* 281–296.

Klass, D. (1986–87). Marriage and divorce among bereaved parents in a self-help group. *Omega, 17,* 237–249.

Klass, D. (1988). *Parental grief: Solace and resolution.* New York: Springer.

Klass, D. (1992–93). The inner representation of the dead child and the worldviews of bereaved parents. *Omega, 26,* 255–272.

Klass, D. (1993). Solace and immortality: Bereaved parents' continuing bond with their children. *Death Studies, 17,* 343–368.

Klass, D. (1996). The deceased child in the psychic and social worlds of bereaved parents during the resolution of grief. In D. Klass, P. R. Silverman, & S. L. Nickman (Eds.), *Continuing bonds: New understandings of grief* (pp. 199–215). Washington, DC: Taylor & Francis.

Klass, D. (1997). The deceased child in the psychic and social worlds of bereaved parents during the resolution of grief. *Death Studies, 21,* 147–175.

Klass, D. (1999). *The spiritual life of bereaved parents.* Philadelphia: Brunner/Mazel.

Klass, D., & Marwit, S. J. (1988–89). Toward a model of parental grief. *Omega, 19,* 1988–1989.

Knapp, R. J. (1986). *Beyond endurance: When a child dies.* New York: Schocken.

Lang, A., & Gottlieb, L. (1993). Parental grief reactions and marital intimacy following infant death. *Death Studies, 17,* 233–255.

Lang, A., Gottlieb, L. N., & Amsel, R. (1996). Predictors of husbands' and wives' grief reactions following infant death: The role of marital intimacy. *Death Studies, 20,* 33–57.

Lauterbach, S. S. (1994). In another world: "Essences" of mothers' mourning experience. In P. L. Munhall (Ed.), *In women's experience* (pp. 233–291). New York: National League for Nursing Press.

Layne, L. L. (1992). Of fetuses and angels: Fragmentation and integration in narratives of pregnancy loss. *Knowledge and Society, 9,* 29–58.

Lehman, D. R., Lang, E. L, Wortman, C. B., & Sorenson, S. B. (1989). Long-term effects of sudden bereavement: Marital and parent-child relationships and children's reactions. *Journal of Family Psychology, 2,* 344–367.

Leon, I. G. (1990). *When a baby dies: Psychotherapy for pregnancy and newborn loss.* New Haven, CT: Yale University Press.

Lewis, H., & Liston, J. (1981). Stillbirth: Reaction and effect. In P. F. Pegg & E. Metze (Eds.), *Death and dying: A quality of life* (pp. 147–156). London: Pitman.

Lister, L. (1991). Men and grief: A review of research. *Smith College Studies in Social Work, 61,* 220–235.

Malkinson, R., & Bar-Tur, L. (1999). The aging of grief in Israel: A perspective of bereaved parents. *Death Studies, 23,* 413–431.

Mandell, F., McAnulty, E., & Reece, R. M. (1980). Observations of paternal responses to sudden unanticipated infant death. *Pediatrics, 65,* 221–225.

Martinson, I. (1991). Grief is an individual journey: Follow-up of families postdeath of a child with cancer. In D. Papadatou & C. Papadatos (Eds.), *Children and death* (pp. 255–265). New York: Hemisphere.

McClowry, S. G., Davies, E. B., May, K. A., Kulenkamp, E. J., & Martinson, I. M. (1987). The empty space phenomenon: The process of grief in the bereaved family. *Death Studies, 11,* 361–374.

Miles, M. S. (1984). Helping adults mourn the death of a child. In H. Wass & C. A. Corr (Eds.), *Childhood and death* (pp. 219–241). Washington, DC: Hemisphere.

Miles, M. S., & Demi, A. S. (1983–84). Toward the development of a theory of bereavement guilt: Sources of guilt in bereaved parents. *Omega, 14,* 299–314.

Miles, M. S., & Demi, A. S. (1991–92). A comparison of guilt in bereaved parents whose children died by suicide, accident, or chronic disease. *Omega, 24,* 203–215.

Mishler, E. G. (1986). The analysis of interview-narratives. In T. R. Sarbin (Ed.), *Narrative psychology: The storied nature of human conduct* (pp. 233–255). New York: Praeger.

Moss, M. S., Lesher, E. L., & Moss, S. Z. (1986–87). Impact of the death of an adult child on elderly parents: Some observations. *Omega, 17,* 209–218.

Nadeau, J. W. (1998). *Families making sense of death.* Thousand Oaks, CA: Sage.

Neimeyer, R. A., & Stewart, A. E. (1996). Trauma, healing, and the narrative emplotment of loss. *Families in Society, 77,* 360–375.

Parkes, C. M. (1972). *Bereavement: Studies of grief in adult life.* New York: International Universities Press.

Paul, N. L. (1986). The paradoxical nature of the grief experience. *Contemporary Family Therapy, 8,* 5–19.

Peppers, L. G., & Knapp, R. J. (1980). *Motherhood and mourning: Perinatal death.* New York: Praeger.

Polkinghorne, D. E. (1988). *Narrative knowing and the human sciences.* Albany, NY: State University of New York Press.

Powell, M. (1995). Sudden infant death syndrome: The subsequent child. *British Journal of Social Work, 25,* 227–240.

Radley, A. (1990). Artefacts, memory and a sense of the past. In D. Middleton & D. Edwards (Eds.), *Collective remembering* (pp. 46–59). London: Sage.

Rando, T. A. (1985). Bereaved parents: Particular difficulties, unique factors, and treatment issues. *Social Work, 30,* 19–23.

Rando, T. A. (1986). The unique issues and impact of the death of a child. In T. A. Rando (Ed.), *Parental loss of a child* (pp. 5–43). Champaign, IL: Research Press.

Rando, T. A. (1991). Parental adjustment to the loss of a child. In D. Papadatou & C. Papadatos (Eds.), *Children and death* (pp. 233–253). New York: Hemisphere.

Raphael, B. (1983). *The anatomy of bereavement*. New York: Basic Books.

Riches, G., & Dawson, P. (1996). "An intimate loneliness": Evaluating the impact of a child's death on parental self-identity and marital relationships. *Journal of Family Therapy, 18,* 1–22.

Riches, G., & Dawson, P. (1998). Lost children, living memories: The role of photographs in processes of grief and adjustment among bereaved parents. *Death Studies, 22,* 121–140.

Riessman, C. K. (1993). *Narrative analysis*. Newbury Park, CA: Sage.

Rosen, E. J. (1988–89). Family therapy in cases of interminable grief for the loss of a child. *Omega, 19,* 187–202.

Rosen, H. (1984–85). Prohibitions against mourning in childhood sibling loss. *Omega, 15,* 307–316.

Rosenblatt, P. C. (1983a). *Bitter, bitter tears: Nineteenth century diarists and twentieth century grief theories*. Minneapolis, MN: University of Minnesota Press.

Rosenblatt, P. C. (1983b). Grief and involvement in wrongful death litigation. *Law and Human Behavior, 7,* 351–359.

Rosenblatt, P. C. (1994). *Metaphors of family systems theory: Toward new constructions*. New York: Guilford.

Rosenblatt, P. C. (2000). Protective parenting after the death of a child. *Journal of Personal and Interpersonal Loss,* in press.

Rosenblatt, P. C., & Burns, L. H. (1986). Long term effects of perinatal loss. *Journal of Family Issues, 7,* 237–253.

Rosenblatt, P. C., & Fischer, L. R. (1993). Qualitative family research. In P. G. Boss, W. J. Doherty, R. LaRossa, W. R. Schumm, & S. K. Steinmetz (Eds.), *Sourcebook of family theories and methods: A contextual approach* (pp. 167–177). New York: Plenum.

Rosenblatt, P. C., & Meyer, C. J. (1986). Imagined interactions and the family. *Family Relations, 35,* 319–324.

Rosenblatt, P. C., Titus, S. L., & Cunningham, M. R. (1979). Disrespect, tension, and togetherness-apartness in marriage. *Journal of Marriage and Family Therapy, 5,* 47–54.

Rosenblatt, P. C., Walsh, R. P., & Jackson, D. A. (1976). *Grief and mourning in cross-cultural perspective*. New Haven, CT: Human Relations Area Files Press.

Rosenblatt, P. C., & Wright, S. E. (1984). Shadow realities in close relationships. *American Journal of Family Therapy, 12* (#2), 45–54.

Rubin, S. S. (1993). The death of a child is forever: The life course impact of child loss. In M. S. Stroebe, W. Stroebe, & R. O. Hansson (Eds.), *Handbook of bereavement: Theory, research, and intervention* (pp. 285–299). New York: Cambridge University Press.

Rubin, S. S. (1996). The wounded family: Bereaved parents and the impact of adult child loss. In D. Klass, P. R. Silverman, & S. L. Nickman (Eds.), *Continuing bonds: New understandings of grief* (pp. 217–232). Washington, DC: Taylor & Francis.

Ruiz, J., & Atwood, J. D. (1996). Backwards scripts. In J. D. Atwood (Ed.), *Family scripts* (pp. 57–100). Washington, DC: Accelerated Development.

Schiff, H. S. (1978). *The bereaved parent*. New York: Penguin.

Schwab, R. (1990). Paternal and maternal coping with the death of a child. *Death Studies, 14,* 407–422.

Schwab, R. (1992). Effects of a child's death on the marital relationship: A preliminary study. *Death Studies, 16,* 141–154.

Schwab, R. (1995). Bereaved parents and support group participation. *Omega, 32,* 49–61.

Schwab, R. (1998). A child's death and divorce: Dispelling the myth. *Death Studies, 22,* 445–468.

Sedney, M. A., Baker, J. E., & Gross, E. (1994). "The story" of a death: Therapeutic considerations with bereaved families. *Journal of Marital and Family Therapy, 20,* 287–296.

Shanfield, S. B., Benjamin, G. A. H., & Swain, B. J. (1988). The family under stress: The death of adult children. In O. S. Margolis, A. H. Kutscher, E. R. Marcus, H. C. Raether, V. R. Pine, I. B. Seeland, & D. J. Cherico (Eds.), *Grief and the loss of an adult child* (pp. 3–7). New York: Praeger.

Shotter, J. (1990). The social construction of remembering and forgetting. In D. Middleton & D. Edwards (Eds.), *Collective remembering* (pp. 120–138). London: Sage.

Shotter, J. (1993). *Conversational realities: Constructing life through language.* London: Sage.

Smart, L. (1993). Parental bereavement in Anglo American history. *Omega, 28,* 49–61.

Sormanti, M., & August, J. (1997). Parental bereavement: Spiritual connections with deceased children. *American Journal of Orthopsychiatry, 67,* 460–469.

Stevenson, R. G. (1988). Parental and grandparental grief for the loss of an adult child. In O. S. Margolis, A. H. Kutscher, E. R. Marcus, H. C. Raether, V. R. Pine, I. B. Seeland, & D. J. Cherico (Eds.), *Grief and the loss of an adult child* (pp. 51–53). New York: Praeger.

Stinson, K. M., Lasker, J. N., Lohmann, J., & Toedter, L. J. (1992). Parents' grief following pregnancy loss: A comparison of mothers and fathers. *Family Relations, 41,* 218–223.

Stroebe, M. (1992–93). Coping with bereavement: A review of the grief work hypothesis. *Omega, 26,* 19–42.

Stroebe, M., Gergen, M. M., Gergen, K. J., & Stroebe, W. (1992). Broken hearts or broken bonds. *American Psychologist, 47,* 1205–1212.

Stroebe, M., van Son, M., Stroebe, W., Kleber, R., Schut, H, & van den Bout, J. (1999). On the classification and diagnosis of pathological grief. *Clinical Psychology Review, 19,* 1–19.

Talbot, K. (1996–97). Mothers now childless: Survival after the death of an only child. *Omega, 34,* 177–189.

Talbot, K. (1998–99). Mothers now childless: Personal transformation after the death of an only child. *Omega, 38,* 167–186

Thomas, V., Striegel, P., Dudley, D., Wilkins, J., & Gibson, D. (1997). Parental grief of a perinatal loss: A comparison of individual and relationship variables. *Journal of Personal and Interpersonal Loss, 2,* 167–187.

Volkan, V. D. (1981). *Linking objects and linking phenomena.* New York: International Universities Press.

Wambach, J. A. (1985–86). The grief process as a social construct. *Omega, 16,* 201–211.

Wheeler, I. (1993–94). The role of meaning and purpose in life in bereaved parents associated with a self-help group: Compassionate Friends. *Omega, 28,* 261–271.

Wheeler, I. (1998–99). The role of linking objects in parental bereavement. *Omega, 38,* 289–296.

Wright, S. E., & Rosenblatt, P. C. (1987). Isolation and farm loss: Why neighbors may not be supportive. *Family Relations, 36,* 391–395.

APPENDIX
Methodological Details

Finding Parents to Interview

The narratives for this book came from two separate studies, one focused on couples who had experienced the death of a child (23 couples) and one focused on farm families who had lost a family member in a farm accident (6 couples). In both studies, interviewees were recruited through classified advertisements, through news releases in magazines, community papers and radio broadcasts, and through flyers sent to social service agencies and distributed at a number of churches. Some people who were interviewed heard about the study from someone else—a friend, relative, neighbor, school nurse, or therapist.

The Interviews

Two people helped with the interviewing, Anna Hagemeister (who interviewed 11 couples with me and five couples on her own) and Terri Karis (who interviewed two couples). I am grateful to them both for careful, astute, and compassionate interviewing. In the interview quotes, Anna is "AH" and Terri is "TK." I am "PR."

Almost all interviews were conducted with the two parents together. Typically, nobody else was present, though some people lowered their voice so children or a resident mother/mother-in-law could not hear some of what they said. For a few couples, children were present during part or all of the interview.

The interview guide for each study was quite extensive. However, my intent was to let the interview go with the narrative flow of the people interviewed. In fact, most people talked for long stretches of time without any interruption from the interviewer. In instances like that, many matters on the interview guide were covered without interviewer questioning or prompting.

The interviewing approach focused on parent narratives. We worked at making room for their stories in their own terms (Chase, 1995); we stayed with their stories and frames of reference rather than pull them toward ours. We tried to understand their stories fully and to be good listeners—encouraging and caring about the details (Chase, 1995), not interrupting, but asking questions for clarification or for more details based on the story we were being told. We carried out what might be called "active" interviewing (Holstein & Gubrium, 1995a) in that we worked at activating "narrative production." We encouraged interviewees with our interest, attentiveness, questions, self-disclosures, and the way we built throughout the interview on what an individual or couple had told us so far. We did not return to our interview guide until a particular line of narrative had been played out in the interaction of interviewee(s) and interviewer(s). Ideally, that return was to a question that fit with interviewee narratives so far, but occasionally the return involved an abrupt shift to a substantially new frame of reference.

When we opened up what could be taken as a new line of questioning, that did not mean stories previously told were left behind. Often the answer to the next question became integrated with one or more previous story lines. For example, a question later in the interview about marital sexuality in bereavement might produce answers that were tied to earlier stories about couple differences in emotionality or about the pain of living with a fully furnished infant room without having an infant.

As an interview progressed, some parents showed the interviewer relevant visual material—particularly photos of the child who had died, news clippings, condolence cards, poems, memorabilia of the funeral, and things the child had made. A few parents showed the interviewer the room the child had occupied.

The two interview studies were not quite comparable in the information they obtained. In particular, the farm study picked up much less about couple sexuality than the "couple" study did but much more about the family's economic situation. The interview guide for the couple study can be found at the end of this appendix.

Couples who were not separated or divorced were always interviewed together. (As a check on what might be lost by interviewing couples together, for two couples we carried out individual interviews after previously having carried out a couple interview. It didn't seem that the individual interviews produced material that differed substantially from the couple interviews.) Most of the interviews occurred at a single sitting. Interviews almost always lasted at least two hours and ran up to about four hours at a single sitting. In a few instances where the partners were interviewed separately or separately as well as together, the total interview time exceeded four hours. In some couple interviews there were times when the interviewer was alone with an interviewee. In one instance an interviewee used that time to whisper something that would not have been said with the spouse present. Almost all interviews were carried out in people's homes, and 27 of the 29 were audiotaped.

Audiotaped interviews were transcribed. [For one couple who did not want to be audiotaped, I did a hand written transcription of as much as I could hear and get onto paper while they talked. For another couple, I botched the audiotaping and instead wrote detailed notes of the interview shortly after I left their house.] If somebody else transcribed an audiotape, I checked the transcription to make it as accurate as possible. For me, "accuracy" in transcribing includes retaining as much as I can of the linguistic complexity and nuance that I can hear on the tape. I include pauses, slurs, repetitions, stutters, throat clearings, heavy breathing, tears, emphases, and the many instances of what Riessman (1993, p. 12) calls "discourse markers" (things like "you know"). Most of this complexity has been edited out of the quotes in this book, to facilitate reading, but I paid attention to all of that in trying to make sense of what people said. I have also smoothed over, as I edited quotes for inclusion in this book, the abrupt changes in direction within sentences. It is ironic that the powerful conventions of presenting language in written form almost demand a lean, linear, smooth text, while the analysis of what people say works best when we make use of the information edited out. This would be a very hard book to read if I left in all that I edited out, and it would be considerably longer.

For the interviews that I did, I often remembered the nonverbal details that went with the verbal. I often remembered smiles and frowns, tense or distracted looks, and so on, and those I also included, when I could remember them, in making sense of the audiotapes. Similarly, I tried to pay attention to the moment-to-moment interactions of the interviewer and the person(s) interviewed in making sense of the transcripts, including the interviewer's frequently voiced sounds of understanding and empathy. However, I omitted those sounds from the quotes in this book.

☐ The Parents in This Book

Fifty-eight parents provided narratives for this book, 29 white, heterosexual couples. (I was eager to include same sex couples and couples in which one or both partners was a person of color, but none volunteered. If I were to start this study over again, one major change would be to include aggressive pursuit of interviewees of color and same-sex couples.) To be eligible to be interviewed in the couple study, both parents had to be willing to be interviewed. The six interviews of farm couples that were incorporated in this study were all the interviews in that study that dealt with the death of a child. Everyone who was interviewed had lost at least one child who had breathed. In addition, whenever parents talked about a stillbirth or miscarriage as a child death, I included what they had to say in the narrative analyses.

The people who were interviewed ranged in age from 33 to 68 years old, with a median age for women of 44 and for men of 46. Women ranged in education from 11 to 18 years (masters degree) with a median of 15 years. Men ranged in education from 8 to 20 years (doctorate or professional degree) with a median of 16 years. The farming couples ranged from those whose farm operation seemed to be quite marginal to those who were well off. Without formal measurement, and judging by housing and occupation, the nonfarming couples ranged in social class from lower working class (e.g., old, tiny house by railroad tracks; employed or retired from low level blue collar or low level service job) to upper middle class (e.g., expensive house in elite suburb, professional or managerial employment). Twenty-six of the 29 couples had another child who was alive at the time of the interview. The 29 couples reported 33 child deaths, including one stillbirth. The children who died ranged in age up to 33 years, with the median age at death being 3. The interviews occurred from 8 months to 35 years after the death, with a median of 7 years after the death.

☐ Narrative Analysis

Narrative analysis was integrated with all phases of this project. Even during interviews, I thought constantly about the analysis and how I might make sense and write about things that I had just been told. At times, this awareness guided my next questions, as I asked for clarification, elaboration, or a spouse's view on something that I was thinking about analyzing in a certain way. Often the additional information fed into my sense of how I would analyze what I had just been told, but sometimes the additional information showed me that I was on the wrong track and had to rethink things.

I also thought a lot about narrative analysis while making or checking interview transcripts. I wanted transcripts that would retain information that I thought I would use in the analysis, and so I worked at making the transcripts information-full. For example, I knew that I wanted to understand as much as I could about emotional complexities, so my transcriptions included sighs, tears, pauses, throat clearings and other nonlexical information that might say something about emotions. Similarly, I knew that I wanted to understand the couple relationship, so I retained information that might speak to that—for example, partner interruption, talking over the partner's words, and laughs and snorts at what the partner said.

After the transcriptions were complete, I read through the transcripts of two cases to make a preliminary outline of book chapters and chapter sections that would deal with what seemed to me to be major areas of couple narrative. Then I used the outline as a basis for analyzing other transcripts. The analysis of the other transcripts involved frequent outline revision and returning to previously coded transcripts as each succeeding transcript that was analyzed led to questioning previous analyses. While writing and rewriting this book, there were many times when I ran into new analysis questions, which led to anything from checking the context of a quote or the next words that somebody said to tabulating something for all cases to be sure that my impression or assertion about something was correct.

I tried throughout the analysis never to lose awareness of the interviewee's realities and of what it was I thought people wanted me to know and to understand. For me, this is a matter of ethics as well as research validity. I respect parent realities and do not privilege my own to the extent of obscuring theirs. But, as you can see at many places in this book, I often move to a level of generalization or commentary that is different from interviewee realities.

Except for the material on sexuality, where Anna Hagemeister joined me in the narrative analysis, I did the analyses myself. The analyses emphasize narrative topic areas that were not unique to one couple or one individual. One of the many ways I tried to discipline my analyses was to count how many individuals and couples said something. Counting not only provided a measure of how widespread something was, it also forced me to define rather clearly what I was counting. Another way of disciplining the analyses was to look within the interviews for interpretations of what I was counting; often parents who were interviewed said things that challenged my interpretations of what they said or of what somebody else said. The scholarly literature that deals with parental bereavement is substantial. I tried to do my initial analyses with my knowledge of that literature set aside, but later on I challenged my analyses with close readings of what Dennis Klass, Kathleen Gilbert, Charles Brice, Reiko Schwab, and all the others whose work I cite had to say.

There is not a clearly defined boundary between narrative analysis and other approaches to qualitative research. In a sense the analysis that led to this book was a thematic analysis carried out on narratives, which is not what some scholars of narrative analysis would consider to be narrative analysis. As I read the parent narratives I paid attention to things that might be attended to in more linguistically sensitive narrative analysis—for example, linguistic connections among and between stories, changes in direction within stories and even sentences, and word choice. But this book is not about linguistic details but about more macro phenomena—grief processes, couple relationships, relationships with others, the cultural contexts of parent bereavement, selectivity and choice in narratives, and what things are linked together in parent narratives. There are many other ways of examining narratives that could be part of narrative analysis (Chase, 1996; Gubrium & Holstein, 1997; Riessman, 1993). I could, for example, have chosen to look more at how parents said things and less at what they said, how parents framed their entire lives, or the parent narratives as stories about the self. Still the exploration of themes seems to be like the exploration of "linkages" in narratives that Gubrium and Holstein (1997, pp. 147–152) see as a potentially central and productive activity in narrative analysis.

I provide quotes at many places that illustrate the points I make. The reader can see from those quotes whether I have any documentation for the points I make and whether the things I say have a conceptual match to what is in the quotes (Rosenblatt & Fischer, 1993). The quotes are typically selections from a larger number of quotes. I almost always selected quotes that were more colorful and easier to understand. A few people who said less, who were less articulate, or whose situation was so unusual that they are hard to quote without revealing who they are are not quoted at all in this book. But their narratives still counted in my determination about what to write.

In the area of couple sexual relationships, coding was done with Anna Hagemeister for an article we published together (Hagemeister & Rosenblatt, 1997). We independently coded the interview transcripts, applying a set of 20 conceptual categories dealing with meanings and couple sexuality which seemed central to what parents said about their sexual relationship. We then discussed areas of disagreement, which sometimes led to clarifying coding categories and sometimes to dropping categories.

☐ Validity

With interviews lasting an average of two to four hours and occurring at a single point in time, we only have a snapshot. I think by the end of the interview parents seemed to have said a large portion of what they could possibly have said at that time. And most seemed to have worked hard to remember and say all that they could that was relevant to the questions and to their sense of what was important to say.

To the extent that their realities, stories, and languages shift over the course of their grief and from situation to situation and to the extent that they can, at a certain time and in a certain situation, only narrate parts of past realities, stories, and languages, the interviews captured a selective and simplified view of things. Still, I think that people's words say a lot that is accurate and valid for them.

Another sense of validity comes from interviewing spouses together. In most couples there seemed to be good agreement (see Chapter 2), but sometimes there were differences:

Tina: (speaking simultaneously with Scott) I'll give mine and then you can give your opinion (laughs).

Another sense of validity comes from the people who were interviewed a second time. Also, some people wrote letters to me or telephoned me after the interview. From these people there was a sense of how much the first interview had stirred up feelings and thoughts, but nobody raised issues that called into question the validity of what was said in the first interview.

Because the most recent death was eight months before the interview and most were years before the interview, this study is not about narratives from early in bereavement. Were this study to be based on what people had to say beginning immediately after the death, I am sure there would be additional findings, particularly about the struggle to find words early in grief, vagueness in answering questions before there are words, intense pain, and confusion. Were this a longitudinal study beginning soon after the death, I am sure there would be much to say about the evolution of parent narratives.

A child's death is so significant and so dominant in a parent's life that I think most parents had previously thought through a great deal of what they said during the interview. There is a validity in researching something so big and important, because the importance may give a great deal of stability, depth, and connectedness to what people have to say. The parents already knew most of it before the interviewer arrived, and what they knew was too important and too tightly linked to too much else to be easily changed by an interview. That parents had so much to say is a measure of how much they had thought about things, how much experience they had to relate, and how nontrivial the death and its aftermath were.

In this book, I generally privilege the realities of the parents. In any area of life, but perhaps particularly when it comes to death and grief, one can argue there are realities people cannot speak, do not know, and will deny (Paul, 1986). So there are perspectives that this book definitely misses.

A case can also be made that validity is not a solid thing but is relative to the frameworks in which interpretation takes place. Gergen (1982, pp. 60–68) has argued that meanings are only verifiable within the framework of another meaning system. And then the meanings generated within that other meaning system can only be verified within another. There is no final place that one can consider the ultimate criterion. So even as I try to write a book of what seems to me to be profound validity, I am aware that I could move to other frameworks which would make what I have to say seem trivial, inadequate, or wrong.

This book focuses on couples, but I want to be clear that I am not in any way trying to diminish the grieving of parents who are not in a couple. There is an enormous amount to be learned about single parents, parents who were divorced, widowed, or separated at the time of a child's death, never married parents, and parent surrogates who are single parenting when a child dies. Research on their grieving would be of immense value. Nor do I want to make it seem as though only a parent's grief is important when a child dies. We need to understand the grieving of people who had other relationships to a child who died than parent.

It is also of great importance to study parent grief in a diversity of populations. Although I think the interviewees represented a broad range in terms of social class (though missing the extreme), it is one of the major limitations of this study that I only have interviews from white, heterosexual, English-speaking couples who are living in one region of the United States.

☐ An Interview Guide

[This interview guide was used with all but three couples in the study]

Interviewees: name, gender, age, years of schooling, occupation

Other household members: name, gender, age, years of schooling, occupation

I. Genealogy

Interviewees' families of origin (including people who are dead, expartners, remarried partners, step-siblings, other perinatal losses experienced by either partner). Were there other losses (than the focal one) that were particularly significant or difficult in your life? Were there any losses that were not deaths—for example, separations, fallings out, break ups of relationships—that were particularly significant or difficult in your life?

II. The Death

Tell me the story of the child's death. Start wherever you want. (Probe, if necessary: How long ago did the loss occur? Was it a sudden death? What was the cause of death?)

Do you still have questions, concerns, or anything else that feels unresolved about the death?

III. Overview of the Aftermath

[Questions that need to be modified depending on the cause of death, how long (if at all) the child was hospitalized before death, how old the child was:] Would you say that each of you had the same relationship with the child, or were there differences in how much contact each of you had or how much each was involved in the day-to-day care of the child? Would you say that you had couple dreams, hopes, or expectations for the child's future or for your future relationship with the child?

While the child was dying or since the death, where, if anywhere, have you gone for information and advice? Did you telephone or visit with your physician? Other medical people? Clergy? Friends? Did you read anything? Did you talk to other parents who had children die?

In what ways is the child in your lives nowadays?

Does the child's death have any particular religious meaning to the two of you? Has it affected your relationship, as a couple, to God? Has it affected your participation in organized religion?

There are support groups for bereaved parents and there are counselors who can help bereaved parents with some issues. Have the two of you been involved in a support group or counseling? (If so, can you tell me about that? Probes: How did you get involved? How long were you involved? What type of support group or counseling was it? Were you and your partner both involved to the same extent? If not, what were the differences?)

IV. Grief and Its Influence on the Couple Relationship

In what ways did each of you grieve the loss? Have you grieved together? Do you think the two of you understood and experienced the loss in the same way? If not, what were the differences? How did those differences affect your relationship with each other? Do the differences still exist? Even partners who understand a death in the same way almost always grieve differently and almost always follow a different time course in grieving. Have you observed that in your own relationship? Has it created any problems in your relationship to grieve differently or over a different time course? (If so, tell me about those problems?) Have you talked about it before today? (If so, what things came up as you talked?)

When do you feel the loss most sharply?

How did the loss affect your relationships with each other and with other family members? (Probes: Do you think your relationship with each other and with other family members was affected by fatigue related to the death? Irritability? Preoccupation with the death? Anger? Economic problems related to the death and its aftermath? Immersion in employment or problems with employment as a result of the death? Health problems related to the death or your grieving? Was your playing together affected by the death? Did the death change how and how much you received or gave attention in the family? Did it change how much time you had to yourself? Did it affect the fairness in workload around the house? Were there hassles with each other about how to think about the death? Were there problems from letting housework and other things go? Were there times when the death drew you closer together? Were there times you felt isolated as a result of the death? Were there times you felt pushed away by another family member?) Did the death affect your peace of mind? Relationships with friends? Did the death affect how you got along at work?

Did the loss affect your use of alcohol, drugs, tobacco, or other chemicals? (If so, how?) If there was a change in usage, how did that affect your relationships with each other and with others in the family? Did either of you use other things to dull the pain—for example, television watching, listening to music, sleep . . .?

In what ways do you think there might have been misunderstandings between you with regard to the loss, misunderstandings about feelings, how to grieve, how the loss happened, or anything else? How did that affect your relationship?

Did you two feel the same way about the ways and amount to grieve? If not, what were the differences? How did those differences affect your relationship?

Have either of you felt guilt about anything connecting to the death? (If so, what?) How has that guilt showed up in your relationship as a couple?

Have either of you found yourself blaming yourself or somebody else about something connected to the death? (If so, tell me about it.) How has that blame showed up in your relationships as a couple?

How, if at all, did you try to support each other following the loss? Was that support appreciated? Was it helpful?

Do you think either of you influenced the other's thinking about the child, the death, grieving, God, or anything else connected to the loss? (If so, what?)

After a child's death, lots of couples have ups and downs. Can you tell me about the most memorable ups and downs in your relationship since the loss?

We suspect that there may be many differences between how women experience and deal with a loss like yours and how men do. Are there (or were there) other differences between the two of you in how you dealt with the loss that we haven't yet talked about? (If so, what are or what were they?)

In what ways, if any, did the loss bring you two closer? In what ways did it strengthen your relationship?

Sometimes a couple is affected by how others in the family react to the death—for example, how other children in the family, parents, siblings, in-laws or other family member grieve or what they say. Were either of you affected by how somebody else in the family reacted to the death? If you were, did that affect your relationship as a couple?

V. Questions about Sexuality

I want to ask you how things have played themselves out in your sexual relationship with each other. But before I do, I want you to tell me what you think of when you think about a sexual relationship. What do you include as part of a sexual relationship? Given that, how has the death and your grieving been played out in your sexual relationship with each other?

Some couples experience a change in their sex life, at least for a while, following a death. Did you? (Probes: What were things like prior to the loss? How have they changed since?)

Some people experience changes in how they think about themselves, their partner, or sexuality after a loss. Did it seem to you that either of you experienced a change in how you thought about self following the death? About the other? About sexuality? About self or other as a sexual being? Do you think that your sexuality or your partner's changed following the loss?

Were there specific encounters that were sexual or might have become sexual that you can remember that were different as a result of the loss? (If so, how?)

Some people talk about needing to be held or to be physically close to someone after a child's death. Did you have those needs (or do you still have them)? (If so, how, if at all, have those needs been met for each of you?)

Do you think your sex life is different even now as a result of the death? (If so, how?)

[Only ask this if it is appropriate given the couple ages and what else they have told you about themselves.] Do you think issues surrounding the possibility of having another child have had any impact on your sexual relationship with each other?

If there were times of sexual distance or abstinence: What happened, if anything, that brought you two back together sexually?

At any time following the death, were there sexual encounters between the two of you that were particularly electric or passionate? (If so, what do you think that was about?)

VI. Other Relationships

With whom have each of you talked the most about the death? Would you say that person knows best where you are at? (If that other person is not the partner: How has the closeness you have had with that other person affected your relationship as a couple?)

Do you feel that one of you got or gets more support from others than the other? (If so, tell me about it?) Has there been any way in which those differences in support affected your marital relationship?

Was there anybody who either of you felt really let you down—for example, being unwilling to listen to you, not being supportive enough, saying hurtful things? (If so, has that changed your relationship with that person/those persons? Have those changes affected your relationship as a couple?)

VII. Concluding Questions

How has the death and what you have had to go through in dealing with it strengthened you as a couple?

What advice would you have for a couple going through what you have had to go through?

INDEX

Printed in the United Kingdom
by Lightning Source UK Ltd.
129294UK00001B/30/A